DISCOVER YOUR *Family History* ONLINE

DISCOVER YOUR *Family History* ONLINE

a step-by-step guide to
starting your genealogy search

Nancy Hendrickson

FAMILY
TREE
BOOKS

Cincinnati, Ohio
shopfamilytree.com

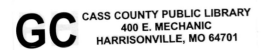

INTRODUCTION 7

CHAPTER 1 BUILDING YOUR FAMILY TREE 8

Your family history research starts with you. In this chapter you'll learn how to gather vital information about yourself so you can branch out to past generations.

CHAPTER 2 COMPUTER BASICS FOR THE ONLINE GENEALOGIST 28

Your computer is your most valuable internet research tool. Learn short-cuts and tricks that will help you make maximize your research efforts.

CHAPTER 3 USING SEARCH ENGINES 42

The internet contains an overwhelming amount of information. Search engines can browse all of that information in seconds and show you exactly where to find what you are looking for. This chapter explains how to use keywords and operators to yield precise results from search engines.

CHAPTER 4 ONLINE DATABASES 53

There are a number of online databases for family historians to explore. This chapter shows you all the subscription and free databases and everything in between.

CHAPTER 5 BIRTH, MARRIAGE, AND DEATH RECORDS 69

Vital records prove family connections. You'll learn where and how to find them online. Probate records can help you make connections as you research ancestors who lived in pre-civil registration eras. After you gather your evidence, you can use it to join a heritage society.

CHAPTER 6 LIFE DURING YOUR ANCESTORS' ERA 89

Your ancestors were affected by the events of their world—war, natural disasters, disease, politics and cultural shifts. Understanding the events of your ancestors' lifetime can help you better relate to them. It may also provide new research leads.

CHAPTER 7 GOOGLE FOR GENEALOGISTS 104

Google is more than a single search engine. Its many functions will prove invaluable in your family history research.

ABOUT THE AUTHOR

Nancy Hendrickson is the author of six books and hundreds of magazine and web articles. A native of St. Joseph, Missouri, she is an internet genealogy consultant and an instructor at Family Tree University <familytreeuniversity.com>. Nancy is passionate about the history that shaped America and spends her vacations photographing and chronicling the historic and pre-historic sites of the American West; ride along with her at <frontiertraveler.com>. To learn more about her genealogy work visit <ancestornews.com>.

DEDICATION

This book is dedicated to my mother's side of the family—the Dearing, Knox, Hume, Bay, Brooks, McClelland, and Broyles. Researching these families has been a challenge and a joy. I've discovered larger-than-life ancestors who were the Daniel Boones of their time—always on the frontier, pushing their way into new territory. They're the adventurers I always wanted to be.

Introduction

Few people had heard of the phenomenon called "the internet" when I first logged onto CompuServe in May of 1986. Back then, family tree information was scarce, unorganized, and hard-to-find.

Since then, millions of genealogy websites have sprung up. Some are well-known commercial sites like Ancestry.com <ancestry.com> and Fold3.com <fold3.com>, but the majority are sites built by everyday genealogy enthusiasts who have a deep desire to share their family history with other seekers.

In truth, the largest percentage of my genealogy breakthroughs have been the result of finding personal websites created by people researching the same family lines.

Thanks to networking with other online researchers, I've made tremendous strides in discovering more about the Dimmitt, Snow, Broyles, and Knox families. And I'm confident that you can do the same, whether you're facing a "Smith" challenge or delving into the mysteries of the pre-1850 censuses.

If you're just starting in internet genealogy, this book will provide dozens of techniques to help you amass names and dates. If you're an old hand you'll discover how to enhance those names and dates with maps, stories, music, news of the day, and photographs. There's no end to what can be found.

In addition to the techniques you'll learn in this book, I've also created several videos that will work you through real-life search scenarios. You'll find the videos at <familytreeuniversity.com/W5972-video>.

Genealogy is a lifetime pursuit, so take your time as you work through each chapter, putting the strategies into practice. In the end you'll be able to merge all that you've learned into a rich history of your family—a history that can be shared today and treasured tomorrow.

I'd love to hear of your successes with the techniques in this book, so please e-mail me your stories at nancy@ancestornews.com.

Happy hunting!

Nancy Hendrickson
San Diego, California
@genealogyteach on Twitter

Building Your Family Tree

You've probably heard a few stories about your family history. You may have been told a distant ancestor arrived on the *Mayflower* or your family's lines go back to European nobility, Scottish rebels, or an Indian princess.

Whatever the stories, they've sent you on a mission of discovery—to find the people who came before you.

If you watched the popular television series *Who Do You Think You Are?*, you may have noticed a common theme running through nearly every story. Each actor gained an understanding of how connected he (or she) is to his past, and often the actor recognized how similar he is to his ancestors.

As a science, genealogy is about proving the link from one generation to the next. As an avocation, genealogy provides hours of fascinating detective work. And as a philosophy, genealogy is, in the end, about self-discovery.

As you make your way through this book, you'll learn the "how-to" of the science as well as the fun of the chase. When you're finished, you'll have a deeper sense of who you really are.

So let's start with the science.

BEGIN WITH YOU

When you climb a tree, you start on the ground, work your way up the trunk, and then move out onto the branches. Use this same approach in genealogy.

Start on the ground (with you); climb up the trunk (your parents and grandparents); then venture out onto the branches (past generations). The higher you go in the tree, the less stable the branches! The further you go back in genealogy, the more challenging the journey. So let's start with you.

You know you were born, but can you prove it with documentation? You probably have a birth certificate, hospital record, or maybe a newspaper birth announcement.

If you begin documentation with yourself and carefully move backward, you'll build a strong foundation from which to work. You may not realize it now, but as your genealogy research progresses you'll see how having a solid (and provable) footing in each generation will lead to the clues that boost you higher up the tree.

1. PLACE OF BIRTH
Registration Dist. No. 3104
Primary Dist. No.
State Board of Health - Bureau of Vital Statistics
DEPARTMENT'S RECORD CITY OF CHICAGO
CERTIFICATE OF BIRTH
County of COOK
Registered No. 11990
City of CHICAGO No. 4627 Lake Pk Av. St.; Ward
2. FULL NAME OF CHILD Margery Helen Brooks (If child is not yet named, make supplemental report, as directed.)
3. Sex of Child F. 4. Twin, triplets, or other? Number in order of birth (To be answered only in event of plural births) 5. Date of birth April 6, 1918 (Month) (Day) (Year)

FATHER
6. FULL NAME Wm N. Brooks.
7. RESIDENCE 4627 Lake Pk Av.
8. COLOR W. 9. AGE AT LAST BIRTHDAY 41 Years
10. BIRTHPLACE (State or Country) Cincinnati
11. OCCUPATION Jewelry Salesman

MOTHER
12. FULL MAIDEN NAME Anna L. Brown
13. RESIDENCE 4627 Lake Pk Av.
14. COLOR W. 15. AGE AT LAST BIRTHDAY 32 Years
16. BIRTHPLACE (State or Country) Chicago
17. OCCUPATION H. W.

18. Number of children born to this mother, including present birth 3
19. Number of children of this mother now living 3

20. CERTIFICATE OF ATTENDING PHYSICIAN OR MIDWIFE.*
I hereby certify that I attended the birth of this child, who was born alive at 3 P. M., on the date above stated.
* When there was no attending physician or midwife, then the father, mother, householder, etc., shall make this return. See Sec. 12 of vital statistics law.
21. (Signature) E. S. Stewart (Physician or Midwife) M. D. Midwife
22. Give name added from a supplemental report, 19
Address 6116 Rhodes Av. Telephone 7153
23. Filed April 12, 1918 M. O. Heckard Registrar

Sample birth certificate, Cook County, Illinois, on FamilySearch.org

Collect Documentation

Start collecting "proof" or documentation of your life in your own home. This might be in the form of:

- a birth certificate
- newspaper clippings
- military documents
- birth certificates for your children
- death certificates for immediate family members
- marriage certificates

As you're looking for documentation about yourself, also look for documentation that provides information about your parents, grandparents, and more distant generations. In addition to the records listed above, look for:

- journals and letters
- family Bibles that list births, deaths, and weddings
- deeds and wills
- awards
- photographs

INTERVIEW THE RELATIVES

Now that you've collected evidence sitting around your house, it's time to interview your relatives. Begin with the oldest and work your way down to the youngest.

Your oldest relative probably remembers tidbits of family lore that no one else knows. These memories can be a tremendous aid in helping with your research—or they may just be scattered bits of trivia like, "This is where your grandfather always bought gas," or "Your grandma's favorite meal was biscuits and gravy." If the latter, save the tidbits for your family history book or scrapbook.

Thanks to computers, it's easy to interview relatives by e-mail. Or, if they don't have e-mail, you can interview them by phone or in person. If possible, capture the oral interview on a digital recorder. Not only will the recording be a helpful resource as your research moves forward, but it also makes for a great family memento.

During the interview process you may hear some fantastic tales like, "The family came over on the *Mayflower.*" For now, the stories are just that—stories until proven. However, family lore often has some basis in fact, although the facts have probably been embellished over time.

For example, your family story may be that you're descended from George Pickett, of the famed Pickett's Charge. This may be true, but it's also possible your ancestor served under Pickett during the Civil War or was a fellow cadet at West Point. Bottom line: there's probably a Pickett connection, but not as a direct descendant.

When interviewing, keep in mind that an elderly relative may not be able to sit and talk for more than an hour at a time.

Before your interview, take time to prepare your questions and your plan of action:

- Have a goal—know what you're trying to accomplish.
- Make a broad outline.
- Prepare questions in advance.
- Check your recording device.
- Be flexible.

If you know the person you're interviewing well, you probably won't need to ask ice-breaker questions. However, for those relatives you don't know very well—perhaps you see them only every few years or maybe you haven't seen them since you were a child—take a little time to get reacquainted.

What can you expect from an interview? Depending on the sharpness of your interviewee's memory, you may uncover a previously unknown path of research. Or you may hear a tiny bit of a story that leads you to another clue and then another. One thing you can count on—you'll always discover more in an interview than expected, particularly from older relatives.

TIP

There are no unimportant details in an interview; one small detail you hear today may be *the* clue you need five years from now.

The key to a great interview is to be a great listener, connecting the pieces of a fascinating puzzle.

For example, if your grandfather tells you he remembers his grandfather talking about prairie fires and buffalo hunts in Kansas, you know you'll be doing some preliminary research about Kansas pioneers. In this case, your interview questions may be along these lines:

1. Do you know when the family was in Kansas?
2. Do you know how old your grandfather was at the time?
3. Where did the family move after Kansas?
4. Do you know why they moved away?
5. Do you know what year this was?
6. Did your grandfather ever mention the name of the town?
7. Did he say how long they lived in Kansas?
8. Did he mention where they lived before Kansas?

This would also be a good time to ask if there are photographs of his grandfather, what he knows about siblings or parents, and what other stories he remembers his grandfather telling.

In addition to asking for photos, ask if the relative has any documents that can help you with your research. Use the list of documents you searched for in your own house as a reference. Ask for photocopies of the records or scan them on your computer.

GedView genealogy application by David A. Knight

GENEALOGY SOFTWARE

You've done a lot of legwork so far, collecting documents in your home and from family members and conducting interviews. It's time to assemble these sources and start building your family tree.

You can record your family history research on paper and in notebooks, or you can record it on your computer using genealogy software. I recommend using a genealogy software program because it provides a built-in repository for your sources, your stories, and your interviews. Plus, as you add more people to your family tree, genealogy software will make it easier for you to track what you've discovered.

Popular software picks for the PC are:

- Ancestral Quest <ancquest.com/index.htm>
- Family Tree Maker <familytreemaker.com>
- Legacy Family Tree <legacyfamilytree.com>
- Personal Ancestral File (PAF) <www.familysearch.org/eng/paf/pafonline.asp>
- RootsMagic <rootsmagic.com>
- The Master Genealogist <whollygenes.com>

and for Mac:

- Family Tree Maker <familytreemaker.com>

- Mac Family Tree <www.syniumsoftware.com/macfamilytree>
- Reunion <www.leisterpro.com>

After you've installed your software, consider adding a genealogy application (app) to your smart phone, iPod, iPad, or other device. This way you'll always have a copy of your family tree with you, even if you don't have your notebook or computer.

Genealogy applications (apps) are available through both the iTunes <www.apple.com/iphone/features/app-store.html> and Droid <https://market.android.com> app stores.

If you want to access your genealogy from any computer with internet access, another option is to create a family tree online. You can build your online trees through sites like:

- Ancestry.com <ancestry.com>
- Genealogy.com <genealogy.com>
- Geni <geni.com>
- MyTrees.com <mytrees.com>
- TribalPages <tribalpages.com>

GETTING STARTED WITH CHARTS

There are two common forms used to document a family tree: a pedigree chart (direct lineage) and a family group sheet (family lineage).

A PEDIGREE CHART begins with one person and documents preceding generations in a direct line. This means the chart will include parents, grandparents, great-grandparents, etc. A pedigree chart does not include siblings or spouses.

For now, your pedigree chart will begin with you as the primary person, then branch back to your parents, grandparents, great-grandparents, etc. Charts vary in size, but typically include four or five generations and fit on an 8.5 × 11-inch piece of paper. There's a blank pedigree chart, labeled Five-Generation Ancestor Chart, in appendix C.

As you progress in your research, you can use genealogy software to print wall-sized charts. Your chart will be generated on several pieces of paper that can be taped together. Or you can purchase a professionally printed chart of your entire family tree.

A FAMILY GROUP SHEET documents one family unit: husband, wife, children, and spouses of children. It has blank spaces to fill in birth, death, and marriage dates as well as place of burial. There's a blank family group sheet in appendix C.

The *pedigree chart* gives you an overall look at where an individual fits into the entire tree, and it's excellent to use as a quick reference. The *family group sheet* focuses on an individual's family. Think of the two charts as wide-angle (pedigree) and zoom lenses (family group sheet).

Tips on Filling Out Charts

When filling in names on charts (either pedigree or family group) use standard (and consistent) naming conventions:

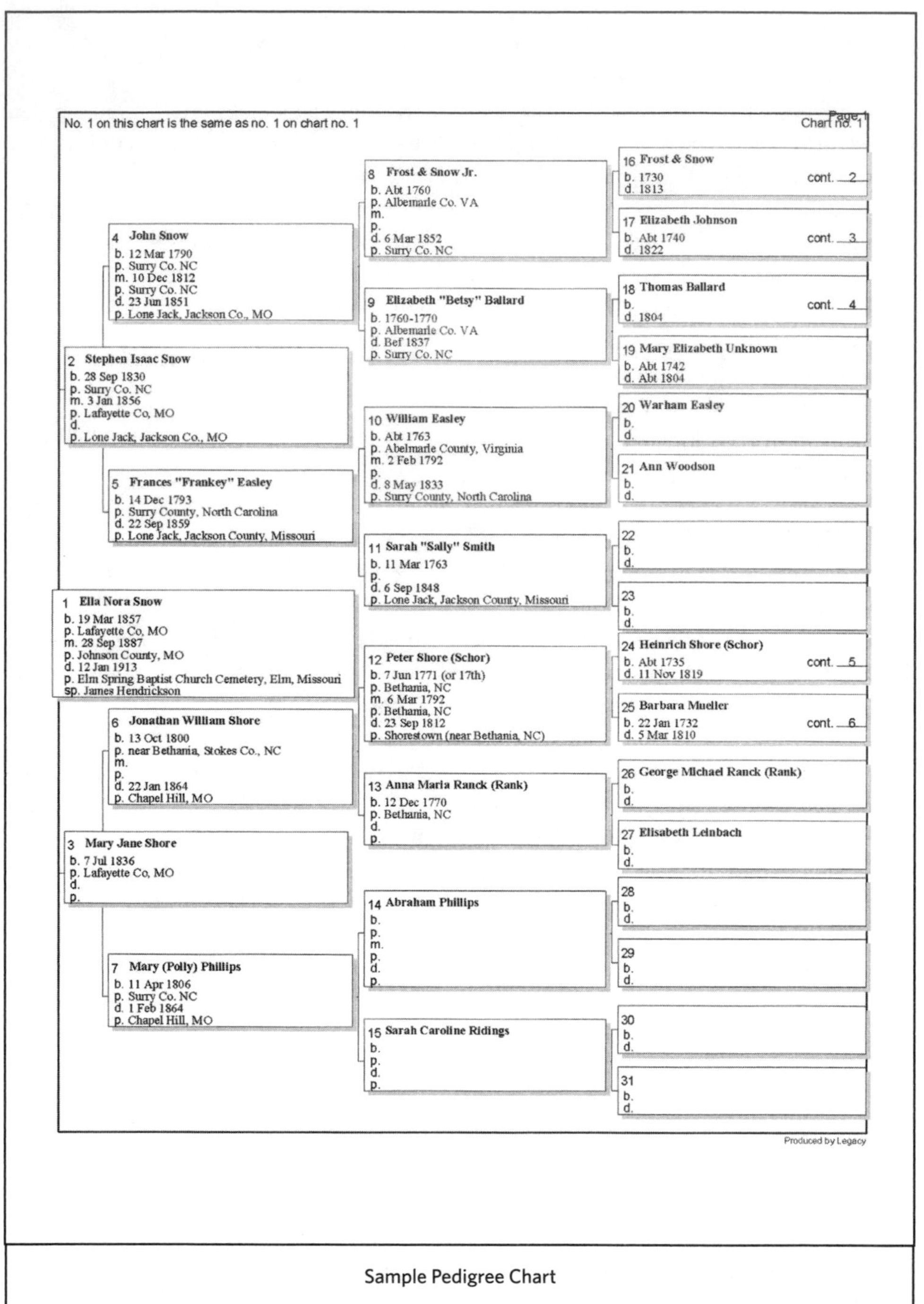

No. 1 on this chart is the same as no. 1 on chart no. 1
Page 1
Chart no. 1
16 Frost & Snow
b. 1730
d. 1813
cont. 2
8 Frost & Snow Jr.
b. Abt 1760
p. Albemarle Co. VA
m.
p.
d. 6 Mar 1852
p. Surry Co. NC
17 Elizabeth Johnson
b. Abt 1740
d. 1822
cont. 3
4 John Snow
b. 12 Mar 1790
p. Surry Co. NC
m. 10 Dec 1812
p. Surry Co. NC
d. 23 Jun 1851
p. Lone Jack, Jackson Co., MO
18 Thomas Ballard
b.
d. 1804
cont. 4
9 Elizabeth "Betsy" Ballard
b. 1760-1770
p. Albemarle Co. VA
d. Bef 1837
p. Surry Co. NC
19 Mary Elizabeth Unknown
b. Abt 1742
d. Abt 1804
2 Stephen Isaac Snow
b. 28 Sep 1830
p. Surry Co. NC
m. 3 Jan 1856
p. Lafayette Co, MO
d.
p. Lone Jack, Jackson Co., MO
20 Warham Easley
b.
d.
10 William Easley
b. Abt 1763
p. Abelmarle County, Virginia
m. 2 Feb 1792
p.
d. 8 May 1833
p. Surry County, North Carolina
21 Ann Woodson
b.
d.
5 Frances "Frankey" Easley
b. 14 Dec 1793
p. Surry County, North Carolina
d. 22 Sep 1859
p. Lone Jack, Jackson County, Missouri
22
b.
d.
11 Sarah "Sally" Smith
b. 11 Mar 1763
p.
d. 6 Sep 1848
p. Lone Jack, Jackson County, Missouri
23
b.
d.
1 Ella Nora Snow
b. 19 Mar 1857
p. Lafayette Co, MO
m. 28 Sep 1887
p. Johnson County, MO
d. 12 Jan 1913
p. Elm Spring Baptist Church Cemetery, Elm, Missouri
sp. James Hendrickson
24 Heinrich Shore (Schor)
b. Abt 1735
d. 11 Nov 1819
cont. 5
12 Peter Shore (Schor)
b. 7 Jun 1771 (or 17th)
p. Bethania, NC
m. 6 Mar 1792
p. Bethania, NC
d. 23 Sep 1812
p. Shorestown (near Bethania, NC)
25 Barbara Mueller
b. 22 Jan 1732
d. 5 Mar 1810
cont. 6
6 Jonathan William Shore
b. 13 Oct 1800
p. near Bethania, Stokes Co., NC
m.
p.
d. 22 Jan 1864
p. Chapel Hill, MO
26 George Michael Ranck (Rank)
b.
d.
13 Anna Maria Ranck (Rank)
b. 12 Dec 1770
p. Bethania, NC
d.
p.
27 Elisabeth Leinbach
b.
d.
3 Mary Jane Shore
b. 7 Jul 1836
p. Lafayette Co, MO
d.
p.
28
b.
d.
14 Abraham Phillips
b.
p.
m.
p.
d.
p.
29
b.
d.
7 Mary (Polly) Phillips
b. 11 Apr 1806
p. Surry Co. NC
d. 1 Feb 1864
p. Chapel Hill, MO
30
b.
d.
15 Sarah Caroline Ridings
b.
p.
d.
p.
31
b.
d.
Produced by Legacy

Sample Pedigree Chart

Family Group Record for John Snow

Page 1

Husband	John Snow			LDS Ordinance Data
Born	12 Mar 1790	Surry Co. NC	B	
Christened			E	
Died	23 Jun 1851	Lone Jack, Jackson Co., MO		
Cause of Death	Cholera			
Buried		Lone Jack Cemetery, Lone Jack, MO		
Father	Frost & Snow Jr. (Abt 1760-1852)		SP	
Mother	Elizabeth "Betsy" Ballard (1760/1770-Bef 1837)			
Marriage	10 Dec 1812	Surry Co. NC	SS	
Wife	**Frances "Frankey" Easley**			
Born	14 Dec 1793	Surry County, North Carolina	B	
Christened			E	
Died	22 Sep 1859	Lone Jack, Jackson County, Missouri		
Buried		Lone Jack Cemetery, Lone Jack, MO		
Father	William Easley (Abt 1763-1833)	Mother: Sarah "Sally" Smith (1763-1848)	SP	
Father	William Easley (Abt 1763-1833)	Mother: Sarah "Sally" Smith (1763-1848)	SP	
Children				
1 F	**Jane Snow**			
Born	Abt 1814	Surry Co. NC	B	
Christened			E	
Died			SP	
Buried				
Spouse			SS	
2 F	**Matilda Snow**			
Born	13 Apr 1818	Surry Co. NC	B	
Christened			E	
Died	20 Apr 1870	Lone Jack, Jackson Co., MO	SP	
Buried		Lone Jack Cemetery, Lone Jack, MO		
Spouse	James G. Golding (-)		SS	
3 F	**Mary T. "Polly" Snow**			
Born	27 Jan 1820	Surry Co. NC	B	
Christened			E	
Died	5 Jul 1912	Winchester, Jefferson Co. KS	SP	
Buried		Hull Grove Cemetery, Jefferson Co. KS		
Spouse	Joshua Bays (1802-1875)	24 Aug 1843	SS	
4 M	**Henry Snow**			
Born	Abt 1820	Surry County, North Carolina	B	
Christened			E	
Died			SP	
Buried				
Spouse			SS	

Produced by Legacy

Sample Family Group Sheet

Input Format

Date Input is: (must be same as computer's date setting)

- (•) month-day-year — 4-5-1853 is considered April 5, 1853
- ( ) day-month-year — 4-5-1853 is considered 4 May 1853
- ( ) year-month-day — 1853-4-5 is considered April 5, 1853

Setting date preference, Legacy Family Tree software

- If the surname spelling has changed over time, record names with the earliest spelling first, the most current last (e.g., Breyhel/Breuel/Broyles).
- Use a woman's maiden name, not her married name.
- If you use all caps for one surname (e.g., HENDRICKSON), be sure to capitalize all surnames.
- Use quotation marks around nicknames (e.g., "Scooter").
- If a woman was married more than once, record her maiden name in parenthesis, followed by married surnames in order of her marriages: Marjorie Grace (Sadler) Hendrickson Dunn.

If you're using genealogy software, some of the naming conventions will be done for you or will be among the program's options. Be aware that the method you use to enter names is how the names will appear when you run reports. If you don't want the report to read something like *John SNOW married Frances EASLEY,* don't capitalize surnames.

Check your program's Options to set your date preference. Dates can be another bugaboo for genealogists. The notation of month/day/year is standard in the United States but not elsewhere. If you're adding dates to a chart by hand, be sure you use a consistent date format.

DOCUMENTING WHAT YOU ALREADY KNOW

Using genealogy software or the blank forms at Family Tree Magazine <familytreemagazine.com/FreeForms>, fill out a pedigree chart using the sources you found in your house and in the interviews you conducted.

Start with you as person number one, your father as person number two, your mother as person number three. As you move up the chart (backward in time), this same numbering convention is used, i.e., each person's father is double his own number and his mother is double his number plus one. You can see this numbering on the image of Ella Snow's pedigree chart in this chapter.

At this point, you may not be able to prove anything on the chart; understand that this is just a starting point.

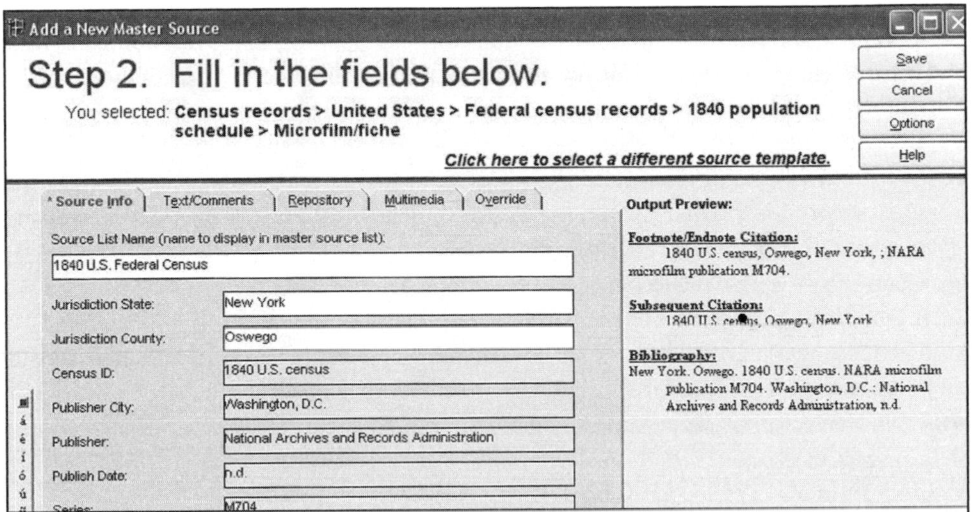

Add a New Master Source

Step 2. Fill in the fields below.

You selected: **Census records > United States > Federal census records > 1840 population schedule > Microfilm/fiche**

Click here to select a different source template.

Save
Cancel
Options
Help

Source Info | Text/Comments | Repository | Multimedia | Override

Source List Name (name to display in master source list): 1840 U.S. Federal Census

Jurisdiction State: New York

Jurisdiction County: Oswego

Census ID: 1840 U.S. census

Publisher City: Washington, D.C.

Publisher: National Archives and Records Administration

Publish Date: n.d.

Series: M704

Output Preview:

Footnote/Endnote Citation:
1840 U.S. census, Oswego, New York, ; NARA microfilm publication M704.

Subsequent Citation:
1840 U.S. census, Oswego, New York

Bibliography:
New York. Oswego. 1840 U.S. census. NARA microfilm publication M704. Washington, D.C.: National Archives and Records Administration, n.d.

Adding a master source to Legacy Family Tree software

As you fill out the chart, you'll quickly notice the gaps; there may be missing generations, unknown maiden names, and no dates or places. Anything you don't know can be a jumping-off place for future research.

CITING SOURCES

Because genealogy is about proving the link between generations, you need to have sources that back up your claims. What are *sources*? They are the "who told me this" or "where I found it" part of genealogy research.

Keep track of sources by properly citing them. (It's not much different from the way you cited sources for research papers you wrote in school.) Like names and dates, your source citations should be consistent and standardized.

As you find each piece of source material (documents, images, certificates, licenses, etc.), enter it into your software or notebook. Many of the genealogy programs use a source "wizard" to walk you through citing sources.

Source wizards already contain templates about most types of source material, including:

- personal blogs
- commercial databases
- websites
- e-mails
- newsletters

If you use the wizard, your sources will always be documented consistently. If your software doesn't have a wizard, or you're documenting your research in a notebook, you'll find information on citing source material at these free sites:

- World Wide Words <www.worldwidewords.org/articles/citation.htm>
- ProGenealogists Citation Guide <www.progenealogists.com/citations.htm>
- Document Your Genealogy on the Polish Genealogical Society of America website <www.pgsa.org/Research/citationArticle.php>
- EasyBib <www.easybib.com>

A sample citation of the 1880 census found online at FamilySearch.org would read:

The Church of Jesus Christ of Latter-day Saints, comp., "1880 United States Census and National Index," FamilySearch (Online: Intellectual Reserve, Inc., 2009), <http://www.familysearch.org/>, accessed 18 January 2012.

WORKING WITH SOURCES

Types of sources you may find are:

A TRANSCRIPT. This is an exact copy of an original document. The transcriber typed it as is, with misspellings, punctuation errors, and all. Places where you may find transcriptions online are census, birth, marriage, and cemetery records.

AN ABSTRACT. This is a summary of an original document. For example, an abstract of a will may include the names and dates and the important facts, but not the entire will.

AN EXTRACT. This is a hybrid version of a transcript and an abstract. It doesn't contain the entire document, nor is it a summary. It's simply an exact copy of a portion of an original document.

AN ORAL HISTORY. This is an audio recording of an interview.

A DIARY OR LETTERS. This is a written account of specific events in an individual's life or remembrance of past events. This may be the entire document or an excerpt.

Evaluating Accuracy and Authenticity

As you add sources based on your research, you're not only noting where the source came from, you're evaluating the source's accuracy and authenticity.

Evaluating information is an integral part of genealogy. How do you know if what you've found is 100 percent correct, 50 percent correct, just a little correct, or completely incorrect?

As you research, one way to evaluate the accuracy of a document is to determine if it's a primary or a secondary source.

A PRIMARY SOURCE is a document created in the time period you're researching and is a first-hand account of what happened. Examples of this are a marriage document signed by the clergyman who performed the ceremony, or a letter or diary written about contemporary events.

A SECONDARY SOURCE is one created after the event and by a person not directly involved in the event. For example, a history book about the Revolutionary War is an interpretation of past events, and as such is a secondary source. Secondary sources are those created after the event happened.

Tombstone that has deteriorated over time

Just to start thinking about evaluating sources, how would you rate the accuracy of the following sources:

1. Transcript of the 1850 federal census
2. Microfilm of the 1850 federal census
3. Your aunt's recollection of your brother's birth
4. Online family tree without sources
5. County history book written fifty to one hundred years after the death of the people about whom biographies were written
6. Book with transcripts of cemetery tombstone inscriptions
7. Information on a death certificate

Which of these seven sources do you think are most accurate? Would you be surprised if I told you that none of them could be considered 100 percent accurate? Here's why:

1. The transcriptionist could have made a mistake, by either misreading a name or transposing numbers or letters.
2. The census taker could have made a mistake, or the informant could have given false information.
3. Your aunt (particularly if she is elderly) could be confusing one brother with another.
4. A family tree without sources may provide clues, but there is no guarantee of accuracy.
5. A book written about people who died fifty to one hundred years before publication relies on secondary information; that is, information recorded or obtained either secondhand or a very long time after an event. Memory falters.
6. Tombstone inscriptions (particularly old ones like the one pictured) can easily be misread.
7. The person giving the information for the death certificate may have been a close family member of the decedent and so upset that she didn't accurately remember dates and places.

So if none of these sources are 100 percent accurate, what's a person to do?

• For starters, be aware that, as a family tree researcher, you're going to constantly evaluate material for accuracy and, in some cases, degrees of accuracy. Some of the information in a document may be correct, some suspect.

• Next, you can't walk the road with the census taker double-checking his work, but you can try to corroborate his information with other sources like birth and marriage records, newspaper articles, or other official records.

• Don't assume something is accurate just because it's in print or on the web. A vital records book, for example, listed the surname on a tombstone as *Frankenberry*. The name on the stone was *Faulkenberry* and it was easily readable. Either the stone was misread, or the transcriptionist made an error when transcribing notes.

If you're using genealogy software, it may even give you the opportunity to apply a "quality" or "surety" rating to the data.

As you find information online, it's important to accurately transcribe what you've found. For example, if you find a census record online and you're transcribing it into your software or notes, transcribe it exactly as it's written, mistakes and all.

If you know there's a mistake in the material (like a stepmother being listed as a mother), add your own notes in brackets [like this]. This denotes the material was not in the original source and is a note you added.

As you can see, the question of accuracy and authenticity is critical. That's one reason why it's important for you to thoroughly document your research. Secondarily, well-documented sources make it easier for other researchers to take up the search where you might have left off.

WHAT TO RESEARCH?

After you've completed your interview(s), you should have quite a collection of data filled in on your pedigree chart and family group sheet. Armed with names, dates, places, and family tales, you can now decide what to research first.

If you're new to genealogy, you may be wondering how to make this decision. Take the new information and add it to your pedigree chart and/or family group sheets. The information is still not proven, but enter it into your software or handwrite it—and be sure to note the source.

Begin by looking back over your pedigree chart. Your options for research include:

- the best-known branch
- your current surname branch
- the branch with the most missing pieces
- the branch you think contains the most records
- the branch someone else in the family is working on
- the branch you learned more about during an interview

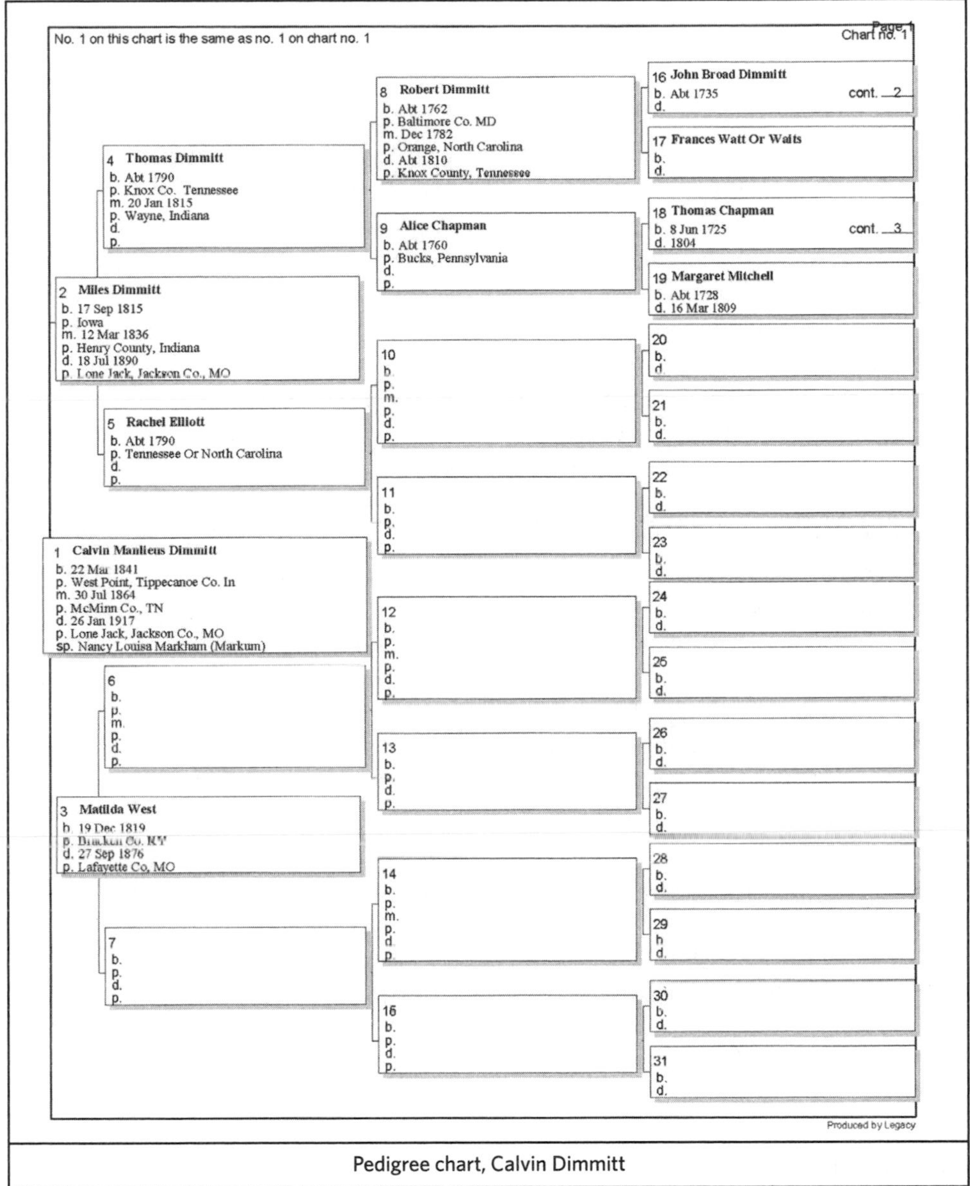

Pedigree chart, Calvin Dimmitt

- the branch that interests you the most
- the branch you think might hold a Revolutionary or Civil War ancestor

Using Calvin Dimmitt's pedigree chart as an example, where would you begin? Questions to ask:

1. If Calvin Dimmitt was born in 1841, he would have been twenty years old at the outbreak of the Civil War. It's possible you'll find him in Civil War records and possibly find his wife in Civil War pension files. Learn how to search for military files in chapter ten.

2. If you pick Matilda West (Calvin's mother), you're facing a challenge. Nothing is known about Matilda's parents. You do have a birth date and place, but nothing more. Maybe something could be found about her if you could find her marriage certificate. Learn how to search for vital records in chapter 5.
3. If you pick the Dimmitt line, you know they were in Baltimore. It's possible you'll find immigration records because Baltimore was a port of entry. Learn how to search for immigration records in chapter 12
4. If you pick the Chapman line (Bucks County, Pennsylvania) it's possible you'll find them in Quaker records because Bucks County had a large Quaker population. Learn how to search for local records in chapter 11.

As you can see, there's a lot to consider when embarking on a research project. Whichever line in your own family tree you choose to research, use the information from the papers you've found in your home, the interviews, and the family stories, and add to your pedigree chart.

Remember: Regardless of which branch you begin researching, start with yourself and work backward. That means you are number one on a pedigree chart, and you are the first person added to either your software or an online tree-building site.

Your goal now is to begin proving the link from you to your parents, then continue to document each generation back. This book will help you identify sources of evidence and show you where and how to find these sources.

TAME THE PAPER TIGER (BEFORE IT EATS YOU FOR BREAKFAST)

If you've been following along in this chapter, here's where you stand so far:

1. You filled in a pedigree chart with what you know.
2. You've interviewed family.
3. You've picked a branch to research.

Time to start actually researching? Almost. First, a word about organizing your research papers. Although you're probably using genealogy software, paper *will* accumulate. For some people, *piles* of paper, for others just a little. Because you're just starting out, now is the time to decide on an organizational system.

An easy way to begin—and one most natural to researchers—is to organize by surname. Either make a file folder or a three-ring binder for each surname, then adopt the habit of filing paper as it arrives—not when it's part of a foot-deep mess on your desk.

Over time, you may run out of space in the folder. At that point you may want subfolders, divided into categories like military, marriages, deaths, etc.

If you've been doing genealogy for a long time, you probably have a filing system (or not!). There are many ways to organize genealogy files, many of which are covered in

Family Tree University's Organize Your Genealogy online course <familytreeuniversity.com>.

Taking time to organize may seem like a waste or paper overkill, but data, documents, images, certificates, and newspaper clippings all add up fast. Ask anyone who's been doing genealogy for a few years, and I'm sure they'll show you the stacks and stacks of paper that has accumulated! In a few months, when your papers are piling up, you'll be glad you started off with a workable organizational system.

TRACK YOUR RESEARCH

If you wanted to, you could jump onto the internet right now, type a name into Google, and see where it takes you. Or you could have a research goal and a plan of action. Earlier in this chapter, you picked a family line to research. Now, looking at your pedigree chart, what information is missing? What's your research goal?

- a place of birth
- a date of death
- a maiden name
- a marriage date
- immigrant ancestor's homeland

Using one of the research forms at Family Tree Magazine <www.familytreemagazine.com/article/ResearchForms> or one you create yourself in Excel, list your goal(s) and then your progress.

Most research logs include the following categories:

- goal—what you want to find or prove

	A	B	C	D	E
1	GOAL	IDEA	SITE	DATE	RESULTS
2	Matilda West parents	Matilda birth record	Kentucky vital records	1/14/2012	Death records only available on this site
3		Matilda marriage record	FamilySearch.org	1/14/2012	Found marriage record, no mention of Matilda's parents, but have microfilm number to order to see original record
4		Any "West" marriage record in Bracken Co, KY in early 1800s	FamilySearch.org	1/14/2012	Dates of marriages were too late to be Matilda's parents
5		Bracken Co. History	Google Books	1/14/2012	Too many instances of "west" as a direction; without first name almost impossible
6		Bracken Co. History	Abebooks.com		
7		Bracken Co. Will	USGenWeb		
8		Was there a Dimmitt in Bracken County?	USGenWeb		
		Were Matilda's parents in Henry Co. Indiana where she and her husband	USGenWeb		

Sample research log

- idea—sources that provide the information you seek
- site—websites you searched (or will search) for sources
- date—when you researched the site
- results

Right now, you may only be able to fill in the Goal and Idea categories, but not websites. Don't worry about it. As you learn about and explore sites in this book, you'll be adding a lot of them to your research form, including:

- free data sites
- commercial sites
- forums
- message boards
- personal blogs and websites
- government sites

Why track the date of your search? Good genealogy websites are constantly adding new information; data that wasn't on a site during your search today may be there a few months from now.

After you've searched a site, add a future date to your calendar, reminding yourself to search the website again. Right about now, you may be shaking your head and thinking, *more paper to deal with*!

True, keeping a research log may seem like a waste of time now. But in reality, it will save you time. And you can always use an Excel document instead of a piece of paper. While you do want to go back and check for new data, you don't want to search through the same data more than once. For example, let's say you searched for your family in the 1860 Cheshire County, New Hampshire, census, but they weren't there. Without documenting this search, what are the odds that two years from now you'll remember that you searched this particular census? Probably low. But a research log will remind you that the census was searched and the family had already moved on.

START A "CLIP FILE"

A clip file is a compilation of "like" things. For writers, it may be a collection of great headlines; for genealogists, a collection of great websites. As you research, you'll begin to find valuable state and local resources that you'll want to add to your clip file. Basically, you'll begin creating a list of the best websites pertinent to the places your ancestors lived. Once you find these sites, they'll become a permanent part of your online arsenal.

Examples of valuable state resources:

- The Handbook of Texas Online <www.tshaonline.org/handbook/online>
- Kentucky Vital Records Project <kyvitals.com>
- Illinois Statewide Marriage Index, 1763-1900 <www.cyberdriveillinois.com/departments/archives/marriage.html>

- New Hampshire Land Surveyor Records <www.sos.nh.gov/archives/archival.html>
- Historic Maps of Delaware <archives.delaware.gov/exhibits/misc/index.shtml>

Where can you find valuable state and local resources?

1. Use a search engine and type in a phrase like: *connecticut genealogy* or *connecticut genealogy records online*.
2. Go to Cyndi's List <cyndislist.com>, a compilation of thousands of genealogy resources. Find your state of interest and follow the list of resources.
3. Go to the website for a state's historical society and genealogical society, e.g., Georgia Historical Society <http://www.georgiahistory.com> or Minnesota Genealogical Society <http://mngs.org>. Not only is it possible to find records on these sites, you'll also discover:

- event announcements
- special exhibits
- link to archives
- photos
- classes
- publications

In addition, some facilities have staff available to do brief lookups for a small fee.

4. Archives:

- photos and images <www.usa.gov/Topics/Graphics.shtml>
- documents <www.archive.org/details/USGovernmentDocuments>
- National Archives classes <www.archives.gov/research/genealogy/events>
- National Historic Landmarks (Was your ancestor involved at events at any of these historic sites?) <www.nps.gov/history/nhl/designations/listsofNHLs.htm>
- USGenWeb <usgenweb.com> More on this site in chapter four, but for now it's enough to say that this is *the* place to collect local and state websites.

HAS SOMEONE ELSE ALREADY DONE THE RESEARCH?

Before you launch into a major research project, take some time to see if someone else has already researched your family line. Thousands of family histories have been published; some you'll find in a local library, others in FamilySearch Centers (FSCs) or the Family History Library (FHL) in Salt Lake City. Even though these histories were produced as printed books, the contents of many have been digitized and a may be available online.

The FHL is owned and operated by the Church of Jesus Christ of Latter-day Saints. The FHL's collections include more than 2.4 million rolls of microfilmed genealogical records, 356,000 books, and more than three thousand electronic resources.

FamilySearch Centers are the 4,500 regional arms of the FHL and are located across the globe. Each FamilySearch Center has its own genealogical collections, both digital and book formats. Patrons of a FamilySearch Center may order microfilms from the FHL for a nominal fee.

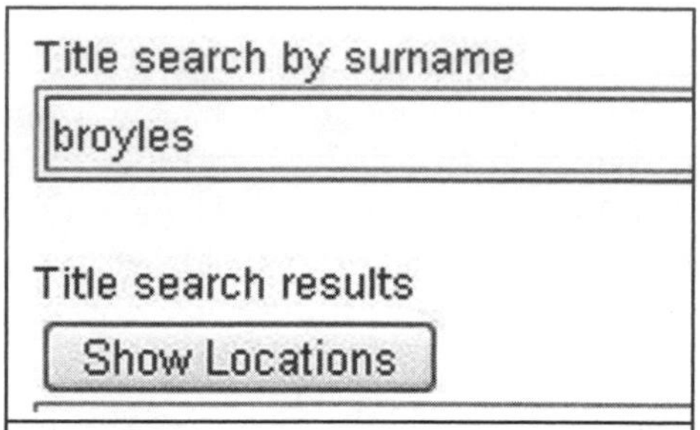

A good place to begin your search is the Family History Library catalog <www.familysearch.org/Search/searchcatalog.asp>. After you've done a surname search, click the Show Locations button to get a list of all of the FSCs that have your book, as well as whether it's available online as part of the Family History Archives <www.lib.byu.edu/fhc>.

Title search by surname
broyles
Title search results
Show Locations

Surname search, Family History Library catalog

You can also click the name of any book to see if it's available on microfilm or microfiche. If the book is on film, you'll see a View Film Notes button in the top right corner of the screen; click this to get the film number, then order it at an FSC.

The subscription site Genealogy.com <genealogy.com> also has an extensive collection of family histories. For a monthly or annual fee, you can search 7.5 million pages from genealogy journals, local histories, and primary sources. In total, this site has sixteen thousand titles from the United States, the British Isles, and Canada.

Ancestry.com <ancestry.com>, another subscription site, lets you search the Periodical Source Index (PERSI), the largest subject index on genealogy and local history periodicals written from 1800 to the present. There are currently more than 1.7 million searchable records in PERSI.

Keep in mind that PERSI is an index of articles, not the article itself. Once you find an article of interest, you can order it online from the Allen County (Indiana) Public Library <www.acpl.lib.in.us/database/graphics/order_form.html>.

Patrons of the Allen County Public Library may search the PERSI database online; others can access the PERSI database through a local library with a subscription to HeritageQuest Online.

Another excellent online source for local history books is Google Books <books.google.com>. Google has digitized millions of books, some of which can be downloaded for free. Most of the digitized books show the table of contents and brief excerpts. If you find a book here that isn't viewable online, check with your local library to see if it's available via interlibrary loan.

You can also search the online catalog at the Library of Congress (LOC) website <catalog.loc.gov>. If the LOC has a book you want, check with your local library to see if it's available through the interlibrary system.

When searching for a family history, it's possible you won't find an entire history about your family, but it is possible that your family will be included as an allied family in another book.

REACHING OUT TO FELLOW RESEARCHERS

At this point, you may be thinking that researching your genealogy is an impossible task. It's not, partly because you won't have to do all the work yourself. In fact, it's likely that someone else has already started researching your family tree. That means you can share files, exchange old photos, and even split up research tasks.

If you've ever been to a genealogy library, you've seen the family history books written by people just like you. These books document a single family (or allied families) through a specific period of time.

Allied families are those who maintained a close connection throughout a lengthy period of time or in a specific locale. For example, the Wilhite and Broyles family both immigrated to America in 1717 from Germany. Over time, they intermarried and traveled together to Tennessee and finally to Missouri. Names of allied family members can often be found as witnesses on wills, on land transactions, in court cases, and in probate files.

Being online is kind of like being in a genealogy library, but instead of being surrounded by family history books, you'll be surrounded by a lot of family history researchers—many of whom are researching your family. The odds of meeting them are better than good.

If this seems impossible, consider this: The number of your direct ancestors (parents, grandparents, etc.) doubles with each generation. By the time you go back ten generations, you'll have 1,024 direct ancestors. Assuming that your 1,024 ancestors had children, think of the number of people today who could be searching for your family. Chances are there's a seventh or eighth cousin out there who would like to find you!

In chapter thirteen you'll learn the best online sites to find genealogy cousins and how to leverage the power of networking. For now though, just be aware that research about your family probably exists somewhere online—it's just a matter of finding it.

YOUR RECORDS CHECKLIST

For the most part you'll be searching for census and vital statistic records (birth, marriage, death), but there are a lot of other types of records to search.

Just so you won't forget to check other, less obvious sources, we've created a Records Checklist for you to use. The checklist is a compilation of record types ranging from World War I draft cards to school report cards and voter registrations.

Make as many copies of the Records Checklist as you'd like, and use one for each person you're researching.

Computer Basics for the Online Genealogist

With each passing year, more genealogy data comes online. Although commercial sites like Ancestry.com, Fold3.com, and Archives.com provide millions of documents for subscribers, smaller personal, county, or state websites are adding data at an astonishing rate.

WHAT'S ONLINE, WHAT'S NOT

In Illinois, you can search a database of the state's Civil War veterans; for those with Texas ancestry, there's a searchable site of people owed monetary or other kinds of restitution from the Republic of Texas. Or your Massachusetts kinfolk might be listed in the Archives Collection that dates back to 1629.

Personal sites (including blogs) may contain data, documents, images, or family stories of the people in one of your surname lines. In chapter three you'll learn how to become an expert searcher, tracking down these personal sites with ease.

Despite the diversity and depth of information found online, you still can't find everything there . . . yet. Why? Because "everything" hasn't been posted online. As you become more experienced with family history research and your search moves further back in history, you'll begin searching for more advanced records, including land records, wills, and probate records because physical belongings and land holdings have been much better documented over time than some other types of records. In your search, you may find an index to wills or an abstract of a will online, but it's rare to find a scan or complete transcript of the will itself. The same holds true for probate files. If you've ever burrowed through a dusty courthouse attic, pulling out handfuls of loose, crumbling papers from a probate file, you'll understand the difficulty of getting these types of records online.

It takes a lot of work to turn a pile of old records into an online database. Transcribing and uploading documents often falls to volunteers. Over the years, Phyllis Fleming, for example, has worked to save old records stored in the Shelby County, Indiana, courthouse. You can see the fruits of her labor at the Shelby County site on USGenWeb.com <www.shelbycountyindiana.org>.

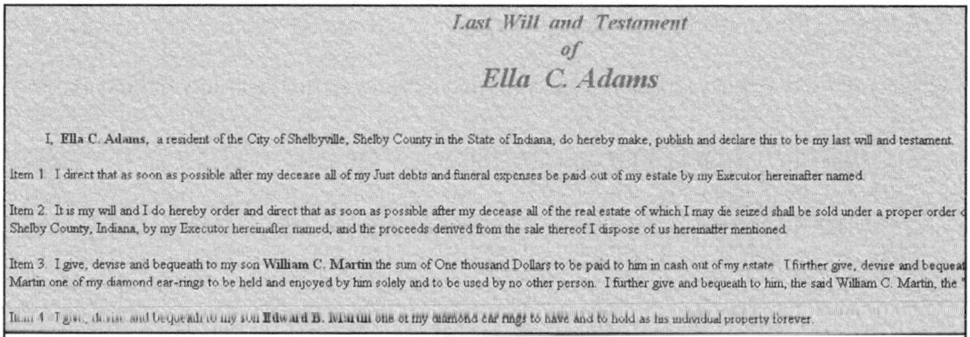

Last Will and Testament
of
Ella C. Adams

I, **Ella C. Adams**, a resident of the City of Shelbyville, Shelby County in the State of Indiana, do hereby make, publish and declare this to be my last will and testament.

Item 1. I direct that as soon as possible after my decease all of my Just debts and funeral expenses be paid out of my estate by my Executor hereinafter named.

Item 2. It is my will and I do hereby order and direct that as soon as possible after my decease all of the real estate of which I may die seized shall be sold under a proper order o
Shelby County, Indiana, by my Executor hereinafter named, and the proceeds derived from the sale thereof I dispose of us hereinafter mentioned.

Item 3. I give, devise and bequeath to my son **William C. Martin** the sum of One thousand Dollars to be paid to him in cash out of my estate. I further give, devise and bequea
Martin one of my diamond ear-rings to be held and enjoyed by him solely and to be used by no other person. I further give and bequeath to him, the said William C. Martin, the

Item 4. I give, devise and bequeath to my son **Edward B. Martin** one of my diamond ear rings to have and to hold as his individual property forever.

Sample will, USGenWeb, Shelby County, Indiana

Because you can't find everything online, at some point in your research, you'll have to turn to books, microfilms, county courthouses, and other researchers to complete your work. But until you reach that time, there's still plenty for you to find online.

Computer-based research makes it easier to save, download, and organize your data. But to take advantage of this, you'll need some basic computer skills. This chapter is designed to help you with the essentials.

FIRST, A FEW TERMINOLOGY BASICS

- **BROWSER:** A browser is a software program that allows you to visit websites. The most common browsers are Internet Explorer, Firefox, Google Chrome, Opera, and Safari. None of these are "the internet"—they're just the software that allow you to access the internet.
- **CLOUD COMPUTING:** Cloud computing is the concept of online storage for all of your documents and files, making it easy to sync to all of your digital devices.

- **DESKTOP:** The desktop is the main background on your monitor (screen). It consists of a background picture or "wallpaper," any program shortcuts you have created, and the taskbar.

Windows desktop

- **DIRECTORY:** Also known as a folder, a directory is a collection of files. Directories can contain subdirectories. For example, "My Documents" is a directory and "My Pictures" is a subdirectory of "My Documents."
- **HARDWARE:** The hardware is the physical part of the computer.
- **PROCESSOR:** The processor is the part of the computer that runs the programs.
- **SEARCH ENGINE:** A search engine is an online service that finds and indexes web pages, then returns the most relevant results based on your search query.
- **SOFTWARE:** Software is the nonphysical part of the computer (your programs).
- **TASKBAR:** The taskbar runs along the bottom of the screen, or you can move it to the side or the top by clicking-and-dragging. You can access the Start menu from the taskbar and add program shortcuts so a single click will open a program.

KEYBOARD SHORTCUTS

Windows users can do specific tasks using either menus or keyboard shortcuts. For example, if you highlight a word and right-click, you have the option to "copy" that word. Instead of using the right-click option, you can also copy the highlighted word by pressing Control-C on your keyboard (CTRL-C).

The most commonly used keyboard shortcuts on PCs:

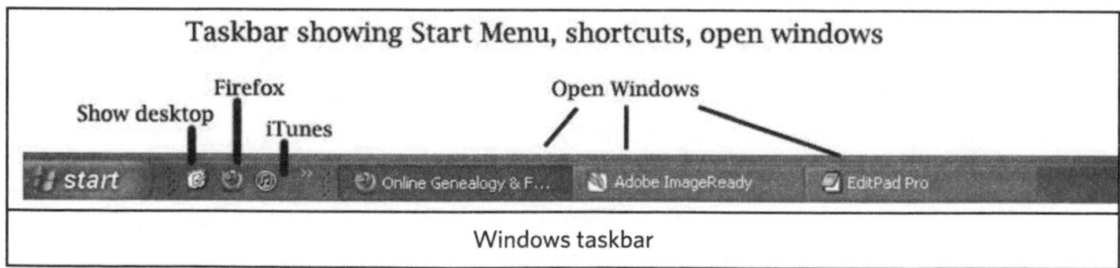

Windows taskbar

- **WINDOWS KEY** = Used to access the Start menu, the Windows key is usually found on the bottom row of the keyboard, between CTRL and ALT (Control and ALT) and has the Windows logo.
- **WINDOWS KEY + F** = Opens the Search window
- **WINDOWS KEY + F1** = Opens the Help and Support Center

The Windows key

- **WINDOWS KEY + E** = Opens Windows Explorer
- **WINDOWS KEY + TAB** = Moves through open windows on the taskbar
- **CTRL + ESC** = Opens the Start menu
- **CTRL + C** = Copy
- **CTRL + X** = Cut
- **CTRL + V** = Paste
- **CTRL + A** = Select All
- **CTRL + Z** = Undo
- **CTRL + B** = Bold highlighted text
- **CTRL + U** = Underline highlighted text
- **CTRL + I** = Italicize highlighted text
- **CTRL + PLUS KEY (+)** = Increases the text size in your browser
- **CTRL + MINUS KEY (-)** = Decreases the text size in your browser
- **CTRL + ALT + DELETE** = Opens Task Manager
- **ALT + F4** = Closes the current window or program
- **ALT + TAB** = Switches between open windows or programs
- **BACKSPACE** = Moves up one folder level
- **HOME** = Go to the start of current line or web page
- **END** = Go to the end of current line or web page
- **F1** = In Microsoft Word opens Help window
- **F2** = Rename selected item
- **F5** = Refresh current window or web page
- **F5** = In Microsoft Word opens Find/Replace window
- **F6** = Move through window panes
- **F8** = In Microsoft Word, used to spell check

Many of the shortcuts for Macs are similar to the shortcuts for PCs. Instead of using the Windows key, use the Command key. Common keyboard shortcuts for Macs are:

- **COMMAND + SHIFT + ?** = Opens Mac Help
- **COMMAND + SPACE** = Opens Spotlight Search
- **OPTION + SHIFT + COMMAND + ESC (HOLD FOR THREE SECONDS)** = Force quit
- **COMMAND + A** = Select all

- **COMMAND + S** = Save
- **COMMAND + C** = Copy
- **COMMAND + X** = Cut
- **COMMAND + V** = Paste
- **COMMAND + D** = Duplicate
- **COMMAND + B** = Bold highlighted text
- **COMMAND + U** = Underline highlighted text
- **COMMAND + I** = Italicize highlighted text
- **COMMAND + E** = Eject
- **COMMAND + K** = Connect to server
- **COMMAND + M** = Minimize window
- **OPTION + COMMAND + M** = Minimize all windows
- **COMMAND + N** = New Finder window
- **COMMAND + O** = Open selected item
- **SHIFT + COMMAND + T** = Add to Favorites
- **COMMAND + Z** = Undo/Redo

NAVIGATING THE WEB

To go from one website to another, type the URL (Uniform Resource Locator—or more commonly known as the website address) into the address bar that runs across the top of your browser.

URLs begin with either *http://* or *https://*. The former is a nonsecure site and is the most common on the internet; the latter indicates a secure ("s") site and is seen when you're using a credit card, logging into your bank, or doing any other kind of financial transaction. After the *http://www.* part, you'll see something like this: familytreemagazine .com/article/Seeking-Rescued-Slaves-1. Here's how URLs are constructed:

- *familytreemagazine.com* is the name of the **domain**
- *article* is the name of a **directory** on the domain
- *Seeking-Rescued-Slaves-1* is a **page** within the article directory

Here's an analogy to help you better understand a URL sequence: In the United States, an address is written from the most local to the most national: Dover, Kent County, Delaware, United States. URLs are constructed in exactly the opposite fashion, going from the broadest (the domain name) to narrowest (the specific web page).

Why does this matter to you? Because websites come and go, pages are moved, and data that was once at one URL may get moved to another. Understanding the site's basic navigation structure may help you recover a lost URL.

If you go to Google and type in something like *roster 4th artillery Civil War* and the link goes to <http://www.4thartillery.com/enlistedmen/civilwar/a-c>, but the link is broken, what do you do?

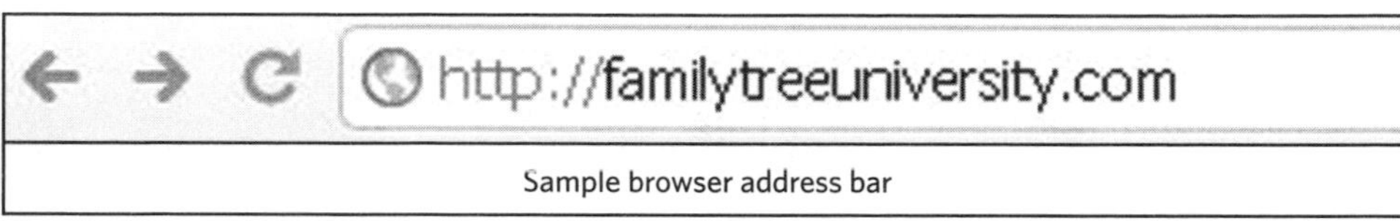

Sample browser address bar

First, go to <http://www.4thartillery.com> and see if the domain name still exists. If it does, explore the navigation links. In the example above, it appears that the original page was organized by enlisted men and then by an alphabetical list (a–c). Maybe the site owner reorganized into pages that don't delineate between enlisted men and officers; or maybe the roster has been divided by a different alphabetical system, e.g., a–f.

In either case, go to the Home page and click on the navigation links to find where rosters are now located.

Sometimes, however, the domain no longer exists; it's possible that the site owner no longer wanted to maintain the site, so he didn't renew the domain name. In this case, you can use a second method to track down your information.

Let's say you're looking for information on the Portuguese immigrants who worked on New Bedford whaling ships. Your search results include a site with a document called "New Bedford Whaling Men from the Azores." But when you click on the link for the site, you discover the domain no longer exists.

Although you can't access the domain, you have discovered the name of the document. So click the Back button on your browser to return to the search engine and enter the document name in the engine; you'll likely find it sitting on another website.

USING BOOKMARKS

You probably have sites that you visit on a frequent basis (like Google, Ancestry, or FamilySearch). Save these sites to your Bookmarks (Chrome, Firefox, and Safari) or Favorites (Internet Explorer). After this site is saved, you'll only need to click the site name in your Bookmarks menu. Each browser has a slightly different way of saving bookmarks:

CHROME: Click the Star icon at the right end of the address bar. Once clicked, the star will turn gold.

Chrome bookmarking star

FIREFOX AND SAFARI: Click the Bookmarks item on the menu bar.

INTERNET EXPLORER: Like Firefox, except click Favorites on the menu bar.

As you research your family tree, you're going to end up with dozens of websites on your bookmarks list. Once this happens, it can be more difficult to find a specific website among your bookmarks than it is to type in the URL! Sidestep this problem by filing bookmarks in groups.

Firefox Bookmarks menu

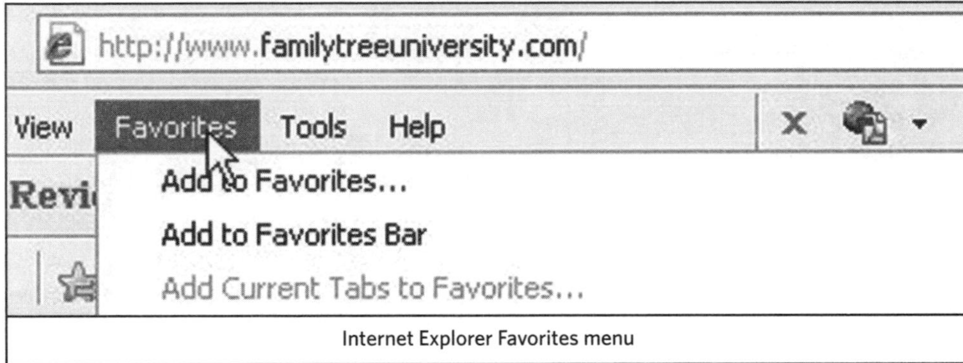

Internet Explorer Favorites menu

All browsers have an "organize bookmarks" function. From this option you can create new folders, i.e., folders for surnames, places, documents, etc. After you've created folders within your bookmarks, start saving your bookmarked sites into the correct folder.

In Internet Explorer, after you click the Organize Favorites link, a new box pops up giving you the option to create folders.

Already have a lot of bookmarks? Not a problem. Just create folders, then drag and drop each item into the appropriate folder.

What if you want to change from one browser to another, but don't want to lose your bookmarks? Importing (or exporting) is typically an option on your Bookmarks menu. Just follow the on-screen directions.

An even easier way to navigate to your favorite websites is a browser add-on called Speed Dial.

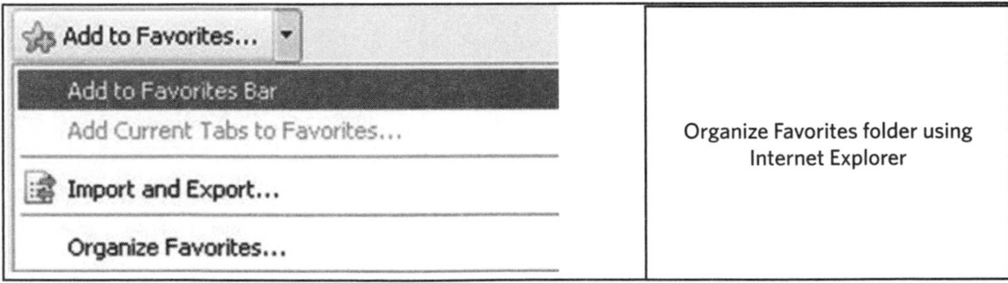

Organize Favorites folder using Internet Explorer

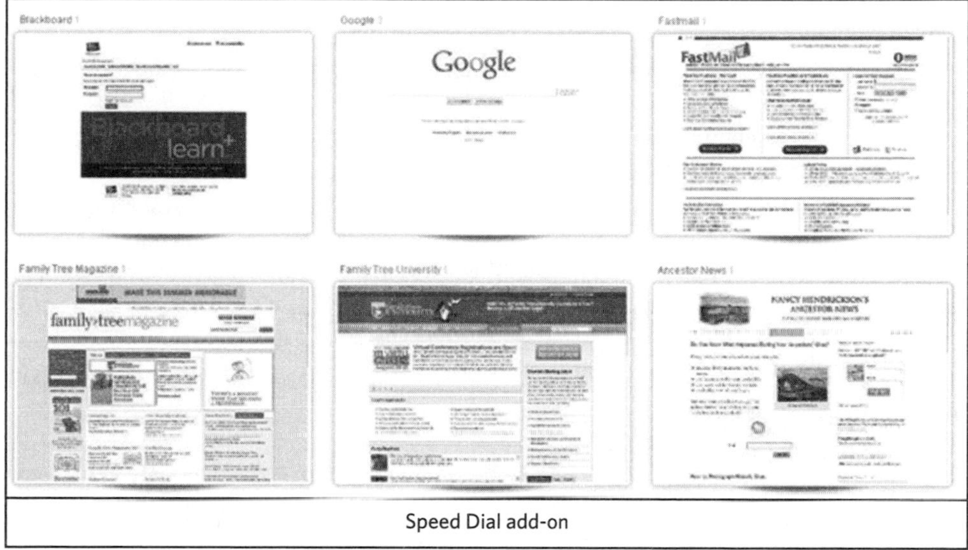

Speed Dial add-on

SPEED DIALING MADE EASY

Speed Dial is a browser add-on—a freebie that you can add to your browser to quickly navigate to favorite websites. After installation, when you click the New Tab plus sign (+), you'll see icons of websites you've added to Speed Dial. Click the icon and the website will load.

Add Speed Dial to your browser:

- Google Chrome <chrome.google.com/webstore>
- Firefox <addons.mozilla.org/en-US/firefox/addon/speed-dial>
- Internet Explorer (Speed Dial is not available for IE, but you may like XMarks) Find lots of cool add-ons <www.ieaddons.com/en>

Safari comes with a top-sites feature in the Bookmarks bar. Click on the Top Sites icon (next to the Bookmark icon) and a window featuring the sites you visit most often will appear.

How to Save Information From the Web

When you find information about your family online, you will want to save it to your computer for offline use, online reference, or use in another program such as your family tree software.

Before you save anything, you should be aware of copyright issues. Unless otherwise specified, you should assume websites, images, documents, etc., are protected by a copyright. While a fact is not subject to copyright law (e.g., Mildred McKinney was born on August 1, 1884, in St. Louis, Missouri), the compilation of information on a web page and commentary on the facts are subject to copyright. If you're going to publish a family tree book and include a copyrighted photo you found online, you'll need to get the owner's permission. Fortunately, there are several sites where you can find photos that aren't subject to copyright law (see below and more in chapter six).

To learn more about copyright issues, follow this link to *Family Tree Magazine*: <familytreemagazine.com/article/Now-What-Copyright-and-Online-Photos>

Copyrighted material can still be saved to your computer for your personal use; you just can't republish it in another form such as your own website or blog, family tree, or family history. You can keep the material for reference in your own research. You can save web pages, documents, images, or text from the internet. Here's how to save what you find:

Web Pages

There are two ways to save a web page:

1. Select the File/Save or File/Save As menu item at the top of your web browser.
2. Copy everything on the page (Control-C or right-click/copy or Command-C for Macs), then save it to your word processing program or a Google Docs account <docs.google.com>. Google Docs accounts are free, and you can access the account from any computer that has an internet connection. While saving, be sure to also save the URL (web address) where you found the information; you'll need the URL when creating a source in your genealogy software.

Photos or Other Graphics

You can save photos by right clicking the photo with your mouse, then (from the menu) select Save Image or Save Picture. The right-click feature on some images may be disabled by the image owner. On Macs you can also click on the image and drag it to your desktop, then move the picture file to the appropriate directory.

SAVE YOUR DATA IN A CLOUD

If you share genealogy documents with other family members or researchers, you can send them information as e-mail attachments or store the information online in a cloud. Data saved in a cloud can be accessed by anyone you authorize.

Using Google Docs, you can not only save information, but also create documents, presentations (like Microsoft's PowerPoint), spreadsheets, and forms. Once created, you can share the file by e-mailing or publishing it to the web.

Another free service (for up to 1GB of storage) is ZohoDocs <docs.zoho.com/jsp/index.jsp>. Here, you can invite others to view and edit documents.

If you're interested in keeping copies of your family tree research online, try one of these sites:

4Shared <www.4shared.com>

iDrive <www.idrive.com>
DropBox <dropbox.com>

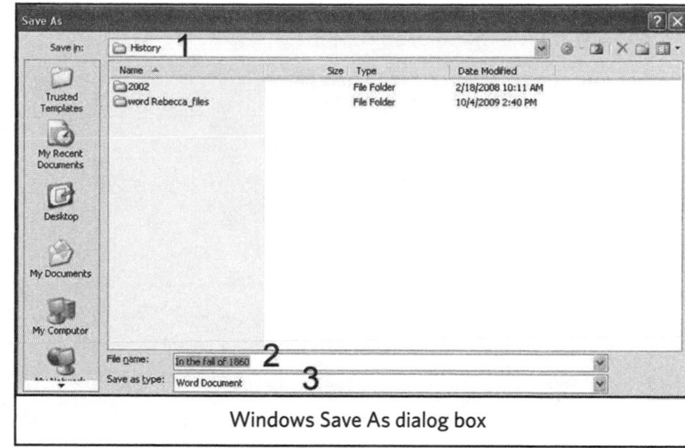

Windows Save As dialog box

SAVE AND SAVE AS

One problem many people have when saving files is inadvertently saving a new file with the name of an existing file, thus wiping out the existing file. This can happen with all types of files, whether documents, GEDCOMs, or photos. How to avoid this disaster? By understanding the difference between Save and Save As. If you create a Microsoft Word file and click the Save icon, you'll have three options:

1. Where to save
2. Name of file
3. File format

After you've saved your file, the next time you save it, you won't be given any of those options. Word will assume you just want to save the file in the same place, using the same name and format.

Because Windows won't let you save two files with the same name in the same location, you'll have to use the Save As option if you want to keep a copy of the original file in the same or a new location. Why would you want to do this?

You may have a family file that pertains to two different surnames and you want a copy of the file in each surname directory. Or you may have an original photo that you don't want to inadvertently overwrite. Make a copy of the photo and use Save As to give the copy a different name.

When you click the Save As option, you'll have the same three options as when you saved the original file: name, place, format.

WHERE DID I SAVE IT?

When you've found something online that you want to keep, you'll need to save it by downloading it to your computer. But once downloaded, do you know where or how to find the item?

Each operating system is set up a little differently, but typically it will save items (by default) to My Documents or the desktop. Finding a downloaded file is an ongoing problem if you don't know the download location. Here's a quick cheat sheet to show you the default location and how to change it:

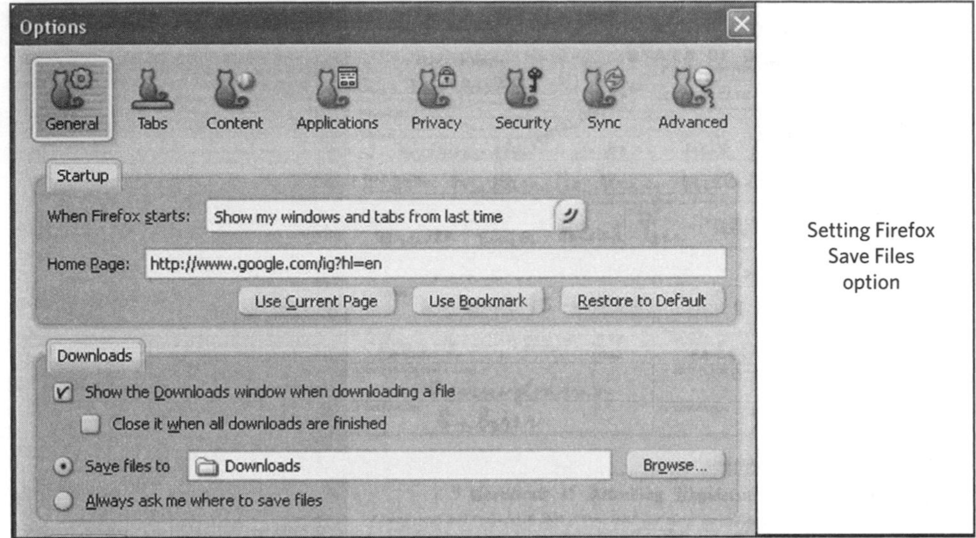

Setting Firefox Save Files option

- In Google Chrome, change the default download location under the Options menu (Options/Under the Hood).
- In Internet Explorer 9 (IE9), click on the Gear icon in the upper right corner, then click on View Downloads. Next, click Options, then Browse. Navigate to and select (highlight) the folder that you want IE9 to use as the default download location, then click on the Select Folder button.
- In Firefox 3, go to Tools, then Options. Under Downloads, click Browse to change the default download location. Or, if you want to decide where to save the download each time, choose the option "Always ask me where to save files."

If you didn't notice the download location, you can always find a document if you know its name by using Windows' Search function.

In Windows XP you'll find the Search function by clicking the Start button. In Windows 7, click the Start button and type a word or part of a word in the search box.

On Macs, click on the Spotlight icon on the Finder menu bar.

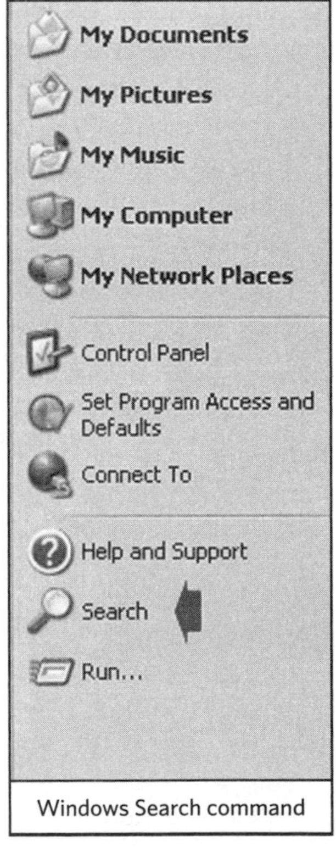

Windows Search command

ORGANIZE YOUR COMPUTER FILES

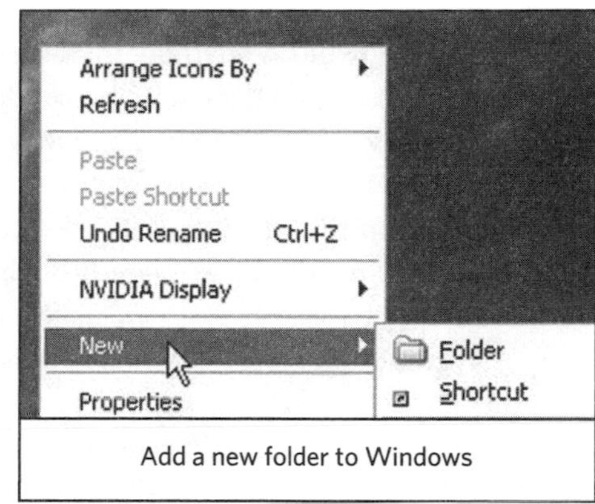

Add a new folder to Windows

Although you can save genealogy files anywhere on your computer's hard drive, it's better to save them within meaningful directories (folders). Set up your directories using the same care and forethought you use when creating a paper filing system. Organized directories keep you from searching your entire computer for a file. Invest some time in organizing and you'll save lots of time in the future.

Directories help organize files; a directory can contain other directories (subdirectories). For example, to organize your genealogy downloads, you can create a directory named *Wilson*, with subfolders of Census, Military, Marriage, Cemetery, etc. By placing subfolders within surname folders, you can easily organize all of your genealogy data.

Although Windows, by default, creates certain directories like My Documents, you can create your own. You can also copy, move, and delete entire directories and individual items within the directories.

Why copy files? One reason is that it's common to have a document or image that pertains to more than one family. For example, you may have a picture of Uncle Joe Johnson and Uncle Sam Wilson, in which case you want the image in both the Johnson and Wilson directories.

How to create directories (folders):

1. Decide what directories you want. For example, do you want an umbrella Genealogy directory, with subdirectories of each surname or place name, and then sub-subdirectories of document types within each surname directory?
2. Navigate to the location (such as a hard drive, directory, or the desktop) where you want to create a new folder. Right-click a blank area on the desktop or in the folder window, point to New, and then click Folder. Type a name for the new folder, and then press Enter.
3. To add a subdirectory (subfolder) to the directory you just created, double click on the name of the new directory, then right-click to create a new folder.

IS IT SAFE TO DOWNLOAD THIS FILE?

At some point you'll want to download a file, such as:

- an historic map
- a GEDCOM file
- a free program

Before you download anything from the internet, it's imperative that you install antivirus software that automatically assesses downloaded files for threats.

Viruses can attack a computer in many different ways. It's called a virus because it infects your computer. Viruses come in many forms, such as a Trojan horse, which is a program that appears harmless but hides malicious functions. Or you may have a worm—a program that spreads like wildfire through your computer and then onto other computers through a network. Viruses can make your computer run very slow, generate pop-up boxes that emulate an official Windows message, and even crash your entire system.

Some of the most popular antivirus programs are:

- Kaspersky <usa.kaspersky.com>
- Norton <norton.com>
- McAfee <mcafee.com>
- Malwarebytes <www.malwarebytes.org> (Free download, this software searches out "malware," malicious software)

Some of the most malicious viruses can crash your computer or erase your hard drive. Others will steal your e-mail addresses and send spam (or worse) to everyone in your contact list. Still others are "keystroke loggers." These won't do anything to your system, but they will sit in the background, logging every keystroke you make—including log-ins to secure sites like your bank.

After you've installed your antivirus program, customize the settings to:

1. Automatically upgrade its virus database. This will ensure that the software knows all about the latest threats. If virus databases are not updated, a new virus can attack your system.
2. Automatically scan your e-mails.
3. Automatically scan downloads.
4. Automatically run complete scans of your system on (at least) a weekly basis.
5. If your software has an internet component (which most do), make sure it's able to scan websites. When an antivirus program detects a virus on a web page, it typically pops up a warning message and won't allow you to access the page.

Five Tips for Staying Virus-Safe

1. Whenever possible, download software from an official site instead of a third-party site. For example, if you need to update your Windows software, you are far less likely to get a virus when you download the update from the official Windows site instead of using a third-party site run by a company you've never heard of.
2. Check the protection policies on the download site. For example, sites like cnet <download.cnet.com> scan every file uploaded to their servers using the latest security software. If you download from a software site, look for information on how the site guards your computer safety.

3. If you've received a file via e-mail, make sure your antivirus software scans it before opening. Even if you receive the file from a trusted friend, scan it because you have no way of knowing if your friend keeps his computer system virus-free.
4. Never open a file sent from someone you don't know. If you receive an e-mail with an attachment from an unknown person, delete it immediately.
5. Watch out for executable files, such as those with names that include *.exe*, *.bat*, *.pif*, and *.scr*. An executable file performs a task, such as opening a program. If you download one of these, you are, potentially opening yourself up to anything on that file once you activate it. Scan it before opening. Sometimes hackers use a double extension on a file to trick you, such as .jpg.exe. Don't be fooled. This is an .exe file.

HOW TO SPOT SPOOFS AND URBAN LEGENDS

Have you ever received an e-mail from a friend, telling you that Bill Gates is sharing his fortune and all you have to do is send him an e-mail to get your share? If so, this is a prime example of an "urban legend"—a spoof or internet rumor that's making the rounds via e-mail. Urban legends range from fake offers to become a mystery shopper to a doctored photo that purportedly shows a frog in a jar of pickles.

Before you start forwarding the "news" to everyone on your contact list, surf over to Snopes.com <snopes.com>, the definitive site for tracking rip-offs, urban legends, and phony photos. Verify that the latest scoop you're about to broadcast across the internet isn't on their spoof list.

WHAT'S NEXT?

Now that you have the computer stuff down cold, time to begin your search! If you want to increase your computer skills, check out Family Tree University's Computer Boot Camp for Genealogists. This four-week course covers all of the basics you'll need to know to gain confidence, learn computer shortcuts, and maximize your online time.

Using Search Engines

There are many internet search engines to choose from, and they are often designed to find and rank web pages in different ways. But for genealogy purposes, all search engines are used in a similar fashion.

HOW SEARCH ENGINES WORK

When you type in a search phrase, results are generated almost instantaneously. But what's happening behind the curtain? Search engines send "spiders" out onto the web that seek pages to add to the search engines' indexes. Once a page is found, the spider follows the links from one page to the next. Then the spiders follow those links to even more pages. Before you know it, billions of pages have been found and indexed.

When you type in a search word or phrase, search engines use their algorithm (mathematical criteria) to determine which pages in its index are most relevant to your search. Criteria can includes things like:

- how many times the search phrase appears on a web page
- if the search phrase was included in the page title
- whether the phrase was part of the URL (website address), i.e. jenkinsfamilytree.com
- if the page contained synonyms matching your search

The search engine then rates the quality of the page based on links coming to the page from other sites. If there are a lot of links from spam-type sites, a page is considered low quality; if there are links from quality sites, the page gets a higher ranking.

After all of the calculations have been made, the search engine serves up your results. For Google, all of this takes about half a second.

Although genealogists rely on large, data-based sites like FamilySearch <familysearch.org>, Ancestry <ancestry.com>, and Ellis Island <ellisisland.org>, sometimes breakthrough results can come from using a simple search engine.

CRAFTING SIMPLE SEARCHES

Search engines have developed different ways to find and index information, but all of them use a basic search box. Amazingly, you can often find exactly what you're looking for by typing what you want into the search box. Try typing:

- *how do I replace a broken faucet*
- *where can I find Cleveland restaurant reviews*
- *are poodles good pets for kids*

You get pretty exact responses.

For genealogy, let's say you want to learn more about the migration routes your ancestors used when they left their Pennsylvania home and headed to Virginia.

Go to Google (or your favorite search engine) and type in *American migration routes Pennsylvania to Virginia*. As you can see from the screenshot, this simple search took 0.2 seconds, and the third result on the page is what you were looking for. Pretty amazing.

american migration routes pennsylvania to virginia

About 4,170,000 results (0.20 seconds)

American Migration Patterns

American Migration has fascinated me from the very beginning of my genealogical research. ... **Pennsylvania to Virginia**, **Migration Routes** ...
freepages.genealogy.rootsweb.ancestry.com/.../**migration**.html - Cached - Similar

Migration Routes, New York, **Pennsylvania**, Maine, Rhode Island ...

In **Pennsylvania**, **Virginia** and Maryland, colonists initiated westward ...
freepages.genealogy.rootsweb.ancestry.com/.../
Ancestral%20**Migration**%20Archives/**Migration**%20Webpag... - Cached - Similar

Migration Routes from **PA to VA**

1) There was a major 18c **migration route** from **PA** through **VA** to the Salem NC ...
www.rootsweb.ancestry.com/~pacumber/**migration**.htm - Cached - Similar

Show more results from ancestry.com

Sample search, Google.com

Did you notice the little magnifying glass to the right of the page title? If you hold your mouse pointer over it, an image will pop up, giving you a preview of the page. Let's try another simple search. Type in *are there historical birth records online for New Hampshire.* The second search result led to free early birth records, including images. Not bad for a quick search.

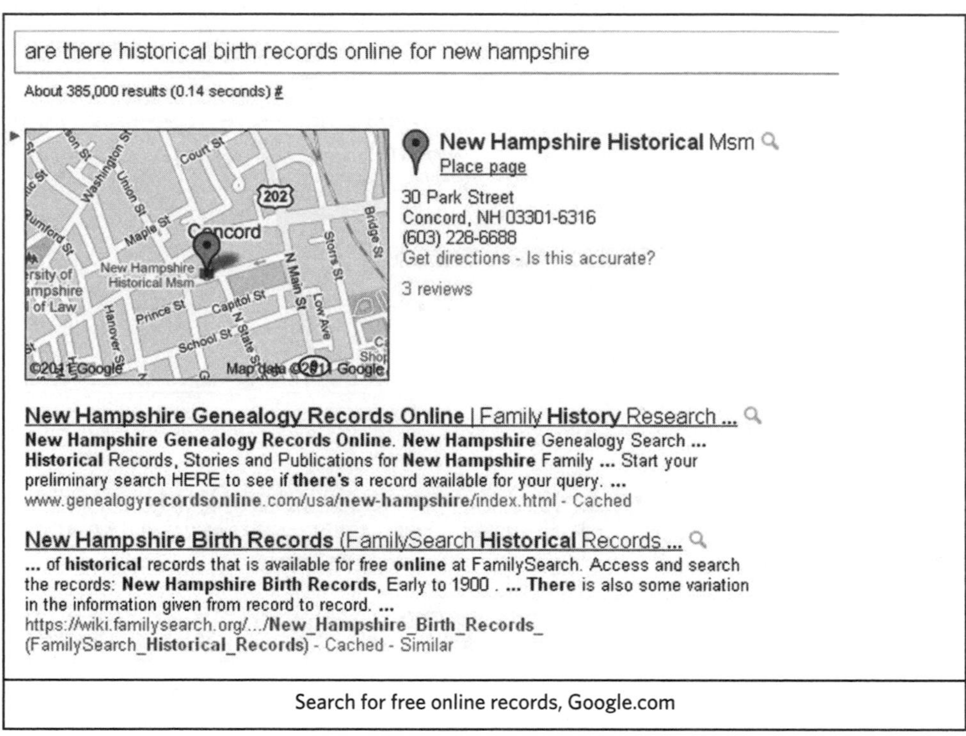

Search for free online records, Google.com

If you use a search engine other than Google, such as Bing or Yahoo!, you'll note that search results differ. Sometimes you won't receive the same result at all; other times you'll receive the same results but in a different order.

Although it's easy to always use the same search engine, when you're doing genealogy research, try to mix it up. If you don't find what you are looking for using one search engine, move to another. Reliable search engines include:

Ask <ask.com>

Bing <bing.com>

Google <google.com>

Yahoo! <yahoo.com>

In addition to general search engines, there are genealogy-specific search engines, which will be discussed later in this chapter.

HOW CAN YOU REFINE SEARCH RESULTS?

Sometimes simple searches can only get you so far. There are times when refining a search is necessary, especially if you're looking for a common surname. One quick and easy way to get desired results is to add the word *genealogy* to your search phrase. Or add *family history*, or the misspelled *geneology*. You can also add more words to your search phrase or put the words together in a different order, i.e., *New Hampshire birth records online*.

Finding ancestors online is a game of flexible thinking; if one approach doesn't work, bend it a little and see what happens. When you're trying to think of helpful search terms, one trick is to imagine that you've built a website that contains the very information you're seeking. As the site builder, what words would you use to describe the information? For example, if your site is about the first families of Pennsylvania, what would you call them?

- first families
- early settlers
- pioneers
- first settlers
- early Quakers
- original settlers
- original Quakers

The terms you would use are probably the same ones the site builder used. If one term doesn't work, try another, then another. Another trick is to start small and go big. Use the least number of words to describe your search. Start with: *Civil War Columbus*. If most of the hits are about Ohio and you want to know about Columbus, Mississippi, add *Mississippi* to your search term.

CONSTRUCTING COMPLEX SEARCHES

When you type a phrase into a search engine, the search engine looks for web pages that have at least one of the words in your phrase, but not necessarily all of them. For example, if you type in *American migration routes genealogy*, the search engine will find pages that have the word *migration* or pages that have the words *American* or *genealogy* but not necessarily pages that have all of the words in your phrase. This search will return millions of pages in the results, many of them irrelevant to genealogy. To receive more relevant results, you'll need to find a way to filter out most of the nongenealogy hits. This filtering is done with operators.

Operators are special words or symbols that force a search engine to filter results in a specific way. Specific operators are:

PLUS SIGN (+): In late 2011, Google changed the plus sign (+) operator to quotation marks (" "); however, the + operator can still be used. A + (plus sign) in front of a word tells the search engine that the word *must* be included in your search results.

Sample search: *American migration routes genealogy* produces 2,130,000 hits; *+American +migration +routes +genealogy* produces 28,300 hits.

QUOTATION MARKS (" "): Quotation marks around a phrase tell the search engine that the *exact* phrase *must* appear on the web page.

Sample search: *American migration routes* produces almost five million hits; *"American migration routes"* produces 26,000 hits.

Use caution when applying quotation marks. If you're searching for William Crawford with: *"William Crawford"*, this search will *not* pick up pages that have *William F. Crawford* or *Bill Crawford*.

MINUS SIGN (-): Use the minus sign when you don't want a word to appear on a web page: *peanut -butter*. This returns hits of pages that have the word peanut but not the word butter.

Why would you want to use the minus sign? If you're looking for records of an ancestor who lived in Massachusetts but the search engine keeps returning results of a person with the same name who lives in Michigan, you'd use the minus sign, i.e., *–Michigan*, to eliminate those results.

Most search engines have a link to an Advanced Search page. Click the link to discover other operators your search engine uses, along with tips for searching.

You can also use the operators in combination with one another to create a complex search. Because this looks so much like an algebraic equation, it's often referred to as "search engine math."

+American +"migration routes" +"from Pennsylvania" -Ohio

Let's breakdown the search equation:

- the plus sign specifies that the search result pages *must* include each word or phrase that has a + in front of it *and*
- the quotation marks indicate that the exact phrases *"migration routes"* and *"from Pennsylvania"* have to appear on the page as well *and*
- the minus sign indicates *Ohio* must not appear on any of the search results pages

ASTERISK (*): An asterisk is a "wildcard" operator. It can be used in place of any other letter or number. Wildcards are useful if you don't know the exact year for an event or if there are a number of alternate spellings for a surname. For example *Sm*th* would bring up results for *Smith* and *Smyth* in the same search.

Using these operators, you can now construct complex searches—a very handy tool when you're searching for a common surname or specific data.

Using Genealogy Search Engines

So far you've learned how to construct simple and complex searches using common search engines. But did you know there are also search engines that only seek out genealogy sites?

One of the newest is Mocavo <mocavo.com>, an exceptionally fast genealogy search engine that searches tens of thousands of genealogy-specific sites including forums, blogs, U.S. state archives, Ellis Island, Find A Grave, Library of Congress, the Internet Archives, and National Archives.

When you search using Mocavo, you'll still receive a lot of hits, but the majority of these hits will specifically relate to genealogy. For example, a Google search for *"Miles Dimmitt"* (using quotation marks) generated 1,170 results, while Mocavo found seventy results, all of which are genealogy-specific.

Mocavo works a lot like other search engines, which means you can use operators to create simple or advanced searches.

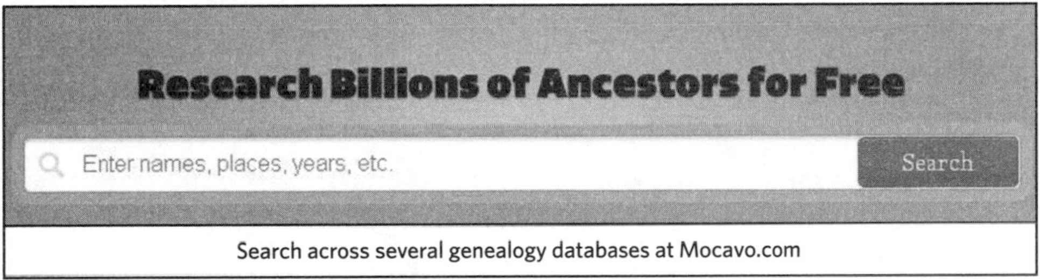

Search across several genealogy databases at Mocavo.com

If you want even more refined results, you can upload a GEDCOM of your family file to Mocavo. Mocavo will then scan the contents of your GEDCOM for better matches all across the web and automatically e-mail the results to you either daily or weekly (your choice).

A GEDCOM (GEnealogical Data COMmunication) is a method of exchanging genealogical data between different software programs. When you export your data as a GEDCOM, the data is put into a format that can be read by all genealogy software programs. All major genealogy programs have the capacity to create a GEDCOM file.

A second genealogy search engine is located at One-Step Web Pages, operated by Stephen Morse <stevemorse.org>.

From this site, you can search sites like Ancestry.com and Ellis Island website <ellisisland.org> using Morse's enhanced search tools instead of searching on the original sites.

The One-Step "Gold Form," for instance, searches the Ellis Island database but uses many more search features than the actual Ellis Island website.

The Gold Form allows you to search for a surname either by the first few letters, a "sounds like," or phonetically. The phonetic option operates like a Soundex but returns far less irrelevant hits. (Soundex is a system devised to index names by first letter and sounds.) You can also check an Ethnicity box in the search form to help filter results even more.

CASE STUDY 1
SEARCHING FOR A COMMON SURNAME

Unless you're searching for unique surnames like Axelquist or Birtwistle, you're going to get millions of irrelevant hits.

Pity the Smith and Jones, as well as the people whose names are based on colors (White), geographical formations (Hill), buildings (Church), or weather phenomenon (Snow).

Search for a John Snow (particularly in winter) and you'll get every weather report on the internet.

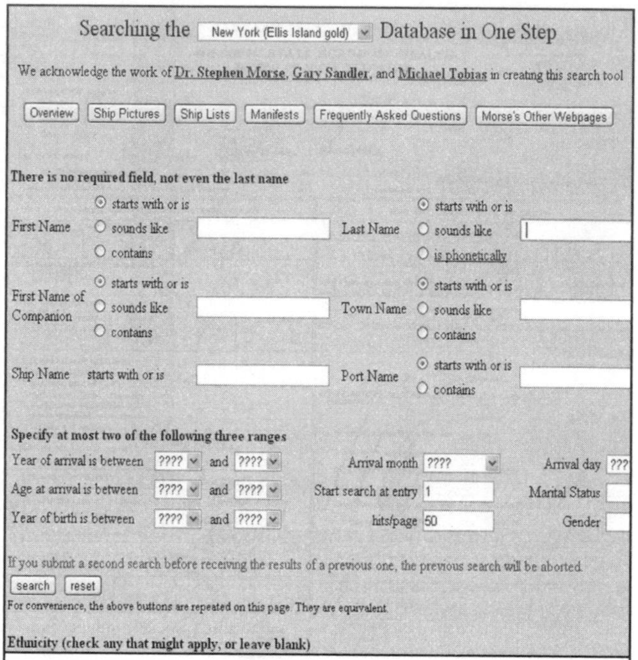

Gold Form search of Ellis Island database, One-Step Webpages <stevemorse.org>

Fortunately the common surname problem is easy to solve using search operators to customize the search your way.

The goal of this case study search is to discover as much as possible about an ancestor named John Bishop, born about 1823 in Somerset, England. He eventually went to Australia in 1855. We particularly want to know where in Somerset he was born.

STEP 1. Go to Google <google.com> and type in the name of your ancestor. This initial search will give you an idea of just how many results for the name are online—and how crafty you're going to need to be to find your family member.

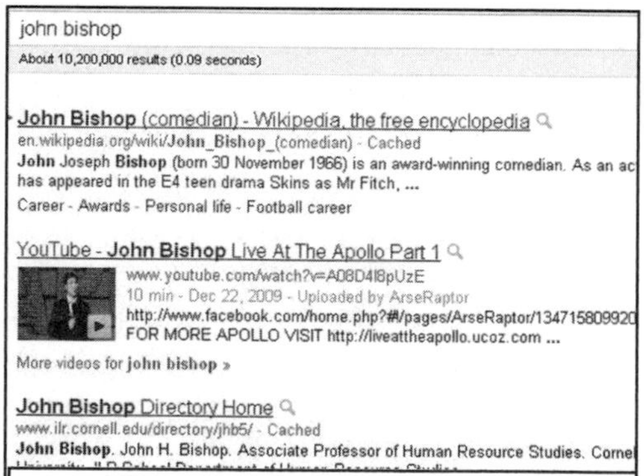

In the case of John Bishop, Google returned 10.2 million results.

A "raw" search (a search that doesn't use operators) will return pages that include either the word *John* or the word *Bishop*—not necessarily the complete name *John Bishop*.

Simple search, Google.com

STEP 2. Put quotation marks around the name. Using quotes forces Google to only return pages that include the exact phrase "*John Bishop.*" In addition to finding the exact phrase, the use of quotes will also allow common words (called stop words) that Google wouldn't typically include, i.e., the, on, where, how.

This time the top results remain the same John Bishop (comedian), but the results narrowed from more than ten million to one million, still a lot of hits—far too many to wade through.

STEP 3. To further refine the results, let's add another operator; this time the plus sign (+). Using the plus sign, we'll add multiple words or phrases to the John Bishop search.

We know that this John Bishop was born about 1823 in Somerset, England. Hopefully, adding the date and place will get us closer to more information.

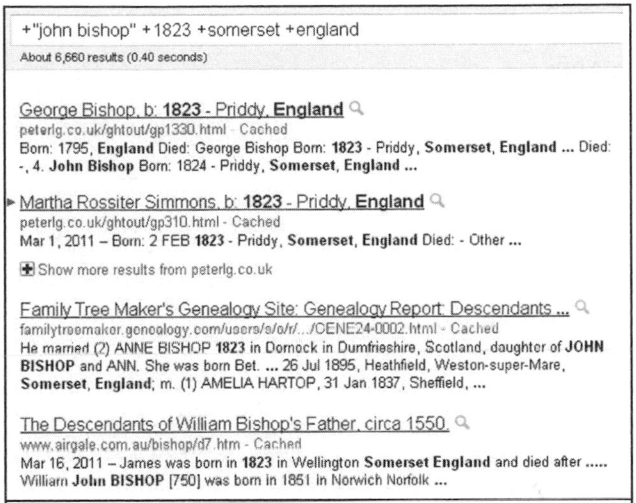

This search yielded 6,660 results. The good news is that most of the top hits are genealogy sites. The bad news is I'm not sure if any of them are the right John Bishop, but I think the first search result might be our guy. If so, "Priddy, England" gets me very close to my goal.

Because this search does yield Bishops in Somerset in about the right time period, I would definitely contact the website owners to see if there's a family connection.

+"john bishop" +1823 +somerset +england

About 6,660 results (0.40 seconds)

George Bishop, b: **1823** - Priddy, **England**
peterlg.co.uk/ghtout/gp1330.html - Cached
Born: 1795, **England** Died: George Bishop Born: **1823** - Priddy, **Somerset, England** ... Died: -, 4. **John Bishop** Born: 1824 - Priddy, **Somerset, England** ...

Martha Rossiter Simmons, b: **1823** - Priddy, **England**
peterlg.co.uk/ghtout/gp310.html - Cached
Mar 1, 2011 – Born: 2 FEB **1823** - Priddy, **Somerset, England** Died: - Other ...

Show more results from peterlg.co.uk

Family Tree Maker's Genealogy Site: Genealogy Report: Descendants ...
familytreemaker.genealogy.com/users/s/o/r/.../GENE24-0002.html - Cached
He married (2) ANNE BISHOP **1823** in Dornock in Dumfriesshire, Scotland, daughter of **JOHN BISHOP** and ANN. She was born Bet. ... 26 Jul 1895, Heathfield, Weston-super-Mare, **Somerset, England**; m. (1) AMELIA HARTOP, 31 Jan 1837, Sheffield, ...

The Descendants of William Bishop's Father, circa 1550.
www.airgale.com.au/bishop/d7.htm - Cached
Mar 16, 2011 – James was born in **1823** in Wellington **Somerset England** and died after ..... William **John BISHOP** [750] was born in 1851 in Norwich Norfolk ...

Structure a complex search, Google.com

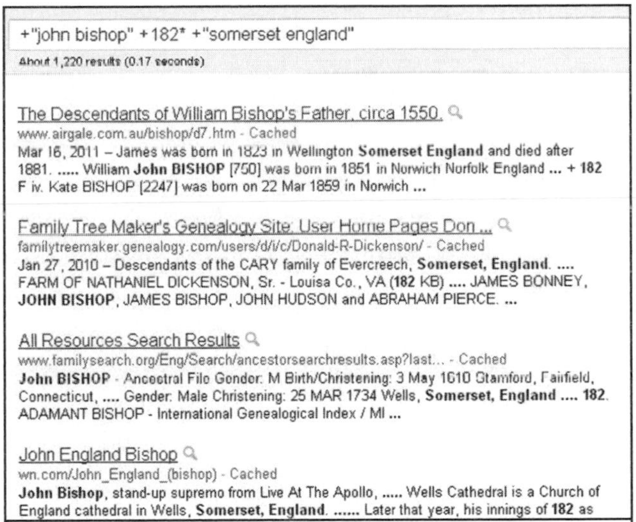

+"john bishop" +182* +"somerset england"

About 1,220 results (0.17 seconds)

The Descendants of William Bishop's Father, circa 1550.
www.airgale.com.au/bishop/d7.htm - Cached
Mar 16, 2011 – James was born in 1823 in Wellington **Somerset England** and died after 1881. ..... William **John BISHOP** [750] was born in 1851 in Norwich Norfolk England ... + **182** F iv. Kate BISHOP [2247] was born on 22 Mar 1859 in Norwich ...

Family Tree Maker's Genealogy Site: User Home Pages Don ...
familytreemaker.genealogy.com/users/d/i/c/Donald-R-Dickenson/ - Cached
Jan 27, 2010 – Descendants of the CARY family of Evercreech, **Somerset, England**. .... FARM OF NATHANIEL DICKENSON, Sr. - Louisa Co., VA (**182** KB) .... JAMES BONNEY, **JOHN BISHOP**, JAMES BISHOP, JOHN HUDSON and ABRAHAM PIERCE. ...

All Resources Search Results
www.familysearch.org/Eng/Search/ancestorsearchresults.asp?last... - Cached
John BISHOP - Ancestral File Gender: M Birth/Christening: 3 May 1610 Stamford, Fairfield, Connecticut, ... Gender: Male Christening: 25 MAR 1734 Wells, **Somerset, England** .... **182**. ADAMANT BISHOP - International Genealogical Index / MI ...

John England Bishop
wn.com/John_England_(bishop) - Cached
John Bishop, stand-up supremo from Live At The Apollo, ... Wells Cathedral is a Church of England cathedral in Wells, **Somerset, England**. ...... Later that year, his innings of **182** as

Use a wildcard (*) in a complex search, Google.com

STEP 4. We don't know for a fact that John Bishop was born in 1823. What if he was born a year or two earlier or later? In that case you'd want to use the wildcard search operator.

The wildcard symbol is an asterisk and can be used in place of any other letter. Typing in *182** would result in pages with any dates that begin with 182. Change the search to use the wildcard and put quotation marks around *"Somerset England"*. The results changed to a little over one thousand hits, with many possibilities of one of them being the right John Bishop.

STEP 5. Now that we've gotten a lot of promising results, let's search based on the Australian immigration.

What interesting results! Lots of convicts named John Bishop were transported to Australia. Could one of these be him? More interesting was the fifth record down, because this result contains a John Bishop with approximately the correct birth date, location, and transport to Australia.

+"john bishop" +1855 +australia

About 12,300 results (0.08 seconds)

Convict Records: **John Bishop**
www.convictrecords.com.au/convicts/bishop/john - Cached
Records 1 - 13 of 13 – Assizes Cambridge, 2nd February, **1855**, Western **Australia**. **John Bishop**, **John Bishop**, one of 176 convicts transported on the America, ...

Convict Records: Transported on ship Stag
www.convictrecords.com.au/convicts/ship-name/stag - Cached
Records 1 - 225 of 225 – Assizes Lewes, 2nd February, **1855**, Western ...

Convict Records: Transported in **1855**
www.convictrecords.com.au/convicts/year/**1855** - Cached
Records 1 - 486 of 486 – Assizes Lewes, 2nd February, **1855**, Western ...

Show more results from convictrecords.com.au

BISHOP William John in SOUTH **AUSTRALIA** Forum
australiansurnamesgroup.yuku.com/topic/.../BISHOP-William-John - Cached
5 posts - 2 authors - Last post: Mar 18, 2009
Karen, children born in South **Australia** for William **John BISHOP** and Sarah TROTT Arthur Hugh b. 20.4.**1855** place not listed SA William John b. ...

B Monk, b: Private -
peterlg.co.uk/ghtout/gp6225.html - Cached
Mar 1, 2011 – **John Bishop** Born: 1824 - Priddy, Somerset, England Marr: 22 JUN **1855** - Fingal, Tasmania, **Australia** Died: 29 JUL 1883 - Longford, Tasmania, ...

Restructure a search to broaden results, Google.com

+"john bishop" +"somerset england" +australasia +1855

9 results (0.19 seconds)

John Bishop of Priddy, Somerset
www.ancestryaid.co.uk/.../23074-**john-bishop**-priddy-somerset.html - Cached
Dec 30, 2010 – Hello All, I am researching **John Bishop**, who emigrated to Tasmania on **Australasia'** in **1855**. He was born in Priddy, ... Where born: Priddy, **Somerset, England** Parish: Priddy County/Island: Somerset ...

RootsWeb: GENANZ-L Re: ship '**AUSTRALASIA**' arr **1855**
archiver.rootsweb.ancestry.com/th/read/GENANZ/.../0986810834 - Cached
Apr 9, 2001 – I believe my ancestor **John BISHOP** b 1827 in **Somerset/England** (and m
... ship '**AUSTRALASIA**' arr **1855** by Jacqueline Symmons <> ...

RootsWeb: GENANZ-L RE: ship '**AUSTRALASIA**' arr **1855**
archiver.rootsweb.ancestry.com/th/read/GENANZ/.../0986809784 - Cached
Apr 9, 2001 – I believe my ancestor **John BISHOP** b 1827 in **Somerset/England** ...

RootsWeb: GENANZ-L ship '**AUSTRALASIA**' arr **1855**
archiver.rootsweb.ancestry.com/th/read/GENANZ/.../0986782723 - Cached
Apr 9, 2001 – I believe my ancestor **John BISHOP** b 1827 in **Somerset/England** ...

Add or delete search words and phrases, Google.com

STEP 6. In this case, additional records the research had on hand shows John was on the ship *Australasia*. Adding this information to the search box returns nine hits, half of them definitely the right John. The sites also have information on his marriage, his wife's maiden name, and his place and date of death.

STEP 7. If your search results continue to generate irrelevant hits, remember to use the minus sign (-) operator. It's an easy way to eliminate hits you know don't relate to your ancestor.

CASE STUDY 2
DISCOVERING A COUNTRY OF ORIGIN

The goal of this search is to learn more about Nancy D. Broyles and the Broyles family, particularly country of origin. What is known: Nancy D. Broyles was born in March 1821 in Tennessee and married Bailous E. Dearing in 1841 in White County, Tennessee.

STEP 1. Raw search (no operators) looking for *Nancy Broyles*.

Result: Too many links to social networking sites like LinkedIn and Facebook.

STEP 2. Search for *+"Nancy Broyles" +Dearing* yielded only 146 hits, but the top ten were exactly what I was looking for.

Among the findings:

Result a: An Ancestry.com message board about this family, noting Nancy was born in Tennessee. It also lists one of her children, whom I had never heard of.

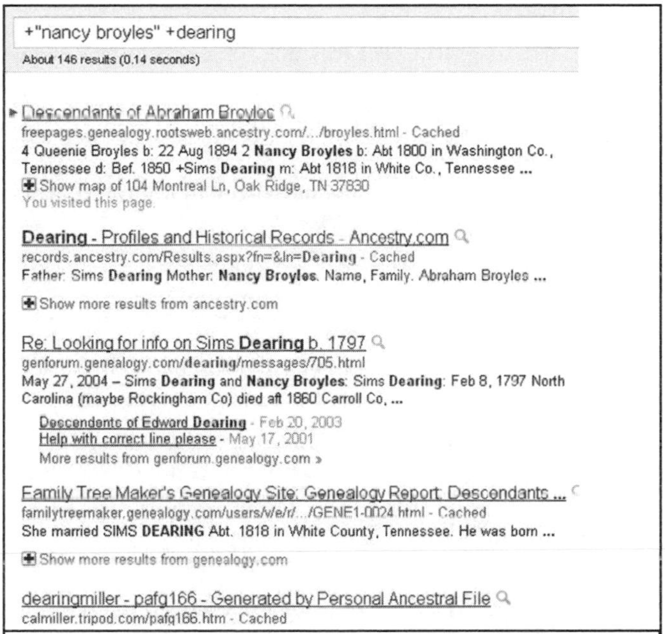

Result b: Another Nancy Broyles-Dearing marriage in White County, Tennessee, but the dates were too early to be the Nancy I'm searching for.

+"nancy broyles" +dearing

About 146 results (0.14 seconds)

Descendants of Abraham Broyles
freepages.genealogy.rootsweb.ancestry.com/.../broyles.html - Cached
4 Queenie Broyles b: 22 Aug 1894 2 **Nancy Broyles** b: Abt 1800 in Washington Co., Tennessee d: Bef. 1850 +Sims **Dearing** m: Abt 1818 in White Co., Tennessee ...
Show map of 104 Montreal Ln, Oak Ridge, TN 37830
You visited this page.

Dearing - Profiles and Historical Records - Ancestry.com
records.ancestry.com/Results.aspx?fn=&ln=**Dearing** - Cached
Father: Sims **Dearing** Mother: **Nancy Broyles**. Name, Family. Abraham Broyles ...
Show more results from ancestry.com

Re: Looking for info on Sims **Dearing** b. 1797
genforum.genealogy.com/**dearing**/messages/705.html
May 27, 2004 – Sims **Dearing** and **Nancy Broyles**: Sims **Dearing**: Feb 8, 1797 North Carolina (maybe Rockingham Co) died aft 1860 Carroll Co, ...
Descendents of Edward **Dearing** - Feb 20, 2003
Help with correct line please - May 17, 2001
More results from genforum.genealogy.com »

Family Tree Maker's Genealogy Site: Genealogy Report: Descendants ...
familytreemaker.genealogy.com/users/w/e/r/.../GENE1-0024.html - Cached
She married SIMS **DEARING** Abt. 1818 in White County, Tennessee. He was born ...
Show more results from genealogy.com

dearingmiller - pafg166 - Generated by Personal Ancestral File
calmiller.tripod.com/pafg166.htm - Cached

Search for a country of origin by first searching for what you already know, Google.com

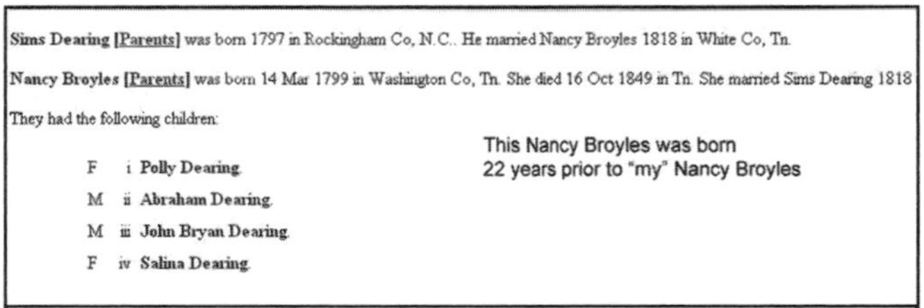

Sims Dearing [Parents] was born 1797 in Rockingham Co, N.C.. He married Nancy Broyles 1818 in White Co, Tn.

Nancy Broyles [Parents] was born 14 Mar 1799 in Washington Co, Tn. She died 16 Oct 1849 in Tn. She married Sims Dearing 1818

They had the following children:

F i **Polly Dearing**
M ii **Abraham Dearing**
M iii **John Bryan Dearing**
F iv **Salina Dearing**

This Nancy Broyles was born 22 years prior to "my" Nancy Broyles

Check dates to be sure you've found the right generation. (Preliminary Results, Descendants of Abraham Broyles, @Robert Edwards)

Result c: Nancy D. has someone named Abraham in her ancestral line.

Note for further research: Who are these other Broyles-Dearings, and do they fit in my family? I later discovered the earlier Nancy was my Nancy's aunt.

Result d: A site listing the descendants of Abraham Broyles. "After the American Revolutionary War Nicholas Broyles moved his family from the Germanna Colony near Culpepper, Virginia to Washington Co., North Carolina/Tennessee. Abraham Broyles, Nicholas' second oldest son, moved to White Co. around 1810 and settled on land about a mile north of Sparta." Per this site, Nancy is the granddaughter of Abraham Broyles.

Result e: Dozens of Broyles family members, with dates and place of birth.

STEP 4. Since the "Abraham" connection mentioned the Germanna Colony, I then did a search for *Germanna Colony*.

Result a: Germanna.org—a treasure of information about two groups of Germans who came to Virginia (1714 and 1717).

Among the second group of colonists was "Breyhel/Breuel/Broyles/Briles/Bruhles, Johann/John and wife Ursula Roup; children: Hans Jacob, Conrad, Maria Elizabetha/Elizabeth": my Broyles family.

When I saw the name of another family in the second group, it cleared up a mystery that had been bothering me for a long time. The other family was Willert/Wilhoit/Wilheit. On a previous research trip to Missouri, I found Dearings buried in the Wilhite Cemetery and always wondered about the connection. The two families probably had been together ever since their arrival from Germany.

Result b: According to the Germanna site, the Broyles came from a town called Schwaigern.

STEP 5. Search for *Schwaigern*. A Wikipedia.org article notes that Schwaigern is a town in the district of Heilbronn, Baden-Württemberg, Germany. According to Wikipedia, this town was first mentioned in writing as early as 766.

Historically, the religion is Protestant. The town church goes back to the thirteenth century. Wikipedia had a photo of the church, and it's probably a view my ancestors knew well.

STEP 6. I returned to Google, searching for the Nicholas Broyles mentioned on the Abraham page. This search resulted in even more information, including land transactions and will and probate records.

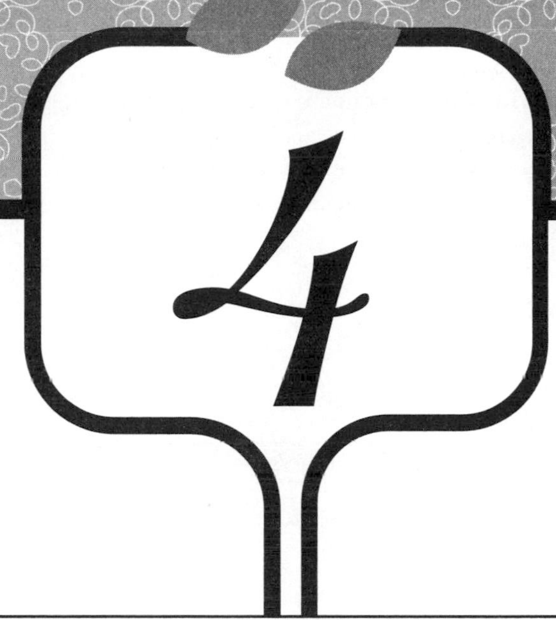

Online Databases

Whether you're searching for birth data, passenger lists, or an old newspaper article, you have a good chance of finding it in an online database. New genealogy information is being posted online daily thanks to tens of thousands of individual websites and large commercial entities. Where to begin your search? In this chapter you'll discover where to find the largest free and for-fee databases.

SUBSCRIPTION SITES

You'll most likely find the greatest depth and breadth of genealogy data on a subscription site. Many of these sites allow you to search for free, but you'll need to pay for a subscription to view the results.

Although subscription sites carry either a monthly or annual fee, they can often save you time because they contain information that you may not be able to access unless you're in a genealogy library. Subscription sites typically have a free trial period; if you're interested in the site, use this trial period to determine if the subscription provides good value for the cost.

ANCESTRY.COM <ancestry.com>

Ancestry.com is the world's largest online collection of genealogy and family history information, with more than six billion records, 24 million reader-submitted family trees, and 60 million photos and stories. Ancestry's holdings include:

- census indexes and images (U.S., Canada, UK)
- military records
- vital statistics
- immigration records
- maps
- newspapers
- voter lists

Ancestry.com users can filter their searches by a specific database or type of document, or they can search across all databases.

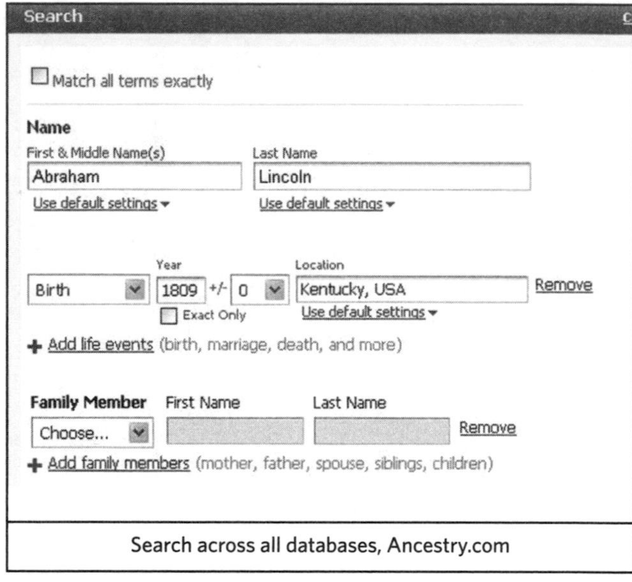

Search across all databases, Ancestry.com

Even if you don't want to pay for a subscription to the site, explore Ancestry.com's community features <community.ancestry.com>, which include free message boards and members directories. User-submitted family trees are available to everyone, not just paid subscribers. Because of the large number of subscribers (1.6 million), there's an excellent chance you can network with another family researcher. When another Ancestry.com user saves data on one of the people in your tree, you'll automatically receive a notification.

FOLD3.COM <fold3.com>

Through a partnership with the National Archives, the Library of Congress, and other institutions, fold3.com has digitized more than 73 million family history records.

In addition to providing subscription services, fold3.com also highlights free databases for anyone to use, such as Continental Congress papers and Matthew Brady's Civil War images.

Inventory and Appraisement of Estate Ed Mortimer
1 Doz Cane bottom chairs $18. 1 Piano Forte $100 $ 118 –
2 Card Tables 1 pair Cut Shades 4 pr Candlestick 20 –
1 Grate Shovel Tongs & fender $20. 1 pr Lustres $5 25 –
1 doz hair bottom chairs $6. 1 Settee $15...... 21 –
1 pr Looking Glasses $4. 1 Brussels Carpet $10. 14 –
1 pr card Tables $10. Tea Table $2. Dinner Sett $12 24 –
Set Glass ware $30. 1 Sett Tea China $4...... 34 –

Estate inventory list, fold3.com

Among fold3.com's most outstanding collections are military records from the Revolutionary War and the War of 1812, as well as Civil War service, pension, and widows records. You'll also find images from the 1860, 1900, 1910, 1920, and 1930 federal censuses.

Like Ancestry.com, users can search fold3.com across all databases or employ a series of filters that include name, place, date, year, and collection. Users can also create their own pages, upload images, create annotations to existing material, and share research findings.

Beginning in late 2011, fold3.com (formerly footnote.com) began focusing on offering the finest and most comprehensive collection of U.S. military records available on the internet. Fold3.com is dedicated to preserving America's military records, some of which are more than two hundred years old.

GENEALOGYBANK <genealogybank.com>

With more than five thousand newspapers—and millions of items—digitized, GenealogyBank has become a premier provider of historical newspaper records. Subscribers can also access historical books and documents as well as old and current obituaries.

The historical newspaper collection dates to 1690 and is fully searchable by name, state, date, and keywords. The collection includes newspapers printed in small towns and big cities throughout the United States.

The genealogy benefits of searching historical newspapers are many. Newspaper obituaries can hold the key to a genealogy puzzle. For example, do you remember Calvin Dimmitt from chapter one? His obituary (found at GenealogyBank.com) includes information about his illness, his marriage, his children, and place of burial. If his wife's maiden name wasn't already known, the obituary makes it clear. Remember this obituary when you get to chapter ten. You'll see why an obituary can be so valuable.

WORLD VITAL RECORDS

<worldvitalrecords.com>

This site offers a monthly or annual subscription rate and a thirty-day money-back guarantee. Search nearly four billion family history names and millions of vital records from the United States and thirty-nine counties.

Although World Vital Records is known for smaller and more unusual collections, like Navy cruise books and high school yearbooks, you'll also find large data collections. Among them is the surname database from more than fifty years of *Everton's Genealogical Helper* magazine. Search results will also include data from free sites like Find A Grave <findagrave.com>.

Calvin Dimmitt died at his home in the south part of town a week ago last Friday night of heart trouble and dropsy. He had been in poor health for almost a year and was not able to lie down for some time before his death. Mr. Dimmitt was born in Indiana seventy-six years ago. He was married to Miss Nancy Marcum August 5, 1860. To this union were born nine children. Besides the wife, five children survive him. They are Watson Dimmitt of Pleasant Hill, Albert Dimmitt of Kansas City, Mrs. W T. Thomas, Mrs. William Rich, Mrs. Josie Faulkenberry of Lone Jack. All were with him when death came, except Albert, who reached here shortly afterward. Mr. Dimmitt came to Missouri in 1869 and settled near Lone Jack and lived the remainder of his life in and around here. The Rev. Fred Hardy made a talk at the home Saturday at 2:30 o'clock, and burial was in the Lone Jack Cemetery.

Calvin Dimmitt obituary, January 1917, *Kansas City Star*, GenealogyBank.com

AMERICAN ANCESTORS <americanancestors.org>

Operated by the New England Historic Genealogical Society (NEHGS), this site is a treasure if you have New England ancestors.

Included in your annual subscription is:

- access to early American newspapers
- discounts on research services
- *American Ancestors* magazine subscription
- Massachusetts vital records
- New England journals
- three thousand online databases

The site has some free databases as well, such as New York Wills, 1626–1836. To access the free databases, you'll need to register with NEHGS (registration is free).

GENEALOGY TODAY <genealogytoday.com>

Genealogy Today is a lesser-known subscription site that specializes in an eclectic collection of family history records. Not sure if this is a subscription would be beneficial for your research? You can conduct a free search of the indexes first and see if the site contains data relevant to your family.

THE ORIGINS NETWORK <www.origins.net>

This is a favorite site for searching your British or Irish ancestry. Search for free, but you'll have to join to view the records. Holdings include birth, death, marriage, and other records, some dating back to the 1400s.

If you're hot on the trail of UK ancestors, check out the three-day membership trial. Even if you can't review and print everything you need in seventy-two-hours, this will give you plenty of time to decide on the value of a monthly or annual plan.

ONE GREAT FAMILY <onegreatfamily.com>

This site is like the world's largest family tree, built with input from genealogists like you. Take the seven-day free trial and see if you can grow your tree. One Great Family automatically searches for new data that fits into your tree, and notifies you when finds are made.

Members come from 170 countries, and the database contains 190 million unique entries.

ARCHIVES <archives.com>

Archives contains more than 1.2 billion genealogical records, including more than 100 million newspaper pages. This subscription site offers a seven-day free trial period, with an annual subscription rate of $39.95. In addition to accessing online data, you can also order (for an additional fee) on-site searches at county courthouses.

Archives' databases span most areas of interest to genealogists:

- vital records
- living people search
- newspapers
- obituaries
- cemetery listings
- census
- military
- immigration

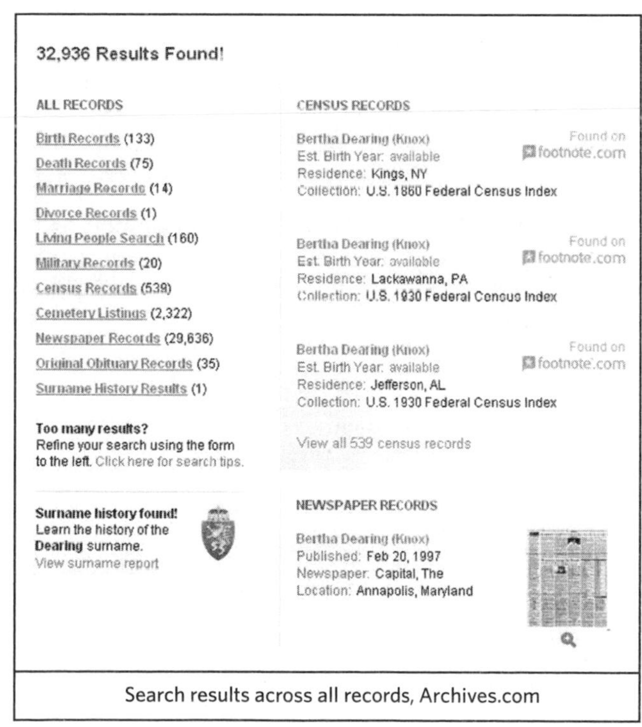

Search results across all records, Archives.com

- surname histories
- public records

A search across all records (verses a specific record type) will return a results page indicating how many hits were found in each type of record.

If you don't know much about the origin of your surname, you'll enjoy reading the Surname History. This includes the country of origin, Americanized spelling, and the number of people with this surname found in databases, i.e., "10 Dearings in immigration records." History will also show you a map of the surname distribution in the United States, as well as variant spellings.

FINDMYPAST <findmypast.co.uk>

With more than 750 million UK records, and more added monthly, FindMyPast is a valuable database for researching your English heritage.

You can begin with a fourteen-day free trial with a search of indexed birth records from 1837–2006, marriage records from 1835–2005, and millions of parish records (baptisms, marriages, burials). You'll also find military records spanning 1656–1994. Can't find your ancestors in U.S. immigration records? It's possible they're here in the passenger lists of people leaving the UK from 1890–1960.

Among the holdings here are "UK Specialist Records"; these are small collections with information you're not likely to find elsewhere. Gems include an 1896 list of clergy, an 1858 medical directory for Ireland, and indexes to 30,000 lists of crew members on board vessels, 1861–1913.

Want an online family tree that you can access from any location? You can create multiple trees (for free) at FindMyPast from scratch or by uploading a GEDCOM file. Users can also store up to 200MB of images and other media along with their online family trees.

FREE DATABASES

The following websites allow you to search their databases and the view results for no charge.

FamilySearch <familysearch.org>

Probably the best known—and largest—of the free sites, FamilySearch has more than one billion names in its databases. Thanks to volunteer efforts, new data is being added on a regular basis.

See chapter fourteen for real-life examples of what you can find at FamilySearch.org

THE DATABASES

You can search across all FamilySearch databases or filter by geographic region, date, and local place. Collections range from state and international censuses to birth record images, probate, Civil War, death, marriage, and migration. Some collections are indexes; others contain images of original records.

If an image is available, you'll see a thumbnail on the left side of the information about the individual. Click the thumbnail to view, print, or save the image. There's even an option to invert the image (from black on white to white on black) if it's of poor quality.

Discover Your Family History

Records Trees Catalog Books

First Names Last Name

Place From Year To Year

Search Advanced search

Browse by Location

Africa
Asia and Middle East
Australia and New Zealand
Caribbean, Central and South America
Europe
Pacific Islands
USA, Canada, and Mexico

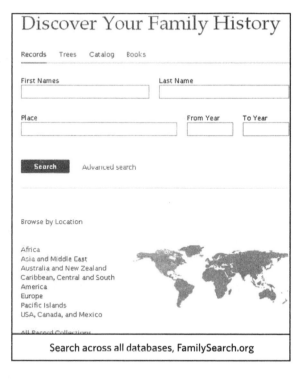

Search across all databases, FamilySearch.org

FAMILYSEARCH RESEARCH WIKI <wiki.familysearch.org/en/Browse_by_Country>
What do you do when you find ancestors from a country across the globe or a research problem concerning an unfamiliar topic? Turn to the FamilySearch Research Wiki. Here you'll find research articles written by experts, and you have the ability to add your own expertise, just like you can at Wikipedia. Some topics have a robust amount of information available, while others have a slim amount.

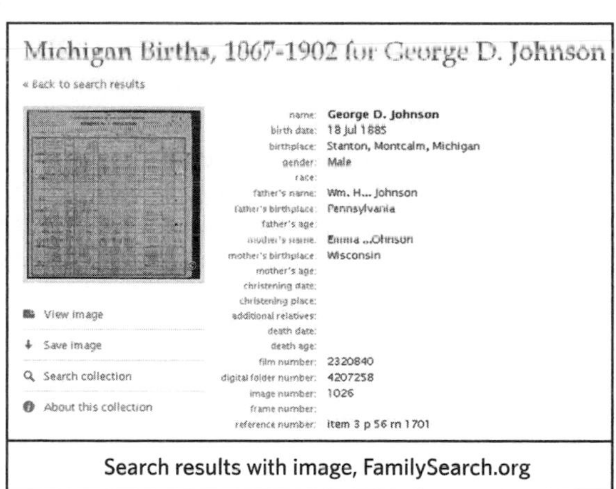

Search results with image, FamilySearch.org

FAMILYSEARCH CATALOG <familysearch.org>
If a genealogical record has been microfilmed, it's probably part of the FamilySearch collections at the Family History Library. For a nominal fee, you can order a microfilm or microfiche through your local FamilySearch Center (FSC) and have it delivered to the FSC for your review.

Use the online catalog for preliminary research into what's available. You can search holdings by surname, place, title, author, subject, call number of film/fiche number, or keywords (beta).

The surname search will tell you if anyone has written a book about your family. Use the place search to see the records available for a specific location. For example, a search for San Diego, California, shows there are more than seventy items, including fifteen on only San Diego history.

Click any entry for availability in either microfilm or fiche. Once you find a film/fiche of interest, copy down the name and call number, then place your order through a FamilySearch Center. It typically takes about two weeks for films to arrive. Unfortunately, books aren't available for loan.

California, San Diego - History - Societies (1)
California, San Diego - History (15)
San Diego and Imperial counties, California : a record of settlement, organization, progress and achievement
author: Black, Samuel F., 1846-
availability: Family History Centers
The history of San Diego County ranchos : the Spanish, Mexican and American occupation of San Diego County and the story of the ownership of land grants therein
author: Brackett, Robert W
availability: Family History Library
San Diego County place-names : yesterday's people, today's geography
author: Stein, Lou, 1908-
availability: Family History Library
History of San Diego County
author: Heilbron, Carl H
availability: Family History Centers
Reproduction of Wallace W. Elliott's history of San Bernadino and San Diego Counties, California, with illustrations, 1883 : Including material on present-day Riverside County
availability: Family History Library
Backcountry annals : records of San Diego County, California, 1850-1981
author: Warner, Susan Merrill

Place search, FamilySearch Library catalog

FAMILYSEARCH LEARNING CENTER <familysearch.org/learn/researchcourses>
Click the Learn link at the top of the home page to see the free genealogy courses offered online. Courses are presented in video format and include a PDF handout or course outline. Online courses are excellent, especially if you're just getting started in researching foreign countries.

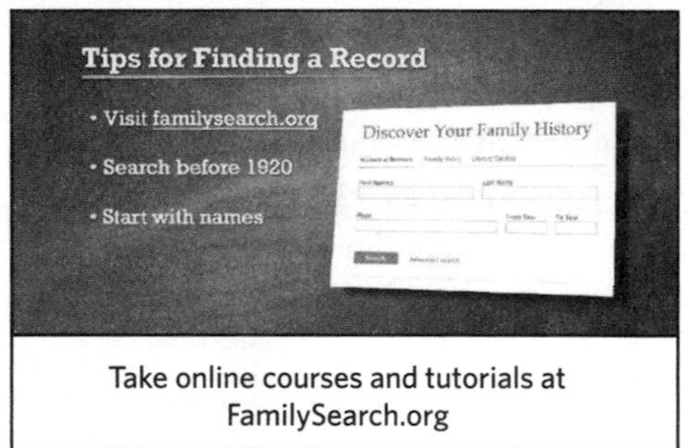

Take online courses and tutorials at FamilySearch.org

RootsWeb <rootsweb.com>

RootsWeb is the oldest free genealogy community on the internet. With more than eight million user-donated records, you will probably find at least one ancestor here.

Although funded by Ancestry.com, RootsWeb has maintained its own identity, maintaining ongoing projects like the 600-million name WorldConnect Project, message boards, and thousands of mailing lists.

If you want to connect with other surname researchers, get on a RootsWeb mailing list. Lists abound for almost every surname and genealogical topic imaginable. When you opt in to the list, you'll get the choice to receive a digest (compilation) of e-mail messages that come into the list or receive each e-mail as it is sent to the list. Mailing lists and message boards offer the opportunity of presenting your brick wall problems to other researchers and hopefully getting some help.

Don't overlook all of the other offerings on this site. A favorite is the U.S. Town/County Database that you can use to quickly look up the county in which a town is located. Or search the Archives for data in a collection that's been growing for more than ten years.

USGenWeb <usgenweb.com>

Established in 1996, USGenWeb is a conglomeration of thousands of websites that are maintained by volunteers. Because this is an all-volunteer organization, the look, feel, and content of each site within the project varies depending on the efforts of the site's coordinator.

Some sites are robust, brimming with databases, biographies, county histories, maps, and transcriptions of church, census, and cemetery records. Others are barebones, providing little more than surname queries and links to the county courthouse, library, and other repositories.

You also may find broken links as you surf the project due to a massive data transfer the project undertook when it moved from its original RootsWeb host to other hosts in 2000. If you encounter a broken link on a USGenWeb site, contact the site's coordinator.

On the left side of the USGenWeb Home page, you'll see an alphabetical list of the fifty states, plus the District of Columbia and Oklahoma/Indian Territory. Click on any of the states to go to that state's home page.

USGenWeb's structure mimics the way genealogists research national-, state-, and county-level records, meaning the most emphasis is placed on local, that is county-level, records. So each USGenWeb state site will prominently feature links to county sites. The key to successfully using USGenWeb is knowing the names of the counties your ancestors lived in. The case study at the end of this chapter will help you find this information if you don't have it.

Massachusetts Counties Selection List

County	Date Formed	Parent County	County Seat	Contact
Barnstable	1685	New Plymouth Colony	Barnstable	Ray Sears
Berkshire	1761	Hampshire	Pittsfield	Dawn Newton
Bristol	1685	New Plymouth Colony	Taunton	Don Wright
Dukes	1683	none	Edgartown	Chris Baer
Essex	1643	none	Lawrence, Newburyport, Salem	Michelle W. Cook Jodi Salerno
Franklin	1811	Hampshire	Greenfield	Sue Downhill
Hampden	1812	Hampshire	Springfield	Dawn Newton
Hampshire	1662	Middlesex	Northampton	Sue Downhill
Middlesex	1643	none	Cambridge, Lowell	Michael Lewis
Nantucket	1695	none	Nantucket	David Sylvester
Norfolk	1793	Suffolk	Dedham	Don Wright
Plymouth	1685	New Plymouth Colony	Plymouth	Dale H. Cook
				Christine Sharbrough

Select a county at the home page of the Massachusetts GenWeb

Almost all records, from tax to property to birth to marriage to death, are kept on the county level, not the state or federal level. You'll also find church, school, social, and newspaper records on the county level.

Again, because the sites are run by volunteers, there's no uniform formula for site content and presentation. But almost all county sites include county formation dates and the names of parent counties from which each was formed, along with other historical background and possibly photos. You'll also find the name and e-mail address of the county coordinator. Counties without coordinators will be indicated as needing "adoption."

You'll probably find:

- a site search engine. For counties with hundreds or even dozens of pages, it's quicker to use the county search engine than go through each set of documents individually. The search engine will query all the record transcriptions for the county, such as newspaper articles and Bible, census, school, and military records.
- names of volunteers who'll do lookups. These volunteers may own county histories or published indexes of local records (census, cemeteries, tax lists), or live near repositories or cemeteries. Look for rules on how to request a lookup.
- surname queries. You can post your own query and read queries from other researchers. Note that contact information on these pages is frequently out-of-date, but it's still worth perusing and posting.
- links to research techniques for other sites.
- links to local repositories and genealogy organizations.

In addition to the States links, the USGenWeb had a number of other helpful links on its Home page:

PROJECTS: The link to special projects is located both on the top menu and the right side of the Home page. One of the projects, for example, focuses on transcribing tombstones across the country. For researchers who live hundreds of miles from a cemetery, being able to track down a burial online is a real time-saver.

Other projects transcribe obituary, census, pension, and marriage records. Explore this link for a list of current projects, along with a link to each.

RESEARCHERS: Also located on the top of the home page is a Researchers link. Click it and you'll land on a page with a hodgepodge of helpful information on topics such as land records, naming conventions, immigration, the census, and more. (Note that on some pages this link is called Research Home.)

PROJECT ARCHIVES: The USGenWeb Archives house thousands of transcriptions of historical documents such as obituaries, biographical sketches, wills, cemeteries, and county histories that volunteers have uploaded to a state or county site. This link lets you search the archives either nationally or by state (or by county, from county sites).

The Project Archives also includes a Special Project section that includes links for Census Images, the Marriages Project, the Maps Project, Newsletter, the Obits Project, the Pensions Project, the Special Collections Project, and Court Cases.

Note that you generally won't see digitized records, so use the transcribed information to track down the original record.

SITE NAVIGATION: This easy-to-miss pull-down menu near the top of the Home page has links to several pages that you'd probably never otherwise find, including brochures you can print for free distribution to your genealogy society, a PowerPoint presentation about USGenWeb, and how to write queries. This menu also has quick links to the pages described under the Projects link.

WorldGenWeb <worldgenweb.org>

If your ancestor search leads you outside the United States, surf the WorldGenWeb. It's structured like the USGenWeb, except for its country-specific divisions (states, counties, regions) rather than state and county.

Although some of the pages have scant information, you will find valuable contact information for the region. This is particularly important when it comes to requesting official records.

Several of the WorldGenWeb sites also have research tips. For example, the Caribbean pages have information on religions in the area by nationality and immigration lists. You'll also learn about "stock books," the local version of slave and indentured servant inventories.

HeritageQuestOnline <heritagequestonline.com>

HeritageQuestOnline is only accessible through public libraries that have a subscription. If your local library has a subscription, you can access the website's six outstanding databases:

- the complete set of federal census records, 1790–1930
- PERSI (Periodical Source Index), a compilation of more than two million articles from genealogy magazines
- Revolutionary War pension and bounty land warrant applications
- Freedman's Bank, an excellent source for information on African-American ancestors
- 28,000 family history books
- U.S. Serial Set, a database of legal documents

Check with your local library to see if it subscribes to HeritageQuestOnline.

Geni <geni.com>

With unlimited, free online space, you can upload your GEDCOM files, photos, videos, and other documents, then share them with other family members or researchers. If you find another tree that relates to your own, you can request permission to collaborate with the tree owner.

Using Geni, you can find connections with other genealogists, as well as become part of the Big Tree—Geni's attempt to create one family tree for the entire world. The Big Tree is built from the collaborative research of millions of genealogists; to date it has connected 57 million profiles.

If you want to boost your chances of finding another person researching your family tree, Geni is a great place to begin.

WeRelate <werelate.org>

With pages on more than 2 million people and families, WeRelate is the largest genealogy wiki—and it's geared primarily toward sharing family tree data. The goal is to encourage people to post their research on specific ancestors for others to find and add to, so everyone benefits from the collaboration.

To get started, sign up for a free account, then either upload a GEDCOM file or begin entering your family tree manually.

After WeRelate creates your pages (this can take up to an hour for large files), you can view your relatives on stand-alone pages, within a pedigree chart, in a timeline, and even on a map.

The site has several excellent video tutorials, each of which walks you through a specific task, such as how to create or edit a family page. Before beginning your wiki expedition, I recommend you watch the "helicopter ride" video (eight minutes), which gives a good overview of how the system works.

GOVERNMENT SITES

Library of Congress <loc.gov>

You can easily spend a day just surfing through the Library of Congress website. Known as America's Library, the Library of Congress was built by Congress in 1800. After the original collection was destroyed by the British during the War of 1812, Thomas Jefferson sold his personal library to the LOC in 1815.

Among the collections are

- sound recordings
- historic newspapers
- photographs
- maps
- manuscripts

Click on any of these "favorite" collections from the home page to search the collection. For example, the digitized newspaper collection ranges from 1836 to 1922 and can be searched by keyword. The Advanced Search allows filtering by state, date, and newspaper name.

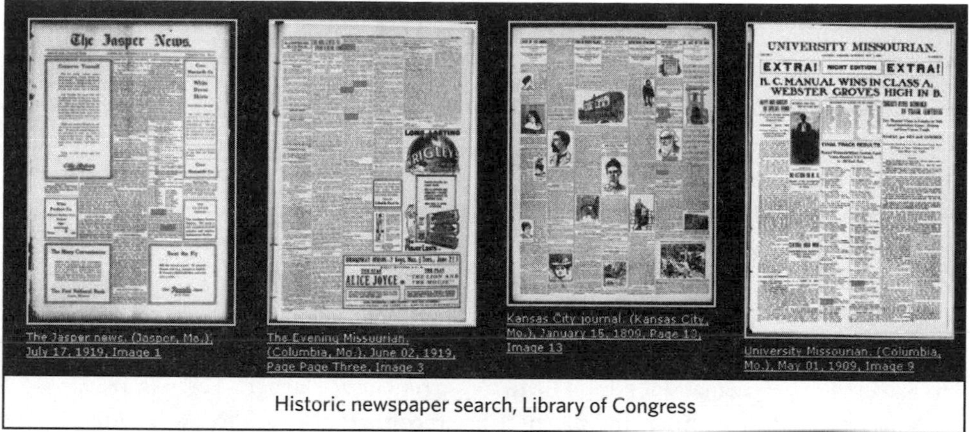

Historic newspaper search, Library of Congress

The Maps Collection is extraordinary, whether you're searching for an historic river route down the Ohio or particulars of a Civil War battle.

Use the on-site search engine to locate specific collections or items in a collection. For example, a simple search for genealogy turned up more than 2,400 listings, including a digitized version of a book written in 1879. This volume is a record of Scotch-Irish Presbyterians who were the first settlers in the "Forks of Delaware."

Click the link to researchers <loc.gov/rr> to find links to all of the digital collections <loc.gov/library/libarch-digital.html>. Keep in mind that each of the major collections can have several other subcollections within them—so there's much more to search than initially meets the eye.

My favorites? Prints & Photographs and American Memory.

National Archives and Records Administration (NARA) <archives.gov/research/genealogy/index.html>

Although many genealogists will never travel to the National Archives, they can visit virtually via the Archives' website. Among the many resources for genealogists are how-to articles, tips on getting started in research, and a section of preserving and storing old photographs.

As the Archives website notes, the focus isn't on providing online data, but rather "on providing research tools, such as microfilm indexes, as well as resources, such as finding aids, articles and information on where to find the records and how to access them, and how to conduct in-person research."

Among those tools are the Access to Archival Databases (AAD) and the Archival Research Catalog (ARC).

The AAD <aad.archives.gov/aad/> is a search engine for 85 million historic electronic records, a tiny fraction of the 10 billion electronic records held by the NARA. You can do a free-text search, or browse by category or subject. One of them might be of great interest to you if your ancestor came to America during the Irish potato famine. It's a list of *Famine Irish Passenger Record Data File (FIPAS), 1/12/1846–12/31/1851*. While you won't find an image of a passenger list, you can see the port of embarkation, manifest number, and arrival date in the United States.

The ARC is the online catalog of all of NARA's holdings, both in Washington, D.C., and the Regional Archives. You can search by keyword, topic, people, and location. A handy filter is the tab that allows a search only of digitized records.

An interesting find, while searching for *Tennessee military* was *Congressman Davy Crockett's Resolution to Abolish the Military Academy at West Point, 02/25/1830*. Another was Robert E. Lee's demand for John Brown's surrender at Harper's Ferry in 1859.

Some of the more popular findings here are records that relate to Native Americans, including *The Final Rolls of Citizens and Freedmen of the Five Civilized Tribes in Indian Territory, 03/04/1907*.

CASE STUDY

FINDING ANCESTORS AT THE USGENWEB

The goal of this search is to learn more about Martin Hendrickson and John Hendrickson when they lived in Kansas. What's known is that both of them lived in Lincoln, Kansas, at an unknown period of time after the Civil War.

STEP 1. I didn't know which county Lincoln, Kansas, was located in, so I used the U.S. Town/County Database at RootsWeb <resources.rootsweb.ancestry.com/cgi-bin/townco.cgi>. Lincoln, Kansas, is located in Lincoln County.

STEP 2. On the USGenWeb Home page <usgenweb.com>, I clicked the link for the Kansas page. The Kansas state page gives you the choice of selecting a specific county on a list or on a map.

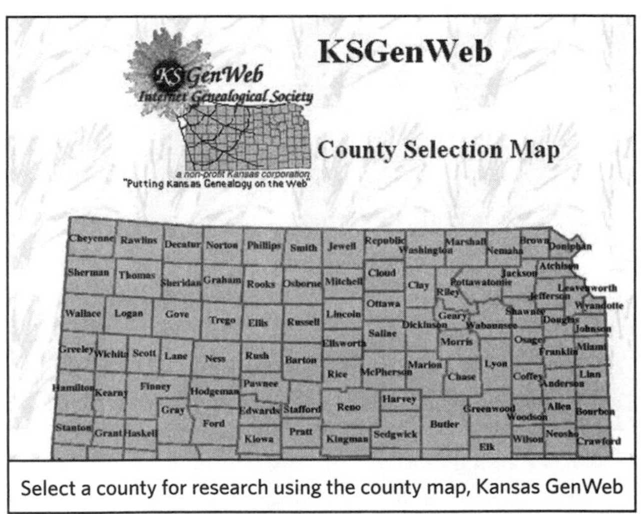

Select a county for research using the county map, Kansas GenWeb

I chose the map option and was able to find and select Lincoln County.

STEP 3. From the Lincoln County Home page, I had the choice of searching the entire Lincoln County site using their on-site search engine, or I could browse through the many sections of the site.

A third choice was to check out the forty links to different Kansas genealogy sites. These include links to:

- online census
- Kansas pioneers
- World War II Kansans
- old maps
- Korean War casualties
- Kansas in the Civil War
- index of an 1895 Kansas state census

Use the on-site search engine to search all of the pages at the Lincoln County, Kansas GenWeb

INFORMATION ON LINCOLN COUNTY		
Agriculture	Biographical information	Books and articles
Businesses	Cemeteries	Census Data
Churches	Courthouse History	Crimes and criminal
Directories and indexes of names	Disasters	Education & school
Lincoln County EMAIL LIST Join others researching Lincoln County	Ethnic sources	Lincoln County famili online
General Lincoln County links	Geography, maps, locations	Geology
Government & Politics	Humor	Libraries & Associati
Lookups	Medicine	Military information
Newspapers	Newspaper gleanings names and information from Lincoln County newspapers	Obituaries and death no
Lincoln County photographs	Queries and Surnames	Lincoln County resea guide
Lincoln County stories	Towns and townships	Vital records

List of Lincoln County, Kansas, genealogy resources

My first choice was to use the search box. Doing a simple search for John Hendrickson and then Martin Hendrickson returned numerous hits, including personal recollections, newspaper articles, and a county history.

In reading through the hits, it was apparent that there was more than one John Hendrickson in the same place and same time period.

However, one of the mentions in the recollection section of the newspaper was about a John Hendrickson who was in Lincoln with his son-in-law, Mike Keller. I knew from previous research that Mike had married Martha Hendrickson, John's daughter. So this was my John.

So, more information about John than I had known before, including:

In the spring of [18]sixty-eight we were joined by others among them was John Hendrickson and his son in-law by the name Mike Keller. Mike settled east of where the Rees mill now stands, about eighty rods east on the south side of the creek and John Hendrickson's claim joined what is now Lincoln Center on the southwest corner. He built his house near where the Alva Wilson house now stands. In August of the same year he and his son in-law had quite a scrap with the Indians. I never did know if they killed any Indians, but they had two of their blankets so they decided they had enough of the west and went back to Missouri that fall and never got back to Kansas only on a visit.

Not only do I have the year of John's arrival in Lincoln, I also have a location where the home stood and the fact that John left Lincoln that same fall. This means taking my research back to an 1870 Missouri census.

What else can I find?

STEP 4. I explored other links on the site and found a photo of the Rees Mill (near where Mike Keller lived) <freepages.genealogy.rootsweb.ancestry.com/~lincolncounty/mill1.jpg> and a link to other Lincoln families who have websites <http://skyways.lib.ks.us/genweb/lincoln/dirfamily.htm>. This is quite a find because at least one of them is connected to the family I'm searching. Most valuable, perhaps, is a Lincoln County Research Guide that details how to find vital records, cemetery and church records, and obituaries.

Is there more to find at the USGenWeb?

STEP 5. Why not check the archives for John? This time, we'll go to the USGenWeb Home page and click Project Archives, then National Search Engine. To search all states at once, click the link to Search all of U.S. <usgwarchives.net/search/searcharchives.html>. Otherwise, click on the link for your state of interest. I picked Missouri and did a search for *John Hendrickson*.

This was pretty much a bust.

STEP 6. How about census images? I also searched the USGenWeb archives for county-level indexes of U.S. census records. (Some USGenWeb pages even have digitized images of the census itself.)

To search through the Census Project, go to the main Census Project page <usgwarchives.net/census> and click your state, then the county. Beneath it, you'll see the available census year(s). Another bust for me, as neither my Kansas nor my Missouri counties were listed. But you may have better luck.

5

Birth, Marriage, and Death Records

In this chapter you'll discover online sites for tracking down birth, death, marriage, probate, court, and cemetery records.

VITAL RECORDS

Vital records are the official records of a person's life maintained by governmental agencies at a city, county, or state level. These include birth and death certificates, marriage licenses, and divorce decrees.

Today, vital records are kept as a matter of course, but that wasn't true in the past. The year each state began mandating vital records varies from state to state. For example, state-level birth records weren't required until 1878 in New Jersey, 1897 in Connecticut, and 1909 in Arizona. Before state-mandated record keeping, vital records were kept by county officials, and the date that record keeping began varied from county to county. Copies of vital records can be ordered from the state or, if the request predates state records, from the county (if available).

You can find a complete list of records available for each state at VitalRec.com <vitalrec.com>. Use the pull-down, Select a State or Territory menu to choose your state, then scroll down the page to view available records, cost, and mailing address of the state agency. You can also order records online by following the links on the state page.

If you order online through the VitalRec.com system, you'll pay an additional handling fee, above the cost required by the state. In the ordering process (whether you order online or by mail), you're required to state the reason you want the record and your relationship to the person the record is for—all measures to protect privacy and security. While some states can process requests quickly, others may take up to six months.

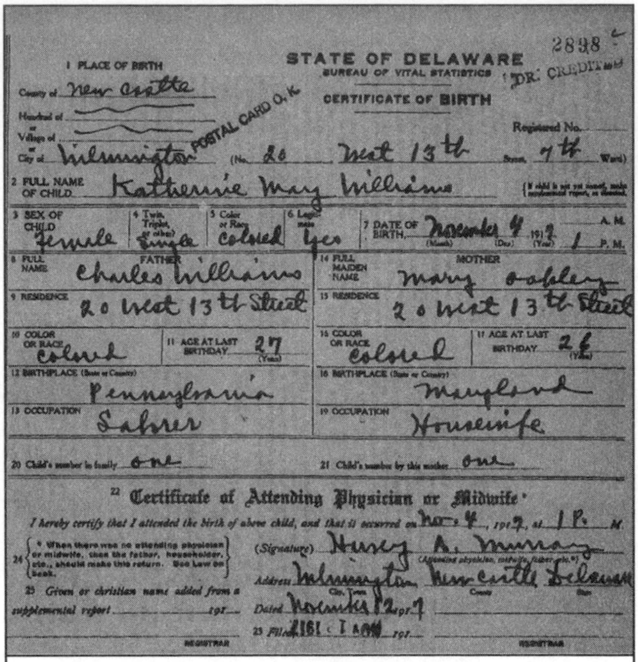

STATE OF DELAWARE
BUREAU OF VITAL STATISTICS
CERTIFICATE OF BIRTH

2898

1 PLACE OF BIRTH
County of New Castle
City of Wilmington (No. 20 West 13th St., 7th Ward)
POSTAL CARD O.K.

2 FULL NAME OF CHILD Katherine May Williams

3 SEX OF CHILD Female | 4 Twin, Triplet, or other Single | 5 Color or Race Colored | 6 Legit. Yes | 7 DATE OF BIRTH November 4 1917

8 FULL NAME FATHER Charles Williams | 14 FULL MAIDEN NAME MOTHER Mary Oakley

9 RESIDENCE 20 West 13th Street | 15 RESIDENCE 20 West 13th Street

10 COLOR OR RACE Colored | 11 AGE AT LAST BIRTHDAY 27 | 16 COLOR OR RACE Colored | 17 AGE AT LAST BIRTHDAY 26

12 BIRTHPLACE Pennsylvania | 18 BIRTHPLACE Maryland

13 OCCUPATION Laborer | 19 OCCUPATION Housewife

20 Child's number in family one | 21 Child's number by this mother one

22 Certificate of Attending Physician or Midwife

I hereby certify that I attended the birth of above child, and that it occurred on Nov. 4, 1917, at 1 P.M.

(Signature) Henry A. Murray

Address Wilmington, New Castle, Delaware

Dated November 12, 1917

Delaware Birth Record, FamilySearch.org

FINDING BIRTH RECORDS ONLINE

FamilySearch.org has one of the largest collections of free birth records. Spanning 1867 to 1931, you can search a name index to birth, baptism, and christening records from a few states. This collection has 20,946 records. Some of these collections include images of the actual birth record.

Birth Records on FamilySearch.org

Using FamilySearch.org <familysearch.org>, you can search for birth records using two different techniques. The first is by doing a global search of all databases using the search boxes on the Home page. Enter name, place (if known), and date range (if known). You can also click the Advanced link to enter more filters, such as an event (i.e., birth, marriage).

Your search may return hundreds or even thousands of results, as federal census records are among the databases. After search results are returned, you can filter further

TIP

Don't forget to check the databases listed under "United States"; some of these contain marriage, birth, and other record types.

by using the filters on the left side of the page. Click any of the filters to narrow search results. In the example at right, clicking the Collections link gives me the option of specifying which group of records I want searched.

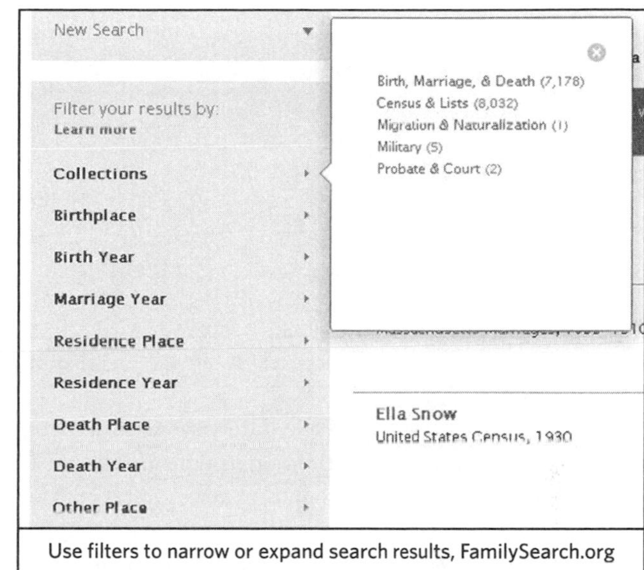

Use filters to narrow or expand search results, FamilySearch.org

Select as many of the filters as needed to improve your search results.

The second method of finding a birth record is by selecting records by location from the link on the Home page. Once clicked, you'll see a list of databases relevant to that locale.

Browse by Location

Africa
Asia and Middle East
Australia and New Zealand
Caribbean, Central and South America
Europe
Pacific Islands
USA, Canada, and Mexico

All Record Collections

Select records by location at FamilySearch.org

If you click the USA, Canada, and Mexico link, you'll see there are more than four hundred databases, listed in alphabetical order. You can easily skim down the list to see if there's a database of marriage records for your state. If you see a camera icon by the name of a database, this means there are images of the original records.

Although it's rewarding to find a birth record online, it's even better if you can find an image of the original record. That's because the digital version may have excerpted only partial data from the original.

In this sample search, I wanted birth information on Lydia Dickinson, born in Massachusetts. Instead of using the simple search form at FamilySearch.org, I chose the second method and searched the database of Massachusetts Births, 1841–1915.

I found Lydia, along with the name of her parents, her date of birth, and the town and county where she was born. Also included were the microfilm number and page number if I wanted to order a copy of the film.

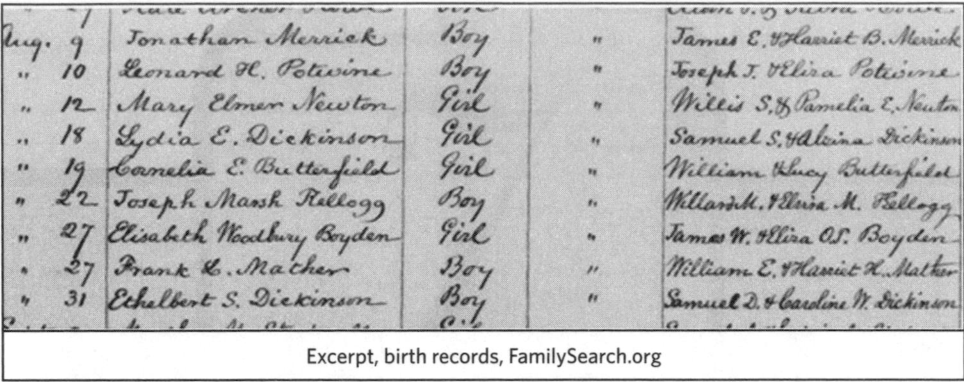

Aug.	9	Jonathan Merrick	Boy	"	James E. & Harriet B. Merrick
"	10	Leonard H. Potwine	Boy	"	Joseph T. & Eliza Potwine
"	12	Mary Elmer Newton	Girl	"	Willis S. & Pamelia E. Newton
"	18	Lydia E. Dickinson	Girl	"	Samuel S. & Alvira Dickinson
"	19	Camelia E. Butterfield	Girl	"	William & Lucy Butterfield
"	22	Joseph Marsh Kellogg	Boy	"	Willard M. & Eliza M. Kellogg
"	27	Elisabeth Woodbury Boyden	Girl	"	James W. & Eliza O.S. Boyden
"	27	Frank E. Mather	Boy	"	William E. & Harriet H. Mather
"	31	Ethelbert S. Dickinson	Boy	"	Samuel D. & Caroline W. Dickinson

Excerpt, birth records, FamilySearch.org

Fortunately, this is one of the databases with images of original records, so I could examine it for more information. You might think that the information listed would be exactly the same as that found on the image. But it isn't.

The original record contained a list of all births in Amherst in 1849 (by exact date), the name of the town clerk, and—better still—the occupation of Lydia's father and the place of birth of both her parents! Although I knew Lydia was a girl, the records also state gender—a handy piece of information when finding names like Emery, Moody, and Slovan.

Not only did I learn far more about the family, but in browsing the list of other births, I saw other Dickinson births. Armed with the names of the other Dickinson babies' parents, I had a lot more research possibilities.

Birth Records on Ancestry.com

If you're using Ancestry.com <ancestry.com> to search for birth records, your search options are similar to that of FamilySearch.org. You can either do a global search across all databases, or you can specify the type of record you want to find.

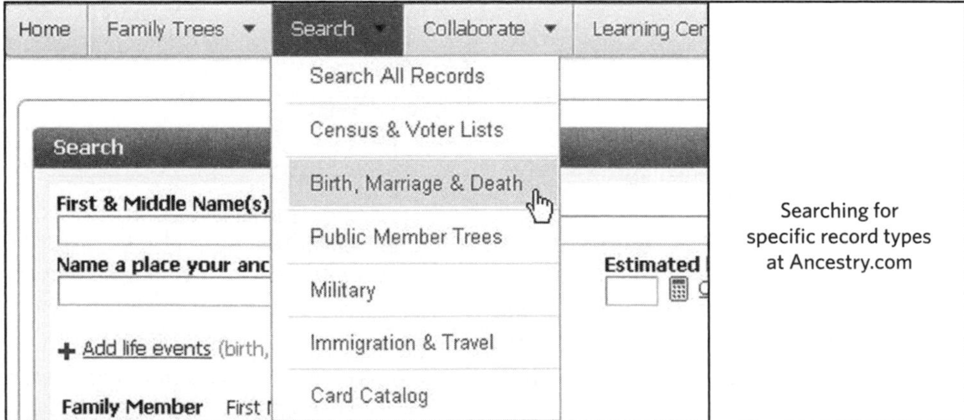

Searching for specific record types at Ancestry.com

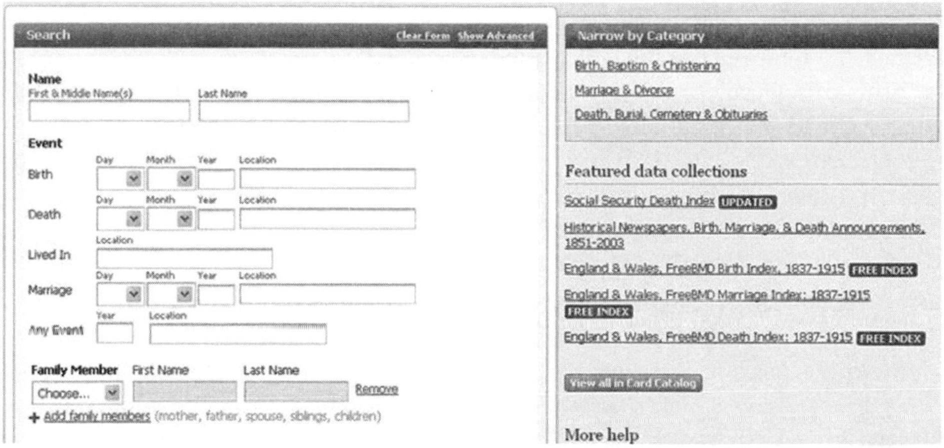

Narrow searches by category or collection, Ancestry.com

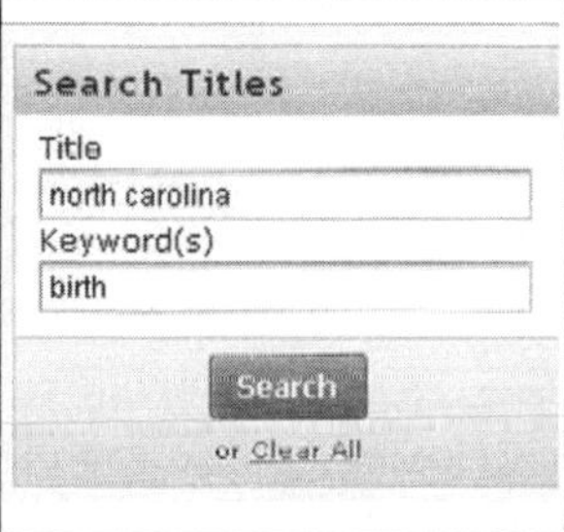

Filter by database, Ancestry.com

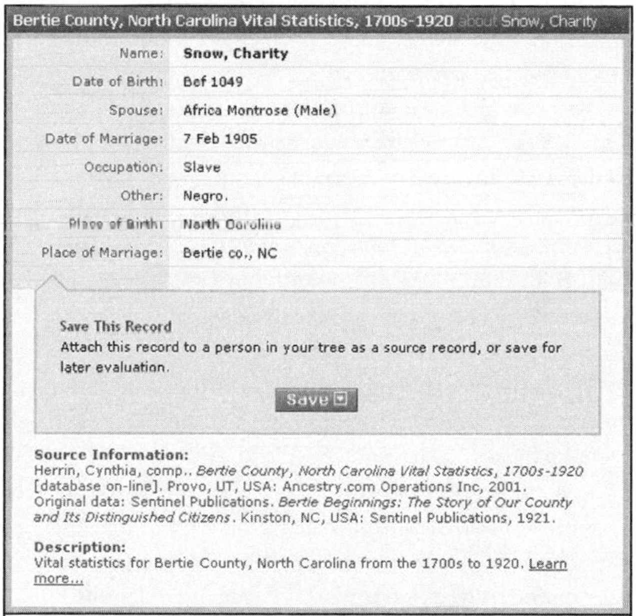

Database source information, Ancestry.com

After you've chosen a broad record group, like Birth, Marriage & Death, you'll see a search screen with several options. There are a couple of ways to filter for best results. One is on the search form itself, which you can filter for birth year, where the person lived, and even the name of another family member. You can also filter by database.

If you search without filtering by database, you'll get records pertaining to all of the birth, marriage, and death databases in Ancestry.com. So before searching, notice the choices in the right column, under the heading Narrow by Category. It's here that you can filter further by specifying Birth, Baptism & Christening.

If this still doesn't filter down enough, click the View All in Card Catalog link, and specify your filters. In this case, I asked for databases with North Carolina as part of the title and *birth* as one of the keywords. Now, instead of wading through records from more than 1,500 databases, my results will be pulled from forty-two relevant databases.

If your filter is too narrow, go back and remove some of your filters.

After you find your ancestor, click on the name and a new box will appear showing basic data, along with source information and a description of the database. Remember to copy the source information so you can add it to your family tree file.

If your results contain an image, click the thumbnail to view the record.

Where Else Can You Find Birth Records?

Because a birth certificate is used to apply for a passport or other official documents, more recent records fall under privacy or security laws. Depending on the state, you can obtain an informational copy of a birth certificate, but not a certified copy.

To find other free online sites, check the links in the Vital Records section of Cyndi's List <cyndislist.com>.

You can also look for birth records on official state websites. The state of Missouri <www.sos.mo.gov/archives/resources/birthdeath>, for example, has a searchable database of pre-1910 births and deaths.

Arizona <genealogy.az.gov> also has a searchable database of births from 1855 to 1935. The results will show the date of birth, county, and name of both parents.

Do a search to see if your state has online birth records. You may have to be creative in your search phrases:

- *Michigan free birth records*
- *birth records online free genealogy Michigan*
- *online free birth records Michigan*
- *Michigan genealogy birth free*

MARRIAGES

Marriage licenses are issued at the county level by the county clerk. The clerk issues couples an application for a license, which

Cyndi's List

Cyndi's List <cyndislist.com> is one of the oldest genealogy portals on the internet. The site contains more than 300,000 links to genealogy websites, organized by category. If you've exhausted a search and aren't sure what to do next, surf over to Cyndi's List and investigate the resources.

You'll find many more links about your topic, including databases, personal websites, and information-rich sites. For example, if you click the categories in the "B" section (for births), you'll see all the related categories, plus links that filter birth records into several subcategories (such as locality-specific). After you are in the U.S. list, click your state of interest. Massachusetts, for instance, has thirteen links, one of them leading to a free database of vital records to 1850.

includes a return—a document signed by the wedding officiate affirming a legal wedding ceremony took place between the man and woman. After the county clerk received the completed return, the clerk filed it in a register and issued the marriage license.

As you research, you may run across the term *marriage bann*. A bann was a public announcement of an intended marriage. The announcement was made shortly before the marriage date to give people time to raise any objections.

You may also see references to *marriage bonds*. A marriage bond was a sum of money an intended groom paid to a relative of his intended bride as a guarantee that there was no legal or moral reason preventing him from marrying. If a legal or moral reason was found or if the intended groom backed out, he forfeited the bond money.

TIP

If you want to be sure your search results are showing hits from official (government) sites, you can add a filter to your search terms. Here's how: *"texas birth records" site:*.gov*

This search tells the engine to look for Texas birth records on sites that have ".gov" as part of their domain name. This trick won't filter out every nongovernment site, but it will lower the irrelevant hits.

Marriage records are some of the easiest vital statistics to find online. Use your favorite search engine and do a search like *marriage records* and *Maryland* (or the name of your state).

Although you'll probably find records on personal blogs, USGenWeb county pages, or archives, many states are now posting marriage records online, including Illinois <cyberdriveillinois.com/departments/archives/databases.html>. This site even lets you request copies of the original records.

Marriage records are available on several of the database sites discussed in chapter four. FamilySearch.org has the largest free collection of marriage records with millions of names in its database. The image from FamilySearch.org's District of Columbia Marriages collection first shows the license as well as the return.

Illinois Statewide Marriage Index, 1763–1900

Click here for information about how to obtain copies of original marriage records.

332 records are displayed.
The maximum number displayed is 500. If a **MORE** button appears below, click for additional records.

Groom	Bride	Date	Vol./Page	License No.	County
KNOX, A R	HATCH, CELIA MRS	1893-07-12	1/ 207	2798	DU PAGE
KNOX, ALBERT	AUSBERGER, ANNIE	1882-12-20	/	507	STEPHENSON
KNOX, ALBERT L	YORK, LIZZIE	1894-09-07	3 /26	10789	VERMILION
KNOX, ALBERT W	SEARLES, HELEN ISABELLE	1893-03-22	/	00198235	COOK
KNOX, ALEX H	BLISS, MAUD	1897-04-22	4 /121	1568	LA SALLE
KNOX, ALEXANDER	LAAGE, MARY J MRS	1870-12-12	/		ADAMS
KNOX, ALEXANDER	LONG, ANN ELIZABETH	1868-02-20	/		ADAMS
KNOX, ALLEN E	HUTLEY, MARY H (SEE UTLEY)	1865-08-10	OMR/0147		CARROLL
KNOX, ALLEN E	UTLEY, MARY H (SEE HUTLEY)	1865-08-10	OMR/0147		CARROLL
KNOX, ALLEN J	KIDD, MARY ANN	1849-12-12	A /	2267	LA SALLE

Search results from Illinois Statewide Marriage Index

You'll also find marriage records on microfilm at FamilySearch Centers.

No. 9626 **Marriage License.**

To Any Minister, or other person, authorized to celebrate marriages in the District of Columbia, Greeting:

You are hereby authorized to solemnize the rites of marriage, between Noah Neale of Washington D.C. and Mary E. Bush of do

and having done so, you are commanded to make return of the same to the Clerk's Office of the Supreme Court of the said District within TEN days, as the law directs.

Witness my hand and seal of said Court, this 6th day of Dec anno Domini 1902

J R Young Clerk.

By [illegible] Assistant Clerk.

No. 9626 **Return.**

I, Rev. John Richard who have been duly authorized to celebrate the rites of marriage in the District of Columbia, do hereby certify that, by authority of license of corresponding number herewith, I solemnized the marriage of Noah Neale and Mary E. Bush named therein, on the 5 day of Jan. 1903, at 1242 1st S.E. in said District.

Rev. John Richard

Marriage license and return, District of Columbia Marriages collection, FamilySearch.org

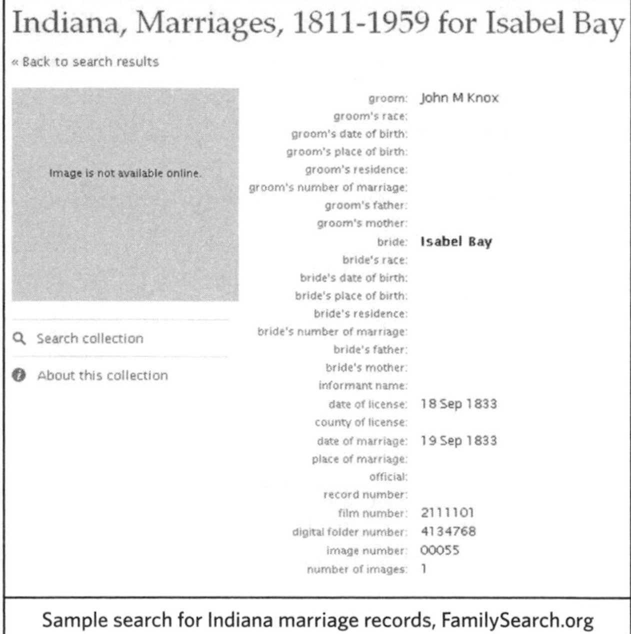

Indiana, Marriages, 1811-1959 for Isabel Bay

« Back to search results

Image is not available online.

Search collection

About this collection

groom:	John M Knox
groom's race:	
groom's date of birth:	
groom's place of birth:	
groom's residence:	
groom's number of marriage:	
groom's father:	
groom's mother:	
bride:	**Isabel Bay**
bride's race:	
bride's date of birth:	
bride's place of birth:	
bride's residence:	
bride's number of marriage:	
bride's father:	
bride's mother:	
informant name:	
date of license:	18 Sep 1833
county of license:	
date of marriage:	19 Sep 1833
place of marriage:	
official:	
record number:	
film number:	2111101
digital folder number:	4134768
image number:	00055
number of images:	1

Sample search for Indiana marriage records, FamilySearch.org

Searching for Marriage Records at FamilySearch.org

Want to try finding a marriage record at FamilySearch.org? I'm looking for the marriage of John Knox and Isabel Bay, married sometime in the early 1800s in Indiana. Instead of using the Home page search engine, I went to the individual databases and selected Indiana Marriage, 1811–1959. From the Home page <familysearch.org> click on USA, Canada, and Mexico, then click on Birth, Marriage, & Death under the Collections heading on the left rail.

Entering *John Knox* (without any other filters) into the search box resulted in ninety-three hits. Rather than go through each one, I went back to the search box and looked instead for *Isabel Bay*. I thought that because her name was less common, I could find the record faster.

This search only had two results, both the same. Per the record, John and Isabel got a marriage license on 18 September 1833 and married the next day. I'd like to get a copy of the record, so I made note of the film and image number so I could place an order at my local FamilySearch Center.

Because I also wanted to include the source information in my genealogy software, I followed the About This Collection link. There I learned more about the collection itself, including the fact that I could also order a copy of the record from the state of Indiana.

Note, too, this collection is an index only; no images are included.

Searching for Marriage Records at Ancestry.com

When searching Ancestry.com, marriage records are searchable in the same manner you searched for birth records: either by a global search across all databases or filtering down to marriage databases.

I did the same search for *John Knox* and *Isabel Bay*, and quickly got the same results, but this time Ancestry.com showed me that the record appeared in four separate databases. One of them (Indiana Marriage Collection, 1800–1941) also specified the record's volume and page number in the original county clerk's record book.

How about one more? This time I filtered by Marriage and Divorce Record Collections rather than Birth, Marriage &Death.

In this search, I'm hoping to find information on the marriage of Francois Bienvenue and Sarah Lesage. Doing a basic search of marriage records quickly showed me the challenges I was facing.

First, Bienvenue is the French form of the name Welcome, so could the marriage be Welcome or Bienvenue?

Second, from what I was told, Francois was born in Montreal, Quebec. This probably means he was Catholic and that the records at Ancestry.com will probably be in French.

Third, people of French ancestry often used "dit names." These are a kind of alias, or additional name, that might have included a place of origin. In getting on the internet and doing a little research, I learned that common dit names for Bienvenue include:

- Fontaine
- Rivière
- LaFontaine
- Delisle
- DeL'Isle

I also learned that Fontaines could be "Fontaine dit Bienvenue."

Now what?

Although there were plenty of Francois Bienvenue listings in Ancestry.com marriages, none were to a Lesage. Hitting this dead end, and facing the three challenges above, tells me that I need to do more research on this Bienvenue family before tracking down the marriage.

Further research might include:

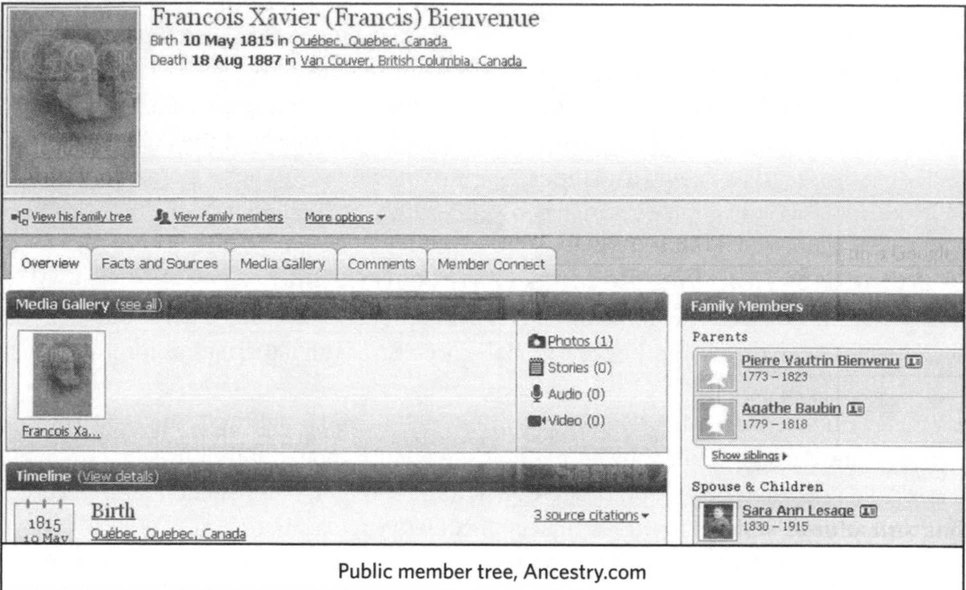

Public member tree, Ancestry.com

- history of the Bienvenue family in Canada
- history of French-Canadian immigrants
- trying to work on finding more about Francois's children
- discovering more about the Lesage family in Canada

Was my Ancestry.com search a total bust? Believe it or not, it wasn't!

I went back and searched the Public Family Trees for any match of *Francois Bienvenue* and *Lesage*. One of the first matches had information on Francois's family tree and included a photo of the man himself.

More important, this tree noted that Francois's marriage to Sara (Sarah) Lesage took place in Syracuse, New York (no source given). If this is true, I can then go back into the Ancestry.com databases and do a new search.

I can also contact the owner of the public family tree to see if they're interested in sharing information.

Where Else to Find Marriage Records?

A valuable source of free marriage records online is USGenWeb <usgenweb.com>. Navigate the links to your desired state and then the desired county. Or check out the USGenWeb Marriage Project <usgwarchives.net/marriages/>.

You'll also find a large list of links to marriage records online at Cyndi's List <cyndislist.com/marriages/>. With more than seven hundred links to marriage and divorce records, it's possible you'll find your ancestral couple on one of the sites.

Like birth records at Cyndi's List, marriage record links are categorized by locale. The links will include both online databases as well as sites where you can order the records.

I also recommend searching Google <google.com> for marriage records. Many genealogy site owners and bloggers have transcribed records and posted them online. Just as you did for birth records, search for a phrase like *"marriage records* [the name of your state]."

Tip

Many online lists of marriages are transcriptions of microfilms or books. Typically, you'll find a listing by groom and then another one by bride. If you don't find your ancestor on one list, try the other. I have found instances when the marriage had been omitted from the groom's list but was on the bride's list.

Death Records

Death records can open up an earlier generation of research. As you can see from the sample death certificate, there are many clues to help in your research:

- parents' names (including mother's maiden name)
- occupation
- cause of death
- where buried
- name of undertaker
- name of informant

Some death certificates also name the funeral home and the length of time the decedent lived in the community.

Online death records rarely include a full transcription of the entire death certificate, but they will give you a date and place of death; using this, you can order a copy of the actual certificate.

As with marriage records, you'll probably find death records on personal blogs and USGenWeb county pages or archives. User-contributed death records are being posted online every day.

Some state agencies are also posting death records online. Illinois's are available at <cyberdriveillinois.com/departments/archives/databases.html>, and Missouri's are at <www.sos.mo.gov/archives/resources/birthdeath>. Missouri has even posted death certificates online <www.sos.mo.gov/archives/resources/deathcertificates/> that you can view or download.

For subscribers at Ancestry.com, you can search through many millions of names, most in death record indexes. Click the Search tab on the Home page and select Birth, Marriage & Death Records.

After you've found a name in the index, you can order a copy of the full death certificate from the appropriate state agency. Ancestry.com will help you start your order, which is completed by VitalChek <vitalchek.com>.

FamilySearch.org has millions of names in their databases of death records, and some copies of death certificates are included in this database.

Another free site to search is Online Searchable Death Indexes & Records <www.deathindexes.com/>. Some of the links on this site will take you to free death record indexes; others go to Ancestry.com or other subscription sites.

Death certificate, 1930, State of Missouri

Social Security Death Index (SSDI)

The SSDI is used to find information on a person who died since 1962, who had a Social Security number, and whose death was reported to the Social Security Administration. This database does include some information going back to 1937, as well as approximately 400,000 railroad retirement records. If you can't find a birth record or date, you may be able to work backward using the information in the SSDI.

What can you learn from the SSDI?

- last name
- first name
- birth date
- death date
- Social Security number
- state of residence where SSN was issued
- last known residence
- location where last benefit payment was sent

You can search the SSDI for free at RootsWeb <ssdi.rootsweb.ancestry.com/cgi-bin/ssdi.cgi>, or you can use the free SSDI search engine created by Stephen Morse <http://stevemorse.org/ssdi/ssdi.html>. Morse's SSDI search engine will search eight different databases at once.

Name	Birth	Death	Age	Last Address of Record	Last Benefit	Issued By
REAGAN, RONALD W	06 Feb 1911	05 Jun 2004 (V)	93	90024 (Los Angeles, Los Angeles, CA)	(none specified)	Iowa

Social Security Death Index, Ronald Reagan

Obituaries

Obituaries are a favorite source for discovering a birth year, marriage date, maiden name, death date, and place of burial. At their best, obituaries will tell you where the deceased was born, the name of his spouse and children (including children's married names), where he worked, when he died, where he was buried, where the service took place (often at home), and the name of the minister who officiated the funeral.

If you're lucky, the obituary will also tell you something more personal. One obituary, for example, told the name of the deceased's cat, and another stated, "She loved animals and enjoyed collecting frogs." Still another notes the deceased had been ill for nearly a year, and when he died, all of his children were with him.

This sample obituary from the January 23, 1984, edition of *The Oregonian* newspaper (found on GenealogyBank <genealogybank.com>) gives you an idea of the varied and valuable information that can be found in an obituary.

Leonora Amelia Hinze, a retired nurse's aide, died Thursday at a daughter's Southeast Portland home. She was 80. Funeral was Sunday in Resurrection Lutheran Church, 1700 N.E. 132nd Ave., with interment in Birchwood Cemetery, Pine City, Minn.

Mrs. Hinze was born in Harris, Minn., and moved to Portland 40 years ago. A resident of Southeast Portland, she retired in 1971 from Hazelwood Nursing Home.

Surviving Mrs. Hinze are three daughters, Elaine Wanous of Portland; Marcella Pangerl of Pine City, and Verna Mae Norris of Albany; two sons, Gerald of Clackamas and Edward of Port Orchard, Wash.; one sister, Ida Pepin of Hinckley, Minn.; 22 grandchildren and 25 great-grandchildren.

Where to find online obituaries:

GENEALOGYBANK <genealogybank.com> Although GenealogyBank has a database of newspaper obituaries dating back to 1977, you can easily find older obits in its Historical Newspaper database. After you have found the obituary, you can print it or save it as a PDF file.

LEGACY.COM <legacy.com> Search more than eight hundred newspapers containing millions of current obituaries in this free database. This website doesn't contain historical obituaries.

OBITUARY CENTRAL <www.obitcentral.com> Obituary Central is a free service that provides an index to obituaries and obituary resources on the internet. Most obituaries are recent. Note that this is an index and not a transcription of the obituary itself. Use the information in the index to find a copy of the full obit, possibly on a newspaper's site.

OBITUARY DAILY TIMES <obits.rootsweb.ancestry.com> This is a no-frills search engine of an index of current obituaries that is updated each day. Typically more than 2,500 entries are added each day. Results will only include name, age, place, newspaper name, and date, not the full obituary.

USGENWEB ARCHIVES OBITUARIES PROJECT <usgwarchives.net/obits> Organized by state and then county, you can find obituaries (current and historic) that have been transcribed by volunteers.

USGENWEB ARCHIVES <searches.rootsweb.ancestry.com/htdig/search.html> Don't forget to check the USGenWeb archives. It's possible the historical obituary you're seeking was transcribed and uploaded by a volunteer. This search engine will check through all of the text-based files.

Locating Cemeteries in the U.S. and Abroad

Finding a burial record online isn't quite as satisfying as visiting a cemetery in person, but if you live hundreds or even thousands of miles away, it's a very close second. Millions of burial records are online, some courtesy of the U.S. government (national cemeteries); others are the product of dedicated volunteers.

Tombstone inscriptions can tell you many things including:

- date of death
- date of birth
- maiden name
- spouse's name
- spouse's date of death
- spouse's date of birth

Some tombstones also include even more description. You can find cemetery information online at these websites:

FIND A GRAVE <findagrave.com> This is a favorite free-content website for finding burials and tombstone photos, and for leaving virtual flowers and a note. Information on the site is generated by volunteers who take photos at their local cemeteries. If you want a tombstone photo, sign up (it's free), then leave a photo request. You can also become a volunteer photographer by leaving information on the cemeteries you are willing to travel to.

Want to know where a famous person is buried? Use the Famous Grave search engine on Find A Grave. Who knows what famous person you'll find buried in your hometown.

INTERMENT.NET <interment.net> This site contains information on millions of burial plots from thousands of cemeteries worldwide. If you don't know where someone is buried, use the search box on the Home page to search across all data. If you have a location, click down through states and then counties. Each county has a listing of cemeteries included in the database.

NATIONWIDE GRAVESITE LOCATOR <gravelocator.cem.va.gov/j2ee/servlet/NGL_v1> Search for burial locations of veterans and their family members in national cemeteries, state veterans cemeteries, and other military and Department of Interior cemeteries. This database also includes veterans buried in private cemeteries when the grave is marked with a government grave marker.

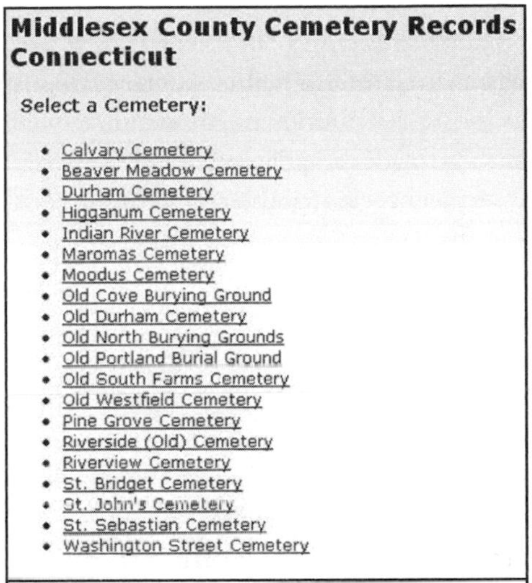

AMERICAN BATTLE MONUMENTS COMMISSION <www.abmc.gov/home.php> Look here for military ancestors buried in U.S. cemeteries abroad. The site covers twenty-four overseas military cemeteries with almost 125,000 American war dead, plus Tablets of the Missing that memorialize more than 94,000 U.S. servicemen and -women.

Middlesex County Cemetery Records Connecticut

Select a Cemetery:

- Calvary Cemetery
- Beaver Meadow Cemetery
- Durham Cemetery
- Higganum Cemetery
- Indian River Cemetery
- Maromas Cemetery
- Moodus Cemetery
- Old Cove Burying Ground
- Old Durham Cemetery
- Old North Burying Grounds
- Old Portland Burial Ground
- Old South Farms Cemetery
- Old Westfield Cemetery
- Pine Grove Cemetery
- Riverside (Old) Cemetery
- Riverview Cemetery
- St. Bridget Cemetery
- St. John's Cemetery
- St. Sebastian Cemetery
- Washington Street Cemetery

List of cemeteries in Middlesex County, Connecticut, Interment.net

CEMETERY SURVEYS INC. <cemeterysurveysinc.org> View nearly 240,000 burial records, many with photos of the actual headstones; the site is richest in coverage for the southeastern United States. You can even import your finds into Google Earth.

MORTALITYSCHEDULES.COM <mortalityschedules.com> Did your ancestor die just before the next federal census? If so, you might be able to find him on one of the free transcriptions of the 1850, 1860, 1870, and 1880 census mortality schedules. These schedules enumerate all people who died within the twelve months preceding the census. It doesn't include all counties.

KENTUCKY HISTORICAL SOCIETY <205.204.134.47/cemetery.asp> This site contains hundreds of thousands of names transcribed from gravestones across Kentucky. Volunteers have documented graves, from urban cemeteries to rural plots, as part of the Kentucky Cemetery Records Project. The site includes cemetery location, i.e., "the new Rose St. Cemetery, on a bluff in the city limits of Clover port, KY Overlooking Hwy 60."

Other cemetery records online:

CEMETERY JUNCTION <www.cemeteryjunction.com>

VIRTUAL CEMETERY <www.genealogy.com/vcem_welcome.html>

PROBATE AND COURT RECORDS

When a person dies, their property is distributed as per their will or trust, and claims against the estate are resolved. The process of resolving an estate in court is called "probate." During probate, the executor follows the directions given in the will.

If someone dies without a will, it is known as being *intestate*, versus leaving a will, which is *testate*. Whether a person died with or without a will, court records are created as to the distribution of the estate. Probate records are valuable to genealogists because probate itself can generate many types of documents:

- inventories (property, including slaves)
- bonds
- petitions
- distributions
- wills

At times, a probate file can hold the only clues as to the name of a spouse or children. A probate file can also have information about guardianship if any of the children were minors at the time of the parents' death.

Probate files can contain surprises as well. You may find that your ancestor had been declared insane, or that there was a claim against his estate for guardianship or care, or even that he owned land in another state. You might also discover that every child except one was left money or that a brother was appointed financial guardian of a married sister. You can discover a lot about family dynamics from the documents in a probate file.

Probate records provide a window into your ancestor's life because they show debt owed to and by him, names of heirs, names of witnesses, residence, the value of his belongings, and a detailed listing of what he owned.

Although probate records are slow to be posted online, there are a few excellent places to search. In addition, local genealogy societies often have on-site researchers who will go to the courthouse for you in search of probate records. Their fees are typically inexpensive.

FAMILYSEARCH <familysearch.org> The best place to look for probate files is FamilySearch. The site currently has posted a total of twenty-eight probate and court collections.

To find other probate files online, type *probate files* and the name of your state, i.e., Maryland, into your favorite search engine.

Some states are posting historical probate records or indexes. The state of Missouri, for example, is indexing judicial files (including probate) <www.sos.mo.gov/archives/mojudicial/#search>. Researchers can search by name and county to see if an ancestor's files have been indexed. If so, the index will provide the microfilm number of the file.

Other places to find probate records:

USGENWEB <www.usgenweb.com> The county pages on USGenWeb are a possible source of probate files. Tulare, California, has an index to probate files until 1920, with instructions on how to order copies of the papers <cagenweb.com/cpl/tulare/tularprb.htm>.

USGENWEB ARCHIVES <rootsweb.ancestry.com/usgenweb> Search for files by state and county.

Live Stock.

Nichols & Home Farm Horses	375	
" " " " Cows & other Live Stock	1162	50
Bitty Farm Horses	200	
" " Cows	1320	
½ Int. - Bartoy Farm Horses	675	
" - " " Cows & other Live Stock	2410	

Farming Tools.

Home & Nichols Farm	283	

Inventory, part of a 1915 Vermont probate file, FamilySearch.org, showing the number and values of horses and cows as well as farm implements

CYNDI'S LIST <cyndislist.com> This website aggregator has links to will and probate websites.

GENEALOGY BANK <genealogybank.com> If you have a subscription to this site, it's possible you'll find a mention of probate in a newspaper article. Although the article won't include all of the details from the probate file itself, it typically provides an overview and gives the name of the executor or the value of the estate.

Using Vital Records to Prove Your Lineage

If you caught the genealogy bug because you thought you were descended from the kings of England or a *Mayflower* passenger, you're not alone. Thousands of genealogists attempt to trace their lineage back to famous individuals or those who figured in the building of the United States. If you can prove direct descent, you can qualify for membership in one of the dozens of lineage societies. And the proof lies in the vital records you've been researching.

To qualify for most lineage societies, you'll need to trace your direct line back to an ancestor who met a specific criteria for membership. Just thinking you qualify for membership doesn't count. In order to join, you'll need to thoroughly document your ancestry back to the qualifying individual.

Mrs. Williams' Will Admitted to Probate

Judge W. P. Kinney of the county court yesterday admitted to probate the will of the late Mary Henry Williams of this city. The estate is valued at more than $100,000. A brother, William C. Henry of Denver, was named administrator with the will annexed. R. H. Hutton, who was named as executor in the will, has been out of the United States and declined to act. Personal property valued at $98,000 and considerable real estate is included in the estate. The will provides for many legacies and bequests and also for a fund of $50,000 for a home for homeless girls.

Probate-related newspaper article, April 1919, *Gazette-Telegraph* (Colorado), GenealogyBank.com

Although the amount of documentation required varies by lineage society, you can expect to provide proof for all places, dates, and relationships. Acceptable sources for proving descent are vital records like birth, death, and marriage certificates, as well as information located in deeds, census, probate, wills, Bibles, and letters. If another individual has already joined the society under the same ancestor, you can often use their research and documentation to the point where your family lines split.

Lineage societies come in several flavors, but the most common are war societies, Old World societies, regional societies, and those associated with colonization or early settlement. A few religious and ethnic organizations also exist.

Here's a look at where you can put your vital records research to work.

War Societies

There are probably more war-related lineage societies than any other type. To qualify for membership, you must be directly descended from someone who served in a specific war, either as a soldier or in some other accepted category.

DAUGHTERS OF THE AMERICAN REVOLUTION (DAR) <dar.org> This group (discussed in more depth in chapter ten) will grant membership to women with "patriot" ancestors; counted among patriots are clergy who gave patriotic sermons, civilians who offered material aid, signers of the Declaration of Independence, members of the military, or those who participated in the Boston Tea Party.

Both the DAR and its fellow organization, Sons of the American Revolution (SAR) <www.sar.org>, have membership applications and worksheet tips on their websites.

THE GENERAL SOCIETY OF THE WAR OF 1812 <www.societyofthewarof1812.org> This organization is limited to males who can prove lineal descent from anyone who participated in the War of 1812. Qualified participants include regular Army, Navy, and Marines, as well as privateers and members of the militia. If you believe you qualify for membership, refer to the society's Web page on how to obtain War of 1812 military records. The site also contains links to other websites that list rosters of soldiers who served.

Qualified females can join the National Society, United States Daughters of 1812 (NSUSD1812) <www.usdaughters1812.org>. NSUSD1812 membership eligibility has a far broader definition than its male counterpart does; to join you must have an ancestor who rendered civil or military service any time from 1784 to 1815, including those who participated in the Lewis and Clark Expedition.

THE ANCIENT AND HONORABLE ARTILLERY COMPANY OF MASSACHUSETTS <ahac.us.com> This is the oldest war society, founded in 1637 and chartered by Governor John Winthrop in 1638. Qualifying members are those with ancestors who belonged to the organization between 1637 and 1737, or those who apply through a member-sponsor, stand before a membership committee, and are accepted by vote.

What's the lineage society with the strangest requirements? Undoubtedly, the Hereditary Order of the Descendants of the Loyalists and Patriots of the American Revolution <loyalistsandpatriots.org>. To join, you must be descended from both a loyalist and a patriot.

Other war societies:

Sons of Union Veterans of the Civil War <suvcw.org>

Daughters of Union Veterans of the Civil War <www.duvcw.org>

United Daughters of the Confederacy <www.hqudc.org>

Sons of Confederate Veterans <www.scv.org>

Old World Societies

If you think Queen Elizabeth is your long-lost cousin, you may want to apply for membership in one of the Old World societies. These are the organizations that require their members to trace the lineage of an immigrant ancestor until noble or royal ancestry is reached.

One of the best-known Old World societies is the Order of the Crown of Charlemagne in the United States of America <www.charlemagne.org>. The society, which was founded in 1939, is limited to members who can prove lineal descent from the Emperor Charlemagne. Two current members must propose potential members, and even after approval, membership is by invitation.

If you're lucky enough to be able to trace your heritage back to the thirteenth century, you may qualify for the National Society Magna Charta Dames and Barons. These folks are descended from the twenty-five sureties (people directly involved with) of the signing of the Magna Charta in 1215. Other qualifying ancestors are knights, barons, prelates, or "other influential people" present on the field of Runnemede in June 1215 on behalf of the charter. You'll find a two-part pedigree form on the website <www.magnacharta.org>; Part I traces the line from you to your immigrant ancestors, Part II from the immigrant to the qualifying ancestor. You'll need to contact the society for more information, because membership is by invitation only.

Other Old World societies:

Baronial Order of Magna Charta <www.magnacharta.com>

The Huguenot Society of America <www.huguenotsocietyofamerica.org>

Colonial Societies

In general, the colonial societies require members to trace their lineage to someone who lived in one of the colonies before a specific date. For example, the National Society Colonial Dames XVII Century <www.colonialdames17c.org> requires you have an ancestor in the colonies before 1701.

Other colonial societies include those with ancestors in specific professions, like a colonial physician, governor, clergy, or tavern keeper.

The General Society of Mayflower Descendants requires lineal descent from a Pilgrim who sailed on the *Mayflower.* If your research proves your lineage, print out a preliminary review form from the society's website <www.themayflowersociety.com> and send it to the appropriate state society (links are on the site). After review, you'll be contacted about moving forward with a formal application.

Other colonial societies:

Descendants of the Colonial Clergy 1620–1776 <my.execpc.com/~drg/widcc.html>

National Society of New England Women <www.newenglandwomen.org>

Pioneer or Early Settler Societies

Early settler societies provide membership to those who can trace their lineage to a specific locale before a specific date. In general, these societies require an ancestor be living in an area before statehood. To join the Sons and Daughters of Oregon Pioneers <www.webtrail.com/sdop>, for example, your ancestor had to be living in Oregon or Washington Territory prior to February 14, 1859.

The oldest historical organization west of the Mississippi is the Society of California Pioneers <www.californiapioneers.org>, which was founded by people who came to California prior to the Gold Rush. If your family settled in the Golden State before January 1, 1850, you qualify for membership.

Many states now offer pioneer certificates to qualifying individuals. Do a search for *pioneer certificate* and the name of your state to see if a pioneer organization exists.

Other early settler societies:

The Society of the Ark and the Dove <www.thearkandthedove.com>

The Sons of the Republic of Texas <www.srttexas.org>

Society of Indiana Pioneers <www.indianapioneers.com>

Holland Society of New York <www.hollandsociety.com>

Life During Your Ancestors' Era

Sooner or later, every genealogist hits a brick wall. Sometimes you can bust through by sheer luck, but other times the clue is found in history—the history of where your family lived and the events of the day.

If you're dealing with a "disappearing" family, one that can't be found where they should be, chances are their whereabouts were influenced by war, mass migration, poverty, famine, an epidemic, or free land out West.

Researching the history of a time or place is as easy as clicking a mouse; tens of thousands of sites are maintained by history buffs, historical villages (like Williamsburg), educational institutes, and historians. In seconds, you can track down a recipe for Roman honey cakes, read the nation's reaction to the Custer massacre, or find plans for a typical Colonial garden.

If you immerse yourself in a county's history long enough, you begin to get a feel for daily life—and that feel will help with some amazingly accurate "intuitive analysis" of where to find the loose brick in your wall. Sometimes the break comes through history itself, and other times through what we call "social history."

Back in school everyone learned history by studying the major events and influential people from George Washington to Franklin Roosevelt's New Deal. What we weren't taught was how those events affected ordinary people. That's the job of social history.

Social history attempts to teach us the everyday details of ordinary people. It's a study of how your North Dakota ancestors recovered from the Schoolhouse Blizzard of 1888 or what foods were served at a Sunday dinner on the farm. Social history adds the flesh to genealogical charts, forms, and data; it brings the names, events, and dates in history to life.

History and social history are two of the most important tools in a genealogist's bag of tricks. That's why I've included this grab bag of outstanding history and social history websites.

And because we all want to know what our ancestors looked like or get a firsthand view of their military regiment, hometown, or mode of dress, I've also included online photo sites where you're most likely to find copyright-free historical images.

HISTORIC TOWNS AND VILLAGES

COLONIAL WILLIAMSBURG <www.colonialwilliamsburg.org>

From eighteenth-century gardening to holiday traditions to common workman's tools, this site breathes life into your Colonial ancestor. You can experience the sights and sounds that may have been familiar to them. The Publications link will take you to an online version of the Colonial Williamsburg journal; recent issues include articles on Colonial dress codes and tavern music. If your ancestor actually lived in Williamsburg, follow the Tour the Town link to view drawings of the historic buildings your family members probably frequented.

OLD STURBRIDGE VILLAGE (OSV) <www.osv.org>

If your nineteenth-century ancestors settled in New England, they might have lived in a town a little like OSV, a re-created 200-acre rural village. The real gem here is a searchable database of primary-source documents on subjects as varied as textiles, music, poetry, public records, health, and transportation. Access the database by clicking Explore & Learn from the Home page.

PLIMOTH PLANTATION <www.plimoth.org>

Visit this site to get a taste of life in the 1627 Pilgrim village, including an historical background of the colonists, Wampanoag culture, the facts about Thanksgiving, and seventeenth-century technology (click the Learn link). Follow the Learn link, then Just for Kids and Just for Teachers to access a wealth of information, including a Pilgrim timeline, maps, recipes, and riddles. If you have a fast internet connection, don't miss the

Interactive Explore the First Thanksgiving feature. Be sure to read the genealogical profiles of many Colonists who arrived in Plymouth Colony between 1620 and 1633.

VIRTUAL JAMESTOWN <www.virtualjamestown.org>
Here you'll find early seventeenth-century maps, a searchable database of more than ten thousand indentured servants, early Jamestown censuses, and firsthand accounts. You can even do a 3D flyover of an Indian village. Over time, documents are being added, including deeds, wills, and court order books.

OLD SALEM <www.oldsalem.org>
Journey through an eighteenth-century Moravian colony at Old Salem. Here you'll find a history of the German-speaking Protestants who arrived in North Carolina in 1755 and built four towns, Salem being the commercial and religious center. If you're interested in the gardens maintained by your colonial ancestors, click Learn at the top of the web page and then click on Garden Workshops.

GENERAL AMERICAN HISTORY

HISTORYBUFF.COM <www.historybuff.com>
Picture the historic events of the last century through the eyes of period newspapers with the help of dozens of articles by Rick Brown, an avid newspaper collector. You'll also find primary source material in the form of newspaper archives and transcripts. Among the holdings are the *London Times* coverage of Jack the Ripper, the July 1876 report of Custer's death, and Andrew Johnson's impeachment acquittal.

AN OUTLINE OF AMERICAN HISTORY <http://bit.ly/rmCvgb>
If you don't remember much of your history, this online version of *An Outline of American History* will make you think you're back in school. Published by the United States International Information Program, the site is divided by time periods and includes thumbnail sketches of the significant events and their causes. Beginning with the migration across the Bering Sea land bridge, the site offers readers an overview of every formative stage in the nation's history, up to 1994.

INDEX OF NATIVE AMERICAN RESOURCES ON THE INTERNET
<www.hanksville.org/NAresources/indices/NAhistory.html>
Because Native American history spans both time and space (a continent, in fact), it's impossible to find a single website that contains the history of every tribe. This index is a portal site that links to more-detailed information on most major tribes. You can also find links to photographs and photographic archives, timelines, and general resources. If you

have Native American heritage, the best place to begin your research is by learning the history of your tribe.

HISTORIC DOCUMENTS FROM REVOLUTION TO RECONSTRUCTION
<odur.let.rug.nl/~usa/D>
There's nothing like reading period documents to understand the burning issues of your ancestors' times. This digital library shelves transcripts beginning with the Magna Charta and privileges and prerogatives granted to Columbus, to the 2008 State of the Union address. Want to know the state of the nation in 1801? Read President Jefferson's address to Congress (things were going well with the Indians, but less so with the Barbary pirates). Was your family among the first to come to the New World? Then be sure to read the Virginia charters or the Charter of Massachusetts Bay.

AMERICAN MEMORY (LIBRARY OF CONGRESS) <memory.loc.gov>
American Memory has enough resources to keep you busy for weeks. Among the on-site holdings are digitized maps, first-person narratives, photographs (many copyright-free), historic manuscripts, music, government documents, and presidential portraits. The easiest way to find something is to do a global search across all collections (click Search from the Home page).

Military History

THE CIVIL WAR <www.civilwar.com>
If you're a little hazy about the battles, songs, timeline, places, or documents that affected your Civil War ancestor, you'll find it all on this site. From the Battles link, search either by date or state for a detailed description of engagements. Information includes date of the battle, the principal commanders, number of casualties, outcome, and a blow-by-blow account. For a lighter look at wartime America, click the Music link to listen to favorite songs of the North and South, among them campfire songs, rallying tunes, and spirituals.

VIRTUAL MARCHING TOUR OF THE AMERICAN REVOLUTION
<www.ushistory.org/march/index.html>
This site traces perhaps the most difficult year of the American Revolution—1777—when Washington's fighting force developed from "Rebels to Mature Army." Click Background to the Campaign to learn about the events in the twelve years leading up to 1776. Then follow each of the links from the Home page to trace the course of the 1777 campaign; read about Howe's landing of 17,000 troops at Head of Elk, Maryland; the Battle of the Clouds; Fort Mifflin; the British looting of Philadelphia; and finally, the Continental Army's debilitating winter at Valley Forge. Click People to learn about the famous and not-so-famous participants of this fateful year.

WORLD WAR II HYPERTEXT <www.ibiblio.org/hyperwar>
What this site lacks in style, it makes up in content. World War II vets and their descendants can read through a huge collection of public domain documents that include official reports, diaries, battle orders, diplomatic messages, logs, and manuals. The collection includes official documents from government agencies of the United States, United Kingdom, and British Commonwealths. You'll find interesting first-person accounts of operations in both the European and Pacific theaters of operation; among them an overview of the Battle of Saipan, the USS *West Virginia's* report of their bombardment in support of the landing on Leyte, and details of Operation Overlord—the invasion of Normandy.

THE WAR OF 1812 WEBSITE <www.militaryheritage.com/1812.htm>
America's forgotten war is brought to life by the sights, sounds, and words on this Canadian multimedia site. Read articles about everyday life in the British Army, their battles, uniforms, and arms. Click Chart of British Regiments for an overview on which regiments fought when and where.

TIMELINES

NATIONAL MUSEUM OF AMERICAN HISTORY: TIMELINE
<americanhistory.si.edu/timeline>
This unusual timeline from the Smithsonian website lets site visitors explore various periods in U.S. history by learning about significant, historic, or iconic objects from previous eras.

ENCYCLOPEDIA SMITHSONIAN: AMERICAN HISTORY TIMELINE
<www.si.edu/Encyclopedia_SI/nmah/timeline.htm>
This timeline is broken down by era, from native cultures of the Americas to an exhibit of the September 11 tragedy, with articles accompanying each period. Of particular interest to genealogists are the articles and exhibits from A New Nation: Exploration and Expansion section, because it chronicles a period when many of our ancestors were on the move.

OUR TIMELINES <ourtimelines.com>
This personalized, interactive timeline is a fun way to gain an understanding of exactly what was going on during the lifetime of your ancestors (or yourself!). Click Timeline, then enter your ancestor's name and birth and death years, then press the Generate Timeline button. The site will automatically generate a new page showing the significant events of that time span, with events color-coded by type (e.g., education, marriages, employment, and military service). You can even enter your own events. Be sure to click the printable box to generate a print-friendly version.

SOCIAL HISTORY

COLONIAL OCCUPATIONS <homepages.rootsweb.com/~sam/occupation.html>
Do you know the difference between a hoggard and a tinctor? Your colonial ancestor did! Scroll through this alphabetically arranged list to discover who did what and what they were called. (Hint: Hoggards dealt with some pretty porky animals; some people would dye to be a tinctor!)

17TH-CENTURY ENGLISH RECIPES <www.godecookery.com/engrec/engrec.html#top>
If you've ever considered treating your family to the same fare as your seventeenth-century ancestors, be prepared for some heavy-duty head scratching—unless, of course, you're already familiar with ingredients like manchets, limbecks, and wild-draggons. Aside from the fascination of trying ancestral dishes, this site will also test your ability to read late-sixteenth and early-seventeenth century language, because all the recipes have been transcribed from original sources.

FEEDING AMERICA COOKBOOKS PROJECT
<www.lib.msu.edu/branches/dmc/collectionbrowse.jsp?coll=78&par=9>
Michigan State University Library and the MSU Museum have put together a searchable collection of what are considered the most influential cookbooks of the nineteenth and twentieth centuries. Search through the digital archives of fifty-seven cookbooks, covering topics of general, ethnic, regional, household management, church/charity, and cooking school publications. You can track down specific recipes or ones that include a certain ingredient. You can even search for household remedies, like the 1869 tip to use black currant jelly for a sore throat.

OLD DISEASE NAMES <www.homeoint.org/cazalet/oldnames.htm>
The next time you see a death certificate or obituary with a bizarre-sounding cause of death, click back to this site to find its equivalent in modern medicine. The names of old diseases in this alphabetically arranged list show both a Latin-based influence (delirium tremens) as well as everyday slang (womb fever).

NEW YORK PUBLIC LIBRARY DIGITAL GALLERY
<digitalgallery.nypl.org/nypldigital/index.cfm>
Interested in images of your ancestors' times? Check out this collection of more than 700,000 images from the library's holdings. Search all collections or browse by broad topic, i.e., Culture & Society or Arts & Leisure. Then drill down further using search options within collections. Gems include images of dress and fashion, Ellis Island immigrants, cigarette cards, landscape photography, floor plans of New York apartments, and scenes of the city from the 1870s.

POETRY AND MUSIC OF THE WAR BETWEEN THE STATES
<www.civilwarpoetry.org>
Unfortunately, this site doesn't have an on-board search engine, but it is organized by category including: Music of the War, Union Poetry, and Confederate Poetry. This collection includes enough heart-rending tunes and sorrowful verse to gain an insight into the true horrors of a brother-against-brother war. *A Cry From Andersonville Prison,* a verse written by a soldier with the 35th New Jersey Volunteers, asks of the nation, "Oh ye who yet can save us . . . will you leave us here to die?" Not surprisingly, Robert E. Lee was the subject of many a creative pen, including one by Julia Ward Howe, author of *The Battle Hymn of the Republic.*

banjo site:www.civilwarpoetry.org
About 16 results (0.12 seconds)

Ring, Ring the **Banjo**
www.civilwarpoetry.org/music/**banjo**.html - Cached
RING, RING THE **BANJO** By Stephen C. Foster (1826-1864). De time is nebber dreary if de darkey nebber groans; De ladies nebber weary wid de rattle of de ...

About "Jine the Cavalry"
www.civilwarpoetry.org/confederate/songs/cav-exp.html - Cached
[Stuart] coveted a **banjo** player in the Appomattox County regiment of Colonel T.T. Munford, one Sam Sweeney, a dark, handsome man in his early thirties who ...

Oh! Susanna
www.civilwarpoetry.org/music/susanna.html - Cached
I came from Alabama, wid my **banjo** on my knee, I'm g'wan to Louisiana my true love for to see, It rain'd all night the day I left, The weather it was dry, ...

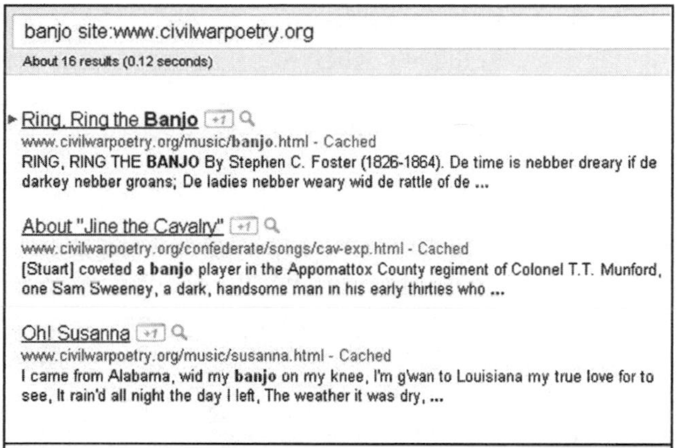

Use a search engine to find period music, Google.com

Even though you can't search the site itself, you can search it using a Google search. Simply type into Google your search phrase, then add *site:www.civilwarpoetry.org* to the equation. In the example, my search returned hits from the site that contained the word *banjo.*

FIDDLE TUNES FROM THE AMERICAN REVOLUTION
<www.halcyondaysmusic.com/colonialmusic>
Get ready to tap your toes when you click over to this site, which contains fifty-four tunes taken from the notebook of an officer in Washington's army. Songs are arranged by type: marches, minuets, airs, country dances, and song tunes. Click on each title to play.

MAKING OF AMERICA <www.hti.umich.edu/m/moagrp>
This searchable collection represents the digitization of ten thousand books and fifty thousand nineteenth-century works, primarily in the fields of education, science, sociology, technology, history, and psychology. You can do a basic or advanced search and locate the texts that are invaluable for genealogists—those that reflect the attitudes and beliefs of our not-so-distant ancestors. For example, an 1877 journal article on "the Indian question" noted, "you can no more expect Crazy Horse to use the shovel and hoe than you could Achilles and Tydides to plant melons or beans."

BETHLEHEM DIGITAL HISTORY PROJECT <bdhp.moravian.edu/home/home.html>
This collection covers the Moravian community of Bethlehem, Pennsylvania, from its founding in 1741 to 1844, when the community first opened to non-Moravians. A community diary recorded everyday and important events. Translations from the German are available for the years 1742 through 1745. Also available are journals, memoirs, and letters.

OHIO MEMORY <www.ohiomemory.org>
Search through primary sources from varied collections covering Ohio life, culture, and history to 1903. You can search all collections by keyword, or browse by subject, place, or contributor. Subjects offer a fascinating look at everyday life, including railroad statistics, a riot following a 1924 Ku Klux Klan rally, and papers for an indentured apprentice.

DIGITAL LIBRARY OF GEORGIA <dlg.galileo.usg.edu/?Welcome>
This site contains material digitized from collections housed in libraries, archives, museums, and other cultural institutions in the state of Georgia. The site offers one million objects in two hundred collections, including letters, military orders, and archeological images created between 1730 and 1842. Civil War material includes a soldier's diary and two collections of letters, one from the wife of an Atlanta lawyer and plantation owner. Search by keyword or browse by topic, county, time period, institution, or media type. Note: Don't miss the Colonial Wills, 1733–1778.

PLYMOUTH COLONY ARCHIVE PROJECT <www.histarch.uiuc.edu/plymouth/index.html>
This site contains documents pertaining to the social history of Plymouth Colony from 1620 to 1691. It includes court records, colony laws, seventeenth-century journals and memoirs, probate inventories, wills, town plans, maps, and fort plans. The site is laid out like a research room; click the room you want to enter, i.e., Grave Art in New England, or Times of Their Lives in Plymouth Colony.

NEW DEAL NETWORK <newdeal.feri.org/>
Search through more than nine hundred New Deal documents and five thousand New Deal photos. Want to ride along on a 1931 road trip? Go to the Archives in the Attic section and read Seven Months of Boyhood Adventures, the narrative of two nineteen year olds who traveled the country during the Depression. Particularly interesting is the cost of food—ten-cents for three eggs and buttered toast.

AMERICAN LIFE HISTORIES: MANUSCRIPTS FROM THE FEDERAL WRITERS' PROJECT, 1936–1940 <memory.loc.gov/ammem/wpaintro/wpahome.html>
This is a treasure house of memories taken from 2,900 interviews conducted for the Works Project Administration (WPA). Interviews include information on income,

occupation, politics, religion, and culture. Search by keyword or search within a specific state. You'll find a fascinating window to social history, sometimes dating back to Civil War and slavery days, i.e., "Slaves in Clinton County very often ran away, but they didn't go far. The pad-a-rollers, men hired to hunt them in the woods at night soon brought them back. We had one man to run off. I was much frightened when they tied him up to lash him, but they never whipped him and he never ran away again."

FIRST-PERSON NARRATIVES OF THE AMERICAN SOUTH, 1860-1920 <memory.loc.gov/ammem/award97/ncuhtml/fpnashome.html>
This site contains about 140 diaries, memoirs, travel accounts, and ex-slave narratives. There is a major concentration on blacks, women, and American Indians. Search by keyword, or browse the subject, author, title, or geographic indexes. There are several topics related to women, including diaries, social life, and customs. One such item is Eliza Ripley's memories of social life in New Orleans, including her experience with "domestic science" (housekeeping), church, plantation life, entertaining, and shopping.

RAID ON DEERFIELD: THE MANY STORIES OF 1704 <1704.deerfield.history.museum>
Read conflicting stories of the famous 1704 raid on Deerfield, Massachusetts, by three hundred French and their Native American allies. At the time of the raid, 112 Deerfield men, women, and children were captured and forced to march three hundred miles to Canada during winter. Material includes seventeenth-century popular songs, and seventeenth- and eighteenth-century French music. It's possible your own colonial ancestors would have raised their voices in singing "Our Forefather's Song"—it's been traced back to 1643 New England.

A PHOTO OF YOUR FAMILY?

Millions of photos are online—but are any of them of your ancestors? It's possible. But even more possible is that you'll find an image of:

- your ancestor's Civil War regiment
- Civil War battles in which he fought
- an ancestor's hometown
- someone with the same occupation during the same time period as your ancestor (like the photo in this chapter of South Carolina firefighters taken in 1855)
- places your ancestors might have traveled
- animals that roamed the forest when your family settled the wilderness
- turn-of-the-century city streets
- hand-drawn maps
- modes of transportation (carts, wagons, Conestogas, stagecoaches, trains, steamers, passenger ships, freighters, canoes, rafts)

After you find a photo—assuming the photos are copyright-free or you have permission from the copyright holder—these images can add depth and personality to your genealogy reports, books, or charts.

WHERE TO FIND COPYRIGHT-FREE IMAGES

According to U.S. copyright law, works published before Jan. 1, 1923, are in the public domain, meaning anyone can use, adapt, or copy them freely. However, there are some odd twists and turns to be aware of. Before you assume an image is copyright-free, read Sharon DeBartolo Carmack's excellent guide to "Copyright for Genealogists" <familytreemagazine.com/article/copyright-for-genealogists>.

Images taken by the U.S. government don't fall under copyright law; in essence, they are the property of "we, the people." However, you may find images on a government site that are owned by a library or archive, and you'll need to get permission or pay a licensing fee for use.

When you've found a photo you want to use, check for copyright notices. As a rule of thumb, almost all personal websites and commercial sites will have a copyright notice. If you want to use an image in your genealogy book, just e-mail the site owner for permission.

If you're on a government site (it will have a ".gov" somewhere in the domain name), there's almost always a link to copyright information. For example, the daguerreotype of the firefighters clearly bears the information: "The Library of Congress is not aware of any restrictions on these photographs." However, it does request a photo credit be given.

Library of Congress, Prints & Photographs Division, LC-USZ6-2211 DLC

1855 Firemen, Library of Congress, Prints & Photographs Division

Conversely, while the History of the American West collection is located on the Library of Congress site, the collection is owned by the Denver Public

Library. The copyright notice states: "The Denver Public Library encourages use of these materials under the fair use clause of the 1976 copyright act. All images in this collection may be used for educational, scholarly purposes and private study. A credit line must be included with each item used." When in doubt, ask.

Ten Websites For Copyright-Free Images

Because you have a better chance of finding copyright-free images on government sites, I recommend starting your search on these ten sites. But again, be sure to check for copyright notices.

AMERICAN MEMORY COLLECTION <memory.loc.gov/ammem/index.html>
This isn't just one collection, but an umbrella site for several photo and map collections. The blend of topics is amazing and diverse:

- early baseball
- homesteaders
- African-Americans in Ohio
- Ansel Adams photos of the Japanese internment camp at Manzanar
- Civil War
- maritime expansion
- American West
- turn-of-the-century America, 1880–1920

BUREAU OF LAND MANAGEMENT <www.blm.gov/wo/st/en/bpd.html>
Search by state or by topic. The Alaska collection may show Denali National Park, Mount McKinley, or river rafters. Eastern states' images range from pelicans and lighthouses to lichen and sand crabs. This is a good site to search if you're looking for photos of natural features, flora, and fauna.

U.S. FISH AND WILDLIFE SERVICE <digitalmedia.fws.gov>
This site is searchable by keyword or by media type (video, audio, documents). If you're not sure what the website's collection includes, click the Browse button to skim through the close to twelve thousand images available in it. Not only can you find photos of wildlife, like migratory birds, but you'll also see images of Fish and Wildlife employees at work.

U.S. GEOLOGICAL SURVEY <gallery.usgs.gov>
This is a tremendous resource that you can search either by collection or by sets within collections. For example, the Native American and Tribal Activities collection has subsets of Miwok and Coast Salish.

NATIONAL PARK SERVICE <nps.gov/pub_aff/imagebase.html>
Did your ancestors pass through national park areas before national parks even existed? It's likely because many national parks were founded in the 1930s. Yellowstone, the first national park, received its designation in 1872. Photos are high resolution, suitable for printing.

Soldiers at rest after drill, Petersburg, Virginia, 1864, National Archives

PUBLIC DOMAIN TORNADO IMAGES <www.spc.noaa.gov/faq/tornado/torscans.htm>
Did your pioneer ancestors live in "tornado alley"? If they did, they likely witnessed at least one twister during their lifetime. This is the collection to search for stormy images.

NATIONAL PARK SERVICE HISTORIC PHOTOGRAPH COLLECTION
<home.nps.gov/applications/hafe/hfc/npsphoto.cfm>
Only two thousand of the two million photos in this collection are online, but they're well worth the look. Search by a number of variables such as photographer, year, or park name. Although some of the photos weren't taken until the 1920s, they captured some historic sites and buildings that are no longer standing.

PICTURES OF THE CIVIL WAR
<http://www.archives.gov/research/military/civil-war/photos/index.html>
Not as large an online collection as you'll find at the American Memory site, but an interesting blend of activities, people, and places. Wonder what it might have been like during the Civil War when battles weren't going on? This photo shows soldiers in Petersburg, Virginia, reading, writing, and playing cards.

MAP COLLECTIONS <memory.loc.gov/ammem/gmdhtml/gmdhome.html>
The map collection is organized by categories of

- cities and towns
- conservation and environment
- discovery and exploration
- cultural landscapes

- military battles and campaigns
- transportation and communication
- general
- places in history
- places in the news

Don't miss the Lewis and Clark maps or the 1766 plan for a farm on "Little Huntg. Creek & Potomk. R.", drawn by one G.W. Yes, that's George Washington.

Note: To view the maps on the site, you'll need to zoom in and out using a less than user-friendly system. It's easier to download the map. Click the link at the bottom of the image page to download.

Most image editing software cannot read a JPEG2000 image. To view the downloaded image, you'll need to install a software program that can read this file format. A free and easy-to-use program is IrfanView, which you can download here: <www.irfanview.net>.

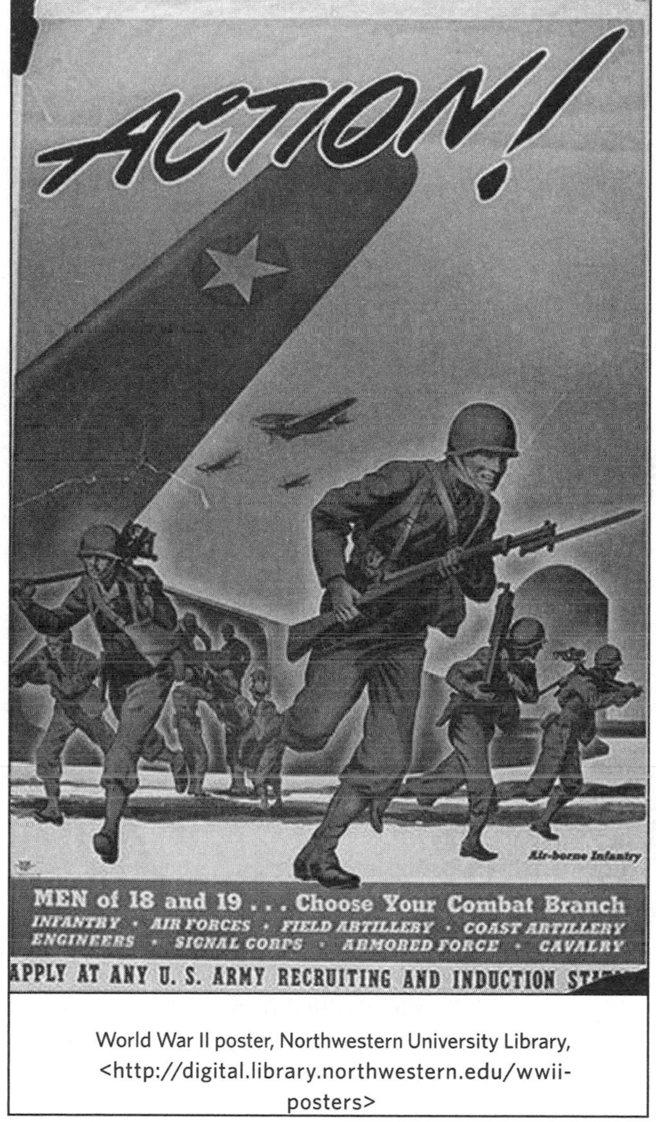

World War II poster, Northwestern University Library, <http://digital.library.northwestern.edu/wwii-posters>

WORLD WAR II POSTER COLLECTION <digital.library.northwestern.edu/wwii-posters>
Although not a government site, this image collection of World War II posters was created in conjunction with the government. These make a fabulous addition to your genealogy book or report if your father or grandfathers served in World War II (or to illustrate mothers and grandmothers who stayed at home). Copyright issues are clearly stated on the site.

GO TO THE AUCTION

An often overlooked source of old photos, maps, or postcards is an auction site like eBay <ebay.com>. You can register for free, then do a search for places that figured prominently in your family tree. Search by keywords and even add a date if you're looking for a postcard, photo, or book from the year you were born or a time that was significant to your family. Because I was born in St. Joseph, Missouri—home of the Pony Express—I like to pick up interesting Pony Express-related postcards. Or because my ancestors worshipped at the Bruton Parish Church in Williamsburg, Virginia, I look for those postcards too. Postcards make for an inexpensive addition to your genealogy scrapbook or family history book. They're almost always available for under ten dollars, sometimes as low as two or three dollars.

FREE PHOTO STORAGE AND EDITING SITES

When you find a digital copy of a great photo, you'll probably want to share it with others via e-mail. However, if you e-mail a large photo, it's likely the recipient's mailbox may reject it.

The solution is to either resize the photo using your own software, or to use one of the free online resizing services. Whenever you plan to alter a photo, make a copy of the original file and work on the copy. Keep the original as is to preclude any possible errors that might ruin the original image.

Free photo-resizing sites include:

- Web Resizer <www.webresizer.com>
- Pic Resize <www.picresize.com>
- Resizr <www.resizr.com>
- Picnik (resize and edit) <www.picnik.com>
- Shrink Pictures < www.shrinkpictures.com>

In this image you can see that Web Resizer reduced the file size of this image nearly 30 percent.

You also may want to do a little fix-up of a not-so-perfect digital image. All of these sites are free and offer several services from quick fixes to major re-dos:

- FotoFlexer <fotoflexer.com>
- Pixlr <pixlr.com>
- Picnik <picnik.com>
- LunaPic <www.lunapic.com/editor>
- piZap <www.pizap.com/>
- Phixr <www.phixr.com/>

And, if you want to share your photos online instead of via e-mail:

- Flickr <flickr.com>
- PhotoBucket <photobucket.com/>

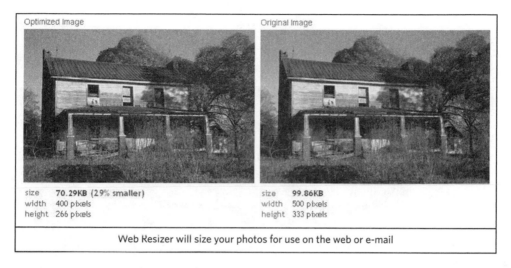

Web Resizer will size your photos for use on the web or e-mail

- Snapfish <snapfish.com>
- Shutterfly <shutterfly.com>
- Picasa <picasa.google.com>

When you want to know more about getting the most from your digital camera and improving your editing skills, Family Tree University offers Digital Photography Essentials <familytreeuniversity.com/digital-photography-essentials>. This course covers many of the tricks of photo editing, including camera selection, rescuing faded images, and restoring accurate color to photos (especially those taken in the 1970s).

Google for Genealogists

In chapter three you learned how to do a simple search and then how to construct a more complex search using search engine operators. You could stop your search at this point, but if you do, you won't discover the many free Google functions that can be so helpful in your online genealogy research.

At the top of the Google Home page <google.com>, you'll find a menu that includes: Web, Images, Videos, Maps, News, and More. Clicking one of these options will change the search criteria Google uses to give you specific results. We explored the Web function in chapter three. The Images function searches for images only, the Videos function searches for video only, and so on. As you can image, these specific focuses can help you quickly find exactly what you are looking for.

GOOGLE IMAGES

Do you remember the search for *American migration routes* from chapter three? In that example, we were looking for a text-based description of various migration routes. Google Images lets you look for photos and maps as well.

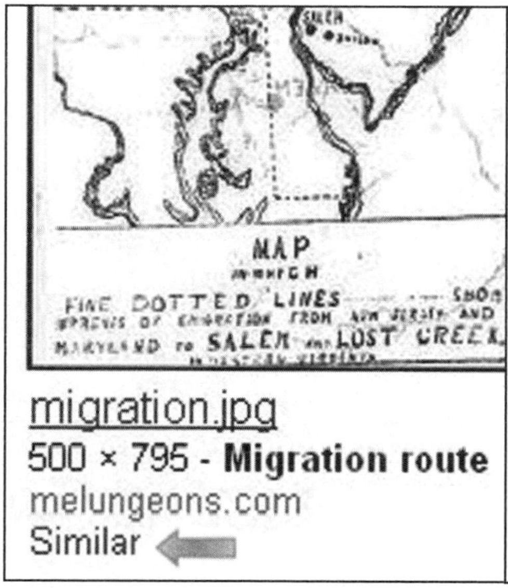

On the Google Home page, click the Images link to go to the Google Images search page. You'll notice it looks almost identical to the Web search page. You can use the same search techniques in Google Images as you use in any other search engine.

Find similar images on Google's Image search

Type in your search words and click Enter. You'll notice the results page is much different than the Web results page. The results are all images. On the left side of the results page, you'll see additional search options. This new menu lets you search images by size, color, and type. If you're searching for a map, click the Line Drawing option; this precludes photos from being included, but does include images that are more likely to be maps.

After you find a map of interest, click the Similar link beneath the thumbnail to generate a new results page full of images that are like the one you're interested in.

Use Google Images to search for pictures and maps of your ancestral state, colony, city, or village. You can also look for historical images of everyday objects, including clothing, tools, foods, housekeeping items, modes of transportation, and more.

Want to find a photo or drawing of an historical occupation? Using the same techniques, search Google Images for an occupation such as blacksmith. Sample images for the search term *blacksmith* included a Victorian-era drawing of a blacksmith at work along with photos and drawings of a blacksmith's tools.

If you want to use an image in your genealogy book or on your blog or website, refer to chapter six for information on copyright law.

Google Images can also be used to search for people, families, or places related to your ancestors. You may not find a 150-year-old image of a great-great-grandparent, but you may locate a photo or drawing that relates in some way.

Using Google Images for this kind of search is an easy way to find pictures that wouldn't appear among text-only search results.

When I searched Google Images for *Calvin Dimmitt*, I didn't find a photo of the man himself, but what did turn up were pictures of his tombstone, his father's tombstone, and his wife's death certificate.

Related searches: **blacksmiths at work** **old** blacksmith **cartoon** blacksmith blacksmith **shop**

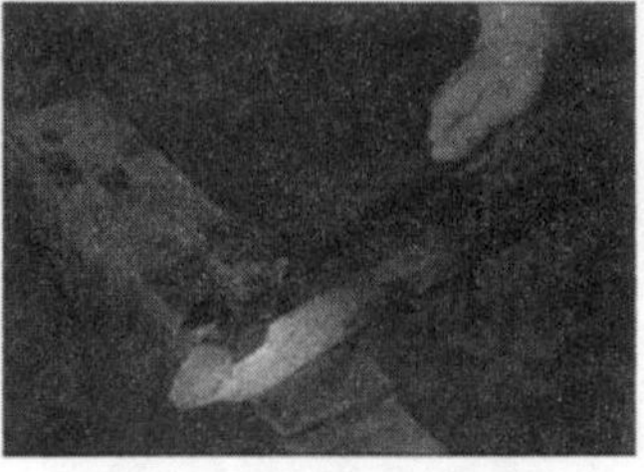

Images of blacksmiths on Google Images

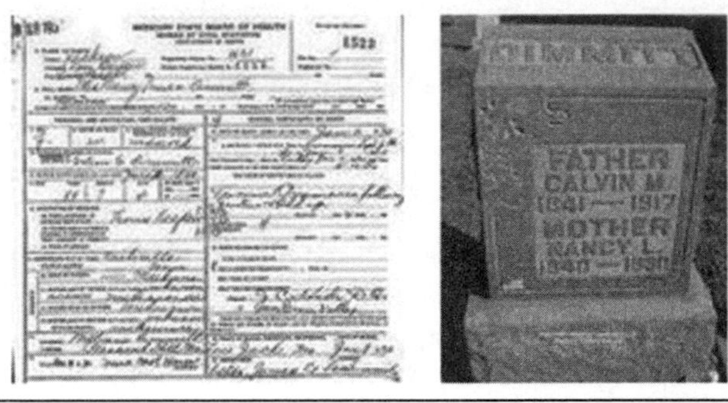

Google images search results for Calvin Dimmitt

In the course of my research, I learned that part of the Faulkenberry family was involved with a famous incident in Texas—the kidnapping of Cynthia Ann Parker from Parker's Fort. (See chapter fourteen for sample searches on unique surnames)

First, I searched for information on the fort, then I went to Google Images to track down photos. Success! The same with another place important to my own family story—Spillman Creek in Kansas. Again, I had no problem finding pictures.

It's possible you can locate photographs or drawings of an ancestor (especially if they were famous), but in lieu of the ancestor, it's guaranteed you'll find plenty of images of the places, occupations, and events he would have experienced.

WHERE WAS THAT PHOTO TAKEN?

One last way to use Google Images is with its photo recognition feature.

Go to Images and look for the Camera icon on the right side of the search box. Click the icon and a box will pop up asking you to either paste in the URL of the image or upload an image from your computer.

Google will now try to match your photo with one in its database. What a boon for genealogists because we can now search for where an old family photo might have been taken.

Click Google's Camera icon to launch the photo recognition feature

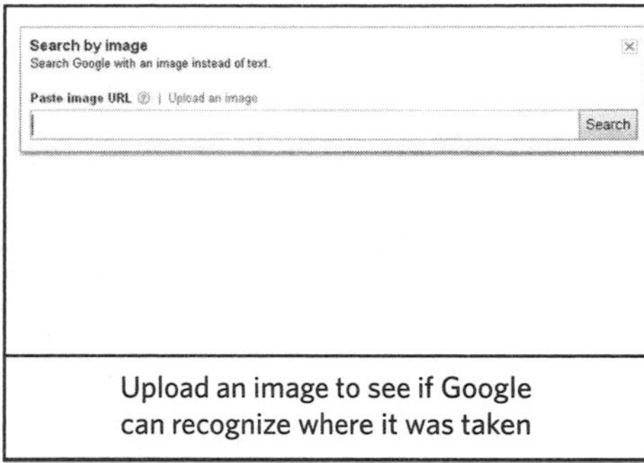

Upload an image to see if Google can recognize where it was taken

Currently, you need a fairly recognizable landmark for the matching feature to work well—but as Google's "brains" grow, so will its database of images. The larger the database, the better chance of matching a photo.

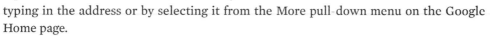

Search within a book at Google Books

GOOGLE BOOKS

Google Books <books.google.com> is a database of millions of books on almost any topic. You can access the Books search by typing in the address or by selecting it from the More pull-down menu on the Google Home page.

Google Books is one of my favorite resources for genealogists because you can use it to search state histories, county histories, published genealogies, directories, and much more without leaving your home.

It's important to note that while Google can often search the entire contents of a book, the book's contents may not be available for viewing online. If this is the case, Google will show you only part of the relevant pages in a book. You may be able to gather enough information from these excerpts. If not, you at least have the title of the book so you can search for it through interlibrary loan or purchase a copy for yourself. You can typically find used out-of-print books on Amazon, eBay, or AbeBooks.com <abebooks.com>.

Let's look at an example. I have ancestors who were early settlers in Jackson County, Missouri, so I searched Google Books for a history of the county using the simple search: *Jackson County Missouri*. One of the first search results was *A History of Jackson County, Missouri*, published in 1881. This book can be downloaded as a PDF or EPUB file and is fully searchable.

Once you've found a book (assuming that the entire book is on the web), use the search box on the left side of the page to search within the book itself.

Search results when looking for mention of an ancestor's name.	Page 113 » tered in the vicinity, and became very much attached to the place. Lone Jack was thus named from a large jack oak tree, which stood alone there in the prairie. It has since been a post-village of considerable importance. Among the early settlers in the vicinity we mention the names of Warham Easley, Galen Cabe, John Snow, Stephen Easley and John Daniel. This was the principal settlement in the southeastern portion of the county, and here their township elections were held. Kansas City was not settled for a long time after Sibley, Independence and Westport. As late as 1830 wild deer, wolves and wild turkeys inhabited those Page 334 » present residence. Not having teams enough to break prairie and to haul rails and fence it, he cleared a field a mile or two north and fenced it with the rails and brush that grew upon it, and there he made his corn for two or three years. In 1856 he sold to Jasper Hopper, and he to Pamphaey Byram. In 1835-6 Galen Cave, Warham Easley and John Snow, three brothers-in-law, came from North Carolina, and entered the land on which the lone Black Jack tree stood, and some hundreds of acres adjoining and contiguous, and being men of energy, some means, and some help in the way of slaves, soon made

In my case, a search within the Jackson County book for my ancestor John Snow resulted in four mentions, including this one that provides clues for future research:

In 1835-6 Galen Cave, Warham Easley and John Snow, three brothers-in-law, came from North Carolina, and entered the land on which the lone Black Jack tree stood, and some hundreds of acres adjoining and contiguous, and being men of energy, some means, and some help in the way of slaves, soon made their mark in the way of good farms . . .

What was learned?

- the family came from North Carolina
- the names of the men John's sisters married
- where in Lone Jack they settled
- their financial status (they owned slaves)
- how much land they acquired

Even if your ancestors aren't mentioned by name, early county histories contain fascinating tidbits that make a great addition to your family tree book, website, or software. The information in a county history will vary, but can include:

- geography
- geology
- pre-white settlement history
- biographies
- extracts of official documents
- maps

How else can Google Books aid in research? A favorite use of Google Books is searching for a published genealogy about your family. Search phrases could be structured like:

- *Dimmitt family tree*
- *Dimmitt genealogy*

- *Dimmitt family genealogy*
- *Dimmitt history*

I used the Advanced Search to filter by "full view" books only, searching for *genealogy of Dimmitt*. What I didn't find was a full-fledged Dimmitt genealogy. But I did find Dimmitts mentioned in several other family history books as well as genealogy publications.

When I changed the search to *Dimmitt family tree*, the first result was a pleasant surprise—a lengthy biography of a Dimmitt in my line in a history of Wapello County, Iowa.

Another use of Google Books is when you have an ancestor with the same name as other people in the area. Using Books, it's possible you'll find a reference that helps untangle the names.

For example, when searching Google Books for the Lance family of the Walnut Valley area of Warren County, New Jersey, one of the names listed was Anthony Lance, a wheelwright. If there were other people in the area with the same name, how would this information help?

First, because the book gives you this Anthony's profession, you can check this against professions listed on a federal census (chapter nine). Next it would tell you that Anthony was a professional man, and it's possible he would be included in a list of business or fraternal organizations in the area. The more you know about an ancestor, the easier it is to distinguish him from others.

GOOGLE ALERTS

Google Alerts <alerts.google.com> is a free news clipping service. In brief, here's how it works: Enter a phrase of interest in the search box, and whenever Google finds that phrase, it e-mails you an alert with a link to the reference.

Don't worry about receiving hundreds of e-mails a day—you won't. You can set the parameters of a) what you want to receive; b) where you want Google to look for it; and c) how often you want Google to e-mail you.

Let's set up a Google alert looking for an obituary for Rachel Knox in Iowa.

1. To ensure the results are precise, we'll use search operators (see chapter three). The search term is *"Rachel Knox" "Iowa" "Obituary"*. Remember, the quotation marks mean those terms must be present and phrases with in quotation marks mean that the exact wording must appear with no other words in it.
2. The pull-down box under Type specifies where you want Google to search. Options include News, Blogs, Videos, Discussions, or Everything. We'll select Everything.
3. The How Often pull-down box lets you specify how often to receive e-mail alerts. Your options are As it happens, Once a day, or Once a week.
4. The Volume pull-down box lets you indicate whether you want Google to determine the relevance of findings (Only the best results) or to send you everything that matches your search criteria.

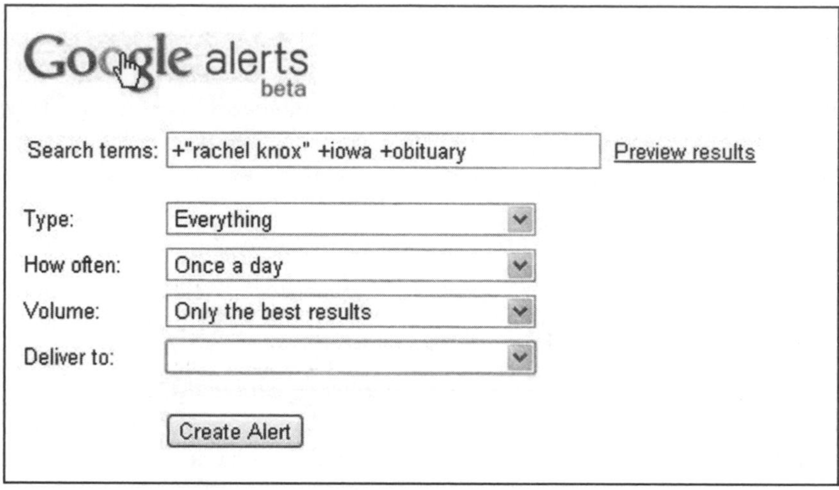

Google alerts beta

Search terms: +"rachel knox" +iowa +obituary Preview results

Type: Everything

How often: Once a day

Volume: Only the best results

Deliver to:

Create Alert

How to set up a Google alert

Not sure if you've constructed the best search? Click the Preview Results link and Google will serve up a sample of findings based on your search term.

GOOGLE NEWS ARCHIVE

Few people are aware that the Google News Archive <google.com/archivesearch> even exists, but it's a valuable source of historic news. Using the archive, you can search historical news archives for topics relevant to your genealogy. This could include:

- name of an ancestor
- obituary
- industries/jobs
- town news
- national or international events
- death notices
- birth notices
- marriages

If something was newsworthy enough to be published in a newspaper, it's possible you can find it in the Google News Archive. What's newsworthy? Back in the early 1900s, almost anything out-of-the-ordinary was fodder for the town newspaper. You might find articles on a trip your ancestor took, out-of-town visitors to your family's home, a prize given to a local student, or a farmer's fall from a horse.

Although Google is no longer adding to the Archives, it's definitely worth a search.

Currently Google's news content comes from three sources:

1. Some of the content comes from companies Google has partnered with to digitize materials.

2. Other content comes from sites that Google's spiders have found on the web. You'll recognize these by the label "Google News Archive."
3. The third group of content is pay-per-view. This means that you'll have to pay to view the content.

GOOGLE MAPS

Google Maps <google.com/maps> isn't just for navigating your way across town. Maps will help you find places, geographic features, GPS coordinates, addresses, and even roads and intersections. How can you use Maps in genealogy?

View of the area near Shiloh Battlefield, Google Maps <maps.google.com>, ©2011 Google

I know that my great-grandfather James Knox fought with the 18th Missouri Infantry at the Battle of Shiloh in Tennessee. Using Google Search, I discovered that the 18th Missouri was camped close to the intersection of Eastern Corinth Road and Peabody Road.

Entering those intersections into Maps, I could see a satellite image of where they had camped. Using the controls on Maps, I can now print this image, e-mail it, or link to it from my website. Depending on location, you can even view and navigate in Google Maps with street-level imagery.

Maps can also be used to plot your genealogy trips. Click Get Directions from the Maps Home page and enter your start location, then each destination you want to visit. Then click Get Directions, and Maps will generate a turn-by-turn list of directions along with a map. You can zoom in on any part of your route for more detailed road information. If you're in the car and have 3G coverage for your electronic device, you can even view real-time traffic, like the image of slowed traffic all around Denver.

Not sure you're in the right place? Maps will show you a street level view at most of the turns in your list of directions.

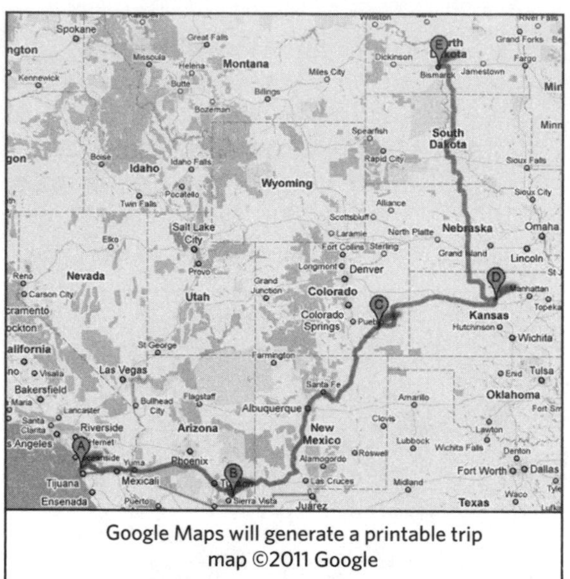

Google Maps will generate a printable trip map ©2011 Google

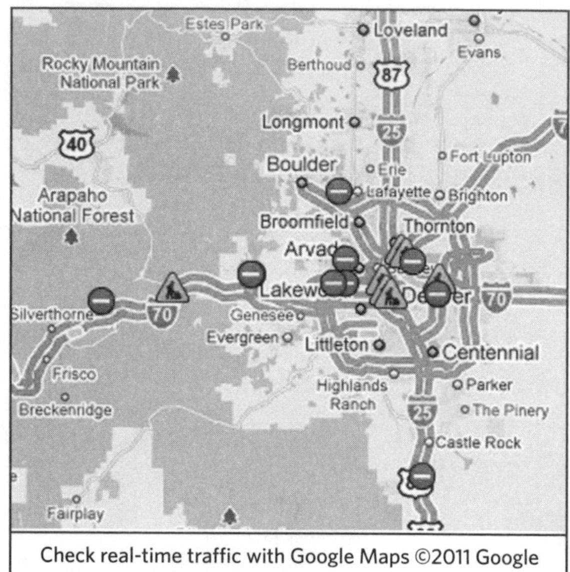

Check real-time traffic with Google Maps ©2011 Google

iGOOGLE—YOUR PERSONALIZED GENEALOGY HOMEPAGE

Do you click over to Google several times during the course of your research? If so, take advantage of the iGoogle function <google.com/ig>. To use iGoogle, you'll need a (free) Google account (follow the steps on the Google Home page to create an account). Go to the Google Home page <google.com> and sign in using your Google username and password.

Next, click the Gears symbol, and on the pull-down menu, click iGoogle. Your screen may look different—it may have an iGoogle link without the Gears symbol.

In the Select Interests area, click the boxes that interest you. Google will then put "gadgets" on your iGoogle page based on the interests you select. You don't have to select any interests because Google places some gadgets on all pages by default.

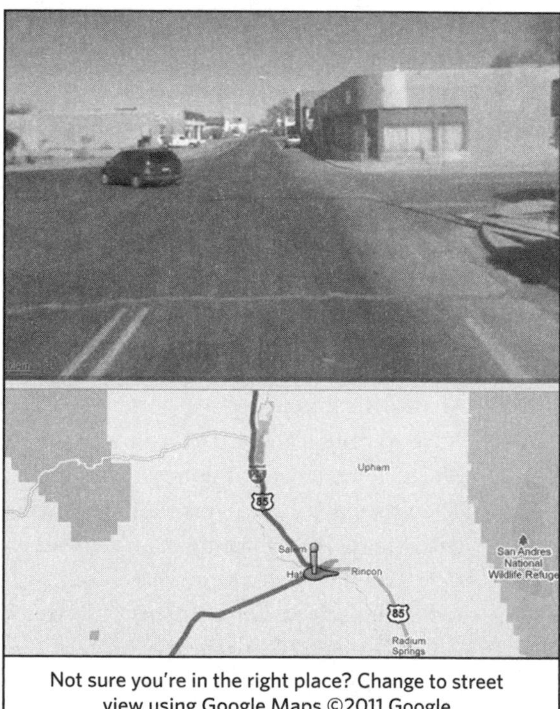

Not sure you're in the right place? Change to street view using Google Maps ©2011 Google

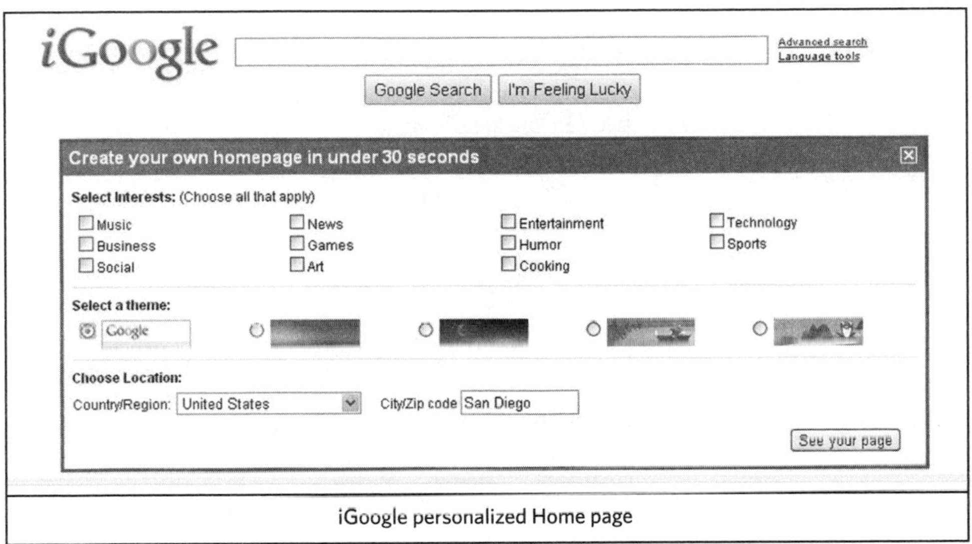

iGoogle personalized Home page

In the same box, you can select a theme—a look and feel for your new iGoogle page.

To remove any gadget you don't want, click the down arrow in the upper right corner of each gadget (like the weather or YouTube video), and then click Delete This Gadget.

Just in case you delete a gadget by mistake, you'll see a yellow Undo box under the Search box.

At this point you may be left with only a few gadgets on your iGoogle, such as the weather and a calendar, or maybe your Gmail. But you can add thousands of gadgets to your iGoogle page, from feeding a pet turtle to playing hangman. Simply click Add Gadgets in the upper right part of your screen and select as many as you want. The choice is yours.

Genealogy Gadgets

Several gadgets will help you with your genealogy research. Two of my favorites are the Bureau of Land Management Patent Search (see chapter eight) and the American Memory Collection Search (Library of Congress). These are two sites I frequently search, so having them on my iGoogle Home page is a real time-saver. Once you find a gadget you want to add, just click the Add It Now button.

Other gadgets you might find helpful to your genealogy are:

- Google Book Search
- MapQuest
- Google Translate (discussed later in this chapter)

iGoogle and Blogs

Another time-saver is adding RSS (Really Simple Syndication) feeds to iGoogle. If you have a favorite genealogy blog that you read daily or weekly, you can automatically display it on iGoogle via a blog gadget. Now you don't have to go to the website to read a post. Here's how it works.

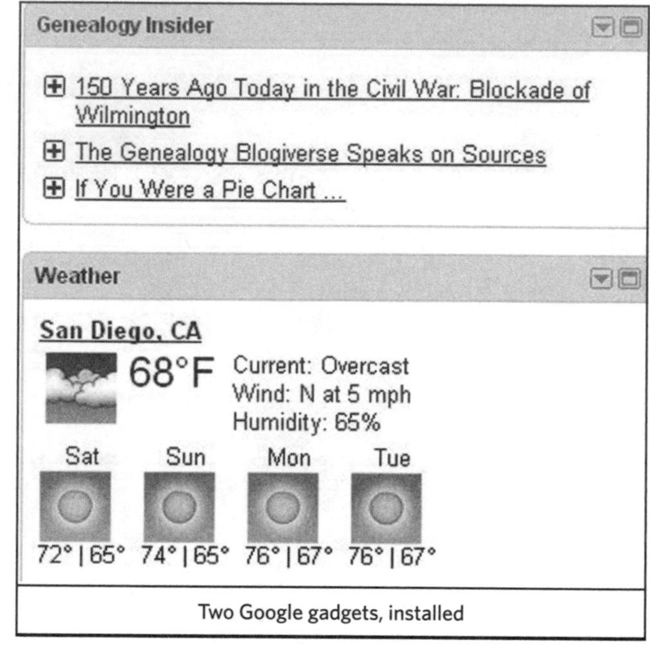

Two Google gadgets, installed

Look on the left side of the Add a Gadget page. You'll see an orange icon and an Add Feed or Gadget link. Click the link, then type or paste the blog address. Go back to your iGoogle Home page and you'll see links to the latest blog posts. Every time a new blog post is added, it will automatically show up on your iGoogle page.

After you have all the gadgets installed, you can customize where they're located on your page by moving them using drag and drop.

A few of my favorite genealogy blogs are:

- Genealogy Insider from *Family Tree Magazine* <blog.familytreemagazine.com/insider>
- Ancestor News (my own blog) <ancestornews.com>
- The Association of Graveyard Rabbits <www.thegraveyardrabbit.com>
- FootnoteMaven <www.footnotemaven.com>
- The Family Curator <www.thefamilycurator.com>

Also, *Family Tree Magazine* <familytreemagazine.com> runs an annual contest to find the best genealogy blogs. The list of the 2012 winners is at <familytreemagazine.com/article/40-best-genealogy-blogs-2012>.

Customize the Look

If the plain white look doesn't suit you, click the Change Theme from Classic link. Here you will find dozens of themes, with categories of animals, nature, food, photography, and games. After you've found the one you want, click Add it Now, and your iGoogle now has a different look.

Making iGoogle Your Home Page

Now that you have everything set up just as you want it, why not make your iGoogle page your home page?

In Internet Explorer: Click Tools, then Internet Options. The first screen you'll see asks what page you want for your home page. If you're already on iGoogle, just click the Use Current link. That's it.

In Google Chrome: You'll find the Set Home Page choice under Options.

In Safari: Select Safari on the Menu bar. Select Preferences. Select General. Type or paste your iGoogle address in the Home Page section or hit the Set to Current button.

In Firefox: Select Firefox on the Menu bar. Select Preferences. Select General. Type or paste your iGoogle address in the Home Page section or hit the Set to Current button.

GOOGLE DOCS

Google Docs <google.com/docs> is a free suite of online office tools. Using Docs, you can create word-processing documents, spreadsheets, presentations, forms, and drawings. If you work from several different computers or do a lot of traveling, you can use Docs to store and access any document you've created or stored online. Using Docs, you can do all of the basic tasks you're used to on your desktop office suite, including creating a new document; making a bulleted list; adding tables, images, and comments; changing fonts, etc. You can also upload existing documents for online storage and access.

Want to create a presentation but don't want to learn Microsoft PowerPoint? You can use a Google Docs feature to easily create your presentation. Google Docs Presentation is easy to use and share. Just choose Presentation from the New menu to launch this feature. After the presentation is complete, you can download your document as a PDF, a PowerPoint, or a text file.

GOOGLE EARTH

I'd be remiss if I didn't mention Google Earth <google.com/earth> in this chapter, but I won't go into detail about it here. Google Earth is a genealogist's dream come true. It's so important, I've made it an integral part of chapter eight.

GOOGLE TRANSLATE

If you ever run across a genealogy website written in another language—or find foreign-language records on Ancestry.com—head over to Google Translate <translate.google.com>. Translate is an easy-to-use, free service that takes words, phrases, or entire web pages written in any of more than sixty languages and translates them to English.

To use the service, just type the words into the box or enter the URL (website address) of the page you want translated, click the button, and you're done. You can also select the native language or let Google automatically detect the language on its own.

Land Records

Land has always been a very valuable commodity, so great care was taken to document ownership. While official birth, marriage, and death records are relatively new, land records have been meticulously kept since the first colonists arrived in America. For this reason, land records are among the most numerous of genealogy records. Land records will show you exactly where your ancestor lived, and armed with that knowledge, you can focus your search on likely locations for census, birth, marriage, and burial records, plus church and social records (i.e., clubs and community activities). While land records are plentiful, they're not always the easiest to find online.

Entire books have been written about genealogy and land records, so if land is your passion, you'll find plenty of books and websites to aid in your education! An excellent source for learning more about land and land records is the E. Wade Hone classic, *Land & Property Research in the United States*. The book is one of the best resources for tracking down old (and hard-to-find) land records in the United States.

TERMS RELATED TO LAND RECORDS

Here are some common terms related to land records along with their definitions.

DEED: An official record of land ownership.

GRANTEE: The buyer.

GRANTOR: The seller.

DEED INDEXES: Indexes of land transactions. These are not the transaction itself. Indexes typically include the date of the transaction, the name of the grantor and grantee, and the deed book and page within the book to find the record, i.e., Deed Book B, page 455.

RECORDED: Most deeds were recorded at the county level in the courthouse.

BOUNTY LAND WARRANT: The federal government provided bounty land as an incentive for military service during the Revolutionary War, the War of 1812, the Mexican War, and Indian wars between 1775 and 1855. Bounty land was provided out of the federal "public domain," although Virginia, New York, and Pennsylvania also set aside bounty land for veterans of the Revolutionary War.

HOMESTEAD: The Homestead Act of 1862 gave settlers up to 160 acres of land, free of charge, with the stipulation that the land had to be improved over the following five years. Not everyone who applied received land; you can find the record of those who did receive land in the General Land Office site (explained later in this chapter); if the application was not completed or denied, you'll find those records in the National Archives <www.archives.gov>.

LAND GRANT: A gift of land such as from a government, a country, or a king. For example, Spain offered land grants to anyone who settled in their colony of Florida, and Mexico gave land grants (ranchos) in California.

LAND SURVEYS

Among some of the most important things to know about land records are whether a state was surveyed using:

- state land states survey system or
- public land states survey system

State Land States

State land states are the original thirteen colonies (Massachusetts, Rhode Island, Connecticut, New Hampshire, New York, Delaware, New Jersey, Pennsylvania, Virginia, Maryland, North Carolina, South Carolina, Georgia) as well as Kentucky, Tennessee, Texas, Vermont, West Virginia, Maine, and Hawaii.

Land distribution was done via a patent or grant, which was the initial transfer of title from the government to the patentee. In many instances, land was given to soldiers in return for military service.

State land states used a survey system known as "metes and bounds." This system used geographical and man-made features such as creeks, fences, and trees to describe the property's boundaries. Boundaries were described by citing the length of each "course" along some line, such as "along a fence" or "ten paces north from the large oak tree." According to the Bureau of Land Management, today's metes and bounds descriptions include the bearings and distances of each course.

Can you "plat" (map out) your ancestor's land using the description in a deed? Yes. In fact, there are two approaches you can take.

The first is to purchase a software program called DeedMapper from Direct Line Software <directlinesoftware.com>, which sells for $99 at the time of this printing.

Using DeedMapper, you can enter the information from the deed, i.e., directions, trees, streams, and distances, and the software will create a plot of your ancestor's land.

The second method entails using tools you probably haven't thought about since high school: a protractor and graph paper. Detailed instructions on platting the land can be found at <genealogy.about.com/cs/land/a/metes_bounds_2.htm>.

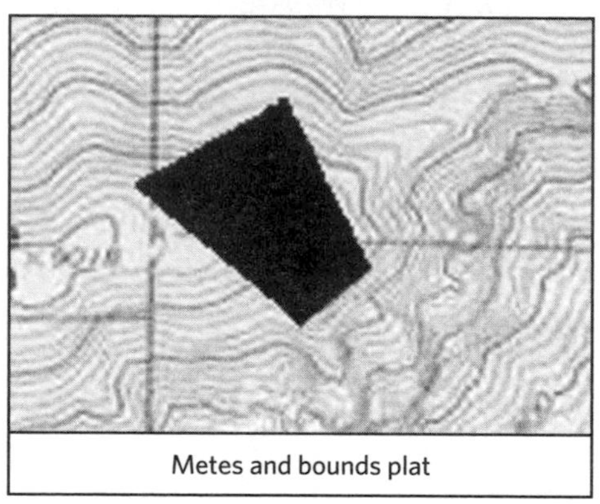

Metes and bounds plat

Public Land States

Public land states were created out of the public domain and are now Alabama, Alaska, Arizona, Arkansas, California, Colorado, Florida, Idaho, Illinois, Indiana, Iowa, Kansas, Louisiana, Michigan, Minnesota, Mississippi, Missouri, Montana, Nebraska, Nevada, New Mexico, North Dakota, Ohio, Oklahoma, Oregon, South Dakota, Utah, Washington, Wisconsin, and Wyoming.

Public land was distributed by acts of Congress, either through sale, homesteads, or military warrants. A primary interest in promoting public land sales was to encourage people to move west.

In the early 1800s, people could buy up to 640 acres of public land for $1.25 an acre. In 1862, the Homestead Act allowed people to settle up to 160 acres of public land if they lived on it for five years and grew crops or made improvements.

Public lands were surveyed using the rectangular system: Lands were divided into townships containing six square miles.

Each township was subdivided into thirty-six sections, each containing approximately 640 acres. Each section was further subdivided into halves and quarters, repeatedly, until the parcel of land was accurately described.

Quick Reference:

- A **township** contains six square miles

- A **section** contains 640 acres
- A **half section** contains 320 acres
- A **quarter section** contains 160 acres
- A **half of a quarter** contains 80 acres
- A **quarter of a quarter** contains 40 acres

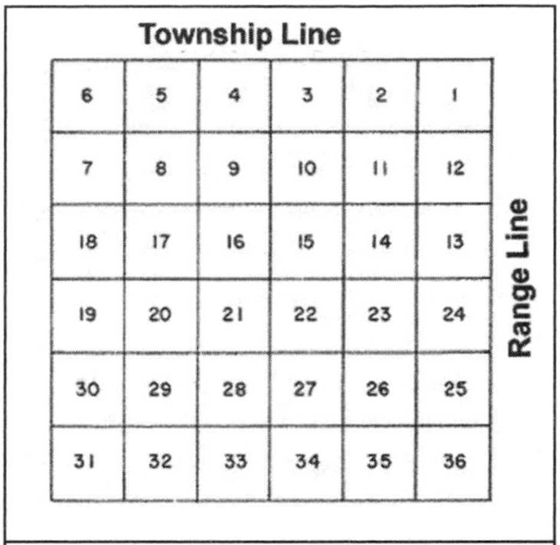

Township Line

6	5	4	3	2	1
7	8	9	10	11	12
18	17	16	15	14	13
19	20	21	22	23	24
30	29	28	27	26	25
31	32	33	34	35	36

Range Line

Township grid

WHERE TO FIND LAND RECORDS ONLINE

Following is a list of websites where you can find land records.

ROOTSWEB LAND RECORDS

<www.searchforancestors.com/records/land.html>

Here you'll find user-submitted land records for Alabama, California, Kentucky, Michigan, Minnesota, Mississippi, Missouri, and Ohio. To search this database, type in the surname and choose a specific state from the pull-down menu, or All States.

Results are returned in a grid, and include the type of transaction, such as homestead or sale, the state, and the parcel description, i.e., 17N, Range 25E, Section 24.

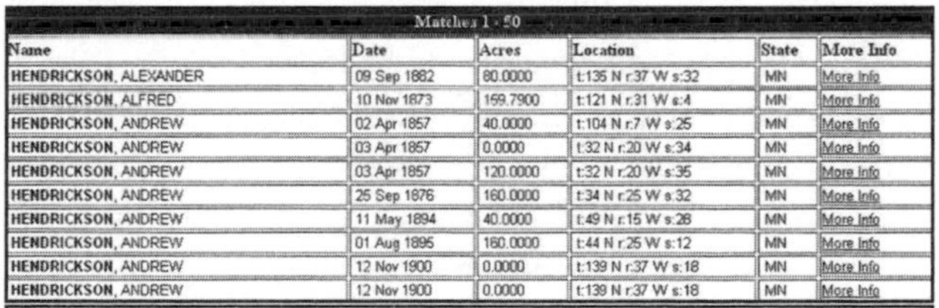

RootsWeb Land Records
User-submitted land records for Alabama, California, Mississippi, Missouri, and Ohio <

Surname: hendrickson
First Name: (optional)
State (optional): All
Search

Search the land records at RootsWeb

Matches 1 - 50

Name	Date	Acres	Location	State	More Info
HENDRICKSON, ALEXANDER	09 Sep 1882	80.0000	t:135 N r:37 W s:32	MN	More Info
HENDRICKSON, ALFRED	10 Nov 1873	159.7900	t:121 N r:31 W s:4	MN	More Info
HENDRICKSON, ANDREW	02 Apr 1857	40.0000	t:104 N r:7 W s:25	MN	More Info
HENDRICKSON, ANDREW	03 Apr 1857	0.0000	t:32 N r:20 W s:34	MN	More Info
HENDRICKSON, ANDREW	03 Apr 1857	120.0000	t:32 N r:20 W s:35	MN	More Info
HENDRICKSON, ANDREW	25 Sep 1876	160.0000	t:34 N r:25 W s:32	MN	More Info
HENDRICKSON, ANDREW	11 May 1894	40.0000	t:49 N r:15 W s:28	MN	More Info
HENDRICKSON, ANDREW	01 Aug 1895	160.0000	t:44 N r:25 W s:12	MN	More Info
HENDRICKSON, ANDREW	12 Nov 1900	0.0000	t:139 N r:37 W s:18	MN	More Info
HENDRICKSON, ANDREW	12 Nov 1900	0.0000	t:139 N r:37 W s:18	MN	More Info

Results of land search, RootsWeb

ANCESTRY.COM <ancestry.com>

Land databases include: U.S. General Land Office Records, 1796–1907; U.S. War Bounty Land Warrants, 1789–1858; U.S. Indexed County Land Ownership Maps, 1860–1918; Historic Land Ownership and Reference Atlases, 1507–2000; and U.S. Southern Claims Commission, Disallowed and Barred Claims, 1871–1880. Ancestry.com also has several databases of land records by state.

Note: The county listed in the Ancestry.com results is not always the county where the land was actually located. For example, results may list the county where the buyer lived, even though the purchased land was in another county.

Pierson Township, Indiana plat map, Ancestry.com

Many land records at Ancestry.com are indexes only. One of my favorites is the U.S. Indexed County Land Ownership Maps, 1860–1918. This database contains images from 1,200 county land atlases—plat maps that show the exact location of land parcels and their owners.

When searching Ancestry.com for land records, you can narrow a broad search by category, selecting Land Records.

Narrow by Category

▸ All Categories

▾ Tax, Criminal, Land & Wills

Land Records	3,125
Tax Lists	2,706
Court, Governmental & Criminal Records	144
Wills, Estates & Guardian Records	191
Bank & Insurance Records	22

Narrow a broad search by category, selecting Land Records, Ancestry.com

Once you've selected Land Records, you'll see a partial list of the databases within this category. Now you can either search across all land databases or make a specific selection.

I had once heard that one of my Faulkenberry ancestors had received Revolutionary War Bounty Land or a pension—so I went directly to the Revolutionary War Pension and Bounty-Land Warrant Application Files, 1800–1900 database. Because the surname is so unusual, I didn't specify anything in the search boxes except the name.

Only one Faulkenberry was in the database, on an 1833 pension filed in Tennessee. When you click on the View Original Image link, the first thing you'll see is an index card. Don't think this is the only record; if you look back at the search results page, you'll see the number of pages in the packet—in this case twenty.

The results in the packet are fascinating: handwritten warrants before a Justice of the Peace by David Faulkenberry, who cannot remember when he was born or much about his military service (although he does remember the first battle in which he fought—Hanging Rock). Also included are affidavits from his son who testified that when his father was younger ("when in his full vigor") he talked in detail about his service. Similar affidavits are given by other neighbors as well as a clergyman. Mentions in the file are of Cashew [Kershaw] County, South Carolina; Georgia; and Rutherford County, Tennessee.

Revolutionary War Pension and Bounty-Land Warrant Application Files, 1800-1900 about David Faulkenberry

Name:	**David Faulkenberry**
Pension Year:	1833
Application State:	Tennessee
Applicant Designation:	Survivor's Pension Application File
Archive Publication Number:	M804
Archive Roll Number:	959
Total Pages in Packet:	20

View original image

Search results for Revolutionary War Bounty Land, Ancestry.com

The amended declaration of David Faulkenbury, in order to obtain a pension for his services as a soldier of the Revolution, under the provisions of the act of Congress passed June the 7th 1832. Personally appeared before me the undersigned, an acting Justice of the Peace for the County of Rutherford and State of Tennessee, David Faulkenberry, who, being duly sworn deposith and saith, that by reason of old age and consequent loss of memory, he cannot swear positively as to the precise length of his services, or the time at which they were performed

Excerpt from a Revolutionary War pension file, Ancestry.com

CYNDI'S LIST
<www.cyndislist.com/land/locality/united-states>
This site includes a comprehensive list of sites that have free or fee-based historical land records. It includes links to deeds, deed books, federal records, and land grants. There are gems among these links, such as the searchable database (and views of original deed books) of Wisconsin Public Land Survey Records: Original Field Notes and Plat Maps <digicoll.library.wisc.edu/SurveyNotes>.

FAMILYSEARCH.ORG <familysearch.org>
The Family History Library (FHL) has microfilmed both deed indexes and deeds themselves for a large number of U.S. counties. Check the FHL catalog online at <familysearch.org> for the county's name to see if the records for your county are available on microfilm. If they are, they can be ordered from your local FamilySearch Center or online (chapter four).

As you can see in this screenshot from the FHL catalog, when searching for land records in Tallahassee, Leon County, Florida, there are four entries. Click on any to read a detailed description of what is included in each title. For example, the second record on the list will include:

The alphabetically arranged entries give the name of the claimant, date of the claim, legal description of the property, and the file number. In many of the approximately 7,300 abstracts, co-claimants, trustees, assignees, or previous grantees are also named
—Back cover

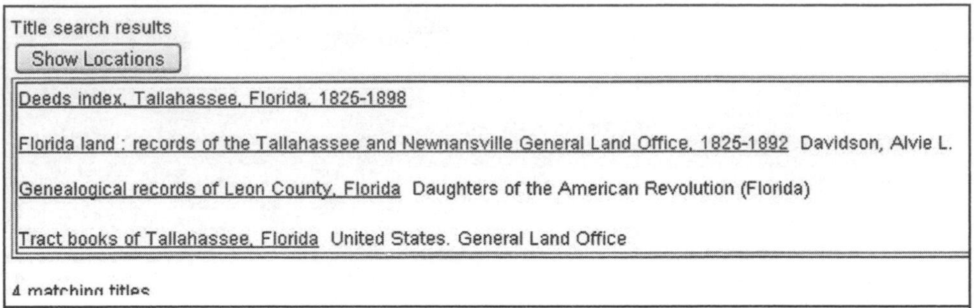

Title search results

Show Locations

Deeds index, Tallahassee, Florida, 1825-1898

Florida land : records of the Tallahassee and Newnansville General Land Office, 1825-1892 Davidson, Alvie L.

Genealogical records of Leon County, Florida Daughters of the American Revolution (Florida)

Tract books of Tallahassee, Florida United States. General Land Office

4 matching titles

Family History Library catalog search for land records

Many of the records of the General Land Office reveal such information as marriage dates, birth dates, death dates, place of residences, place of birth, and lists of possible relatives who signed as witnesses on documents—Intro

SEARCHES ENGINE OPTIONS

Don't forget to search Google or your favorite search engine for terms such as:

- [name of your state or county] *land records*
- [name of your state or county] *historic deeds*
- [name of your state or county] *land records*
- [name of your state or county] *military land*
- [name of your state or county] *land bounty*

BUREAU OF LAND MANAGEMENT, GENERAL LAND OFFICE (GLO)

<www.glorecords.blm.gov>

The BLM-GLO site is the crème de la crème of public land records, with more than two million searchable patents. GLO records are more than an index. They contain the name of the person the land was transferred to (patentee), the legal land description (where it is), the land office that had jurisdiction over the title transfer, and the congressional act or treaty under whose authority the land was transferred.

The site also contains scanned images of the original patents. Although millions of records are available on the site, the GLO collection does not currently contain every federal title record issued for the public land states.

Note: The GLO records are for the initial transfer of land from the government to an individual; they do not include records for subsequent sales.

SEARCHING FOR FEDERAL PATENTS

Let's use the BLM-GLO site to search for a federal land patent. From my research, I know that on August 5, 1834, the federal government transferred title of 80 acres of public lands

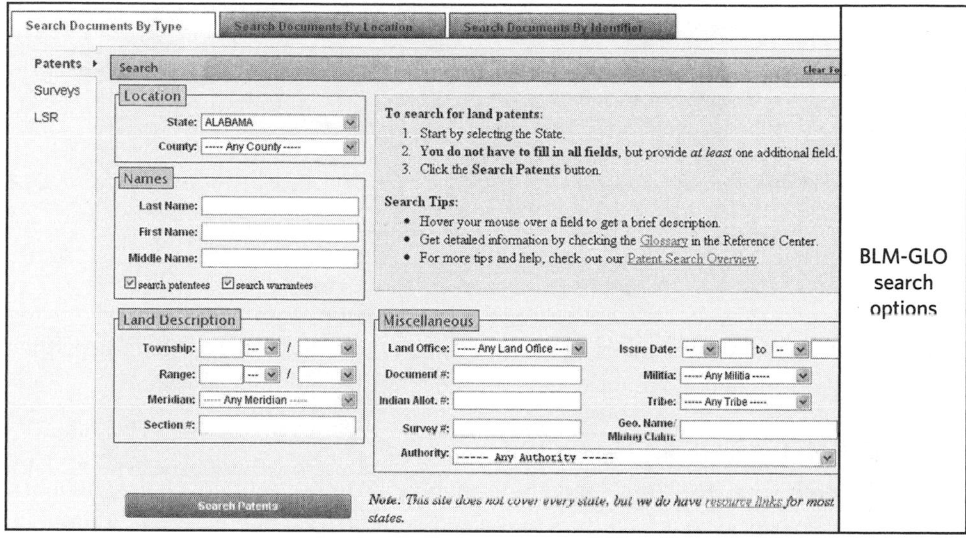

BLM-GLO search options

to my third-great-grandfather, Aaron Hendrickson. Aaron's acres were located in Shelby County, Indiana, just southeast of the land owned by his brother, William.

STEP 1. From the GLO Home page <www.glorecords.blm.gov>, click on Search Documents. This will open a search screen.

STEP 2. At the search screen, select a state, then fill in at least one of the search fields, such as the patentee's name. If you know the county your ancestor lived in, select it from a pull-down list; otherwise, let the system search statewide.

Searching for Aaron's records, I went to the Indiana screen, entered *Hendrickson* and chose Shelby County. Within a few seconds I had a list of twelve Hendrickson land patents.

If you don't get the results you expected, read the Search Tips or broaden your search by using wildcards in the name. The wildcards on this site differ from the standard asterisk (*); use a percent sign (%) to match any number of characters in the search field (e.g., *Sm%th* for Smith or Smyth or *183%* for 1831, 1832, etc.), and the underscore (_) to match any one single character. In other words, the percent sign is a wildcard when you need to cover your bases on more than one character, while the underscore is used for a single character only. *Smith%* could find Smithson, Smithsons, Smithington, while *Smit_* [underscore] will only find names such as Smith, Smite, Smito, or Smita.

STEP 3. After your search returns a patent of interest, click on the link to see the general patent description. The Legal Land Description tab provides specifics about the land, including the township, section, meridian, and range.

The Patent Image tab takes you to scanned images of the patent. You can save the image as a PDF file or click for a printer-friendly version (this will not include the actual

Certificate. No. 12076 **The United States of America,**

To all to whom these presents shall come, Greeting:

Whereas, Aaron Hendrickson of Decatur County Indiana has deposited in the General Land Office of the United States, a certificate of the Register of the Land Office at Indian whereby it appears that full payment has been made by the said Aaron Hendrickson according to the provisions of the act of Congress of the 24th April, 1820, entitled "An act making further provision for the sal the East half of the South West quarter of Section Thirty five in Township Range Seven East in the District of lands subject to sale at Indianapolis Eighty acres

Sample land patent, General Land Office

image). To print the image, choose a TIFF or Adobe Acrobat (PDF) format. A certified copy, printed on either bond or parchment paper, is available for $2.

GET TO KNOW THE NEIGHBORS

As you research your ancestors' land holdings, be sure to take note of their neighbors. These were the people your ancestors interacted with on a regular basis, and therefore, they'll likely show up as in-laws, witnesses on wills, and spouses. If you know who owned land around your ancestors', you'll have more clues about your family.

Land patents won't tell you who owned the surrounding land, but you can use the coordinates on the patent to search for surrounding patents.

Let's do this using the example of Aaron Hendrickson.

STEP 1. Using your search results on the BLM-GLO site, go back to the Legal Land Description screen and write down the aliquot parts (such as "E ½ SW ¼"), the section, township, range, and meridian of your ancestor's land.

STEP 2. Return to the search form and click the Clear button. Choose the county, but instead of filling in a name, go to the bottom of the form and fill in the section, township, range, and meridian fields. One click and you'll get the names and land descriptions of everyone who owned land in that section.

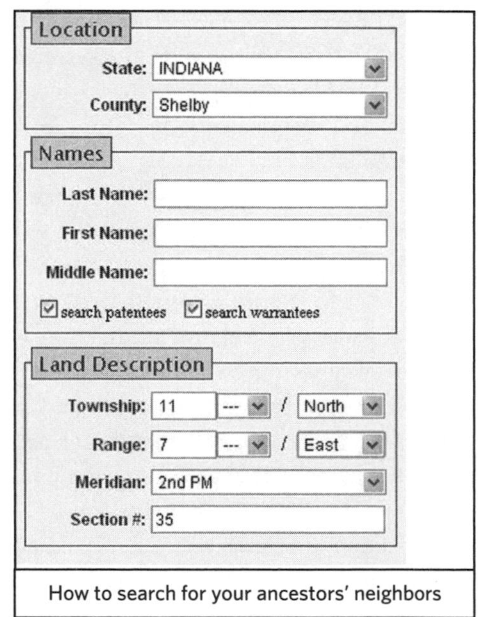
Location
State: INDIANA
County: Shelby
Names
Last Name:
First Name:
Middle Name:
search patentees
search warrantees
Land Description
Township: 11 --- / North
Range: 7 --- / East
Meridian: 2nd PM
Section #: 35

How to search for your ancestors' neighbors

As you can see, William Hendrickson, Aaron's brother, appears in the results. There are also a number of Moores. From my research, I knew Moores and Hendricksons had been marrying each other for a couple of generations prior to the

Image	Accession	Names	Date	Doc #	State	Meridian	Twp - Rng	Aliquots	Sec. #	County
	IN0710 .321	HARDY, ELIZABETH A	9/30/1835	18466	IN	2nd PM	011N - 007E	W½SE¼	35	Shelby
	IN0710 .320	HARDY, NANCY S	9/30/1835	18465	IN	2nd PM	011N - 007E	E½SE¼	35	Shelby
	IN0580 .294	HENDRICKSON, AARON	8/5/1834	12076	IN	2nd PM	011N - 007E	E½SW¼	35	Shelby
	IN0580 .042	HENDRICKSON, WILLIAM	10/1/1833	11824	IN	2nd PM	011N - 007E	W½NW¼	35	Shelby
	IN0650 .197	MOORE, JOHN	10/30/1834	15479	IN	2nd PM	011N - 007E	E½NE¼	35	Shelby
	IN0670 .226	MOORE, JOHN	11/6/1834	16517	IN	2nd PM	011N - 007E	E½NW¼	35	Shelby
	IN0710 .092	MOORE, JOHN	9/30/1835	18234	IN	2nd PM	011N - 007E	NW¼NE¼	35	Shelby
	IN0610 .064	MOORE, THOMAS	9/2/1834	13340	IN	2nd PM	011N - 007E	W½SW¼	35	Shelby
	IN0760 .443	WILSON, WILLIAM	9/30/1835	21108	IN	2nd PM	011N - 007E	SW¼NE¼	35	Shelby

Results of "neighbor search"

1830s. I've found marriage records in Kentucky. The fact that the families own land in the same section leads me to suspect that they moved together from Kentucky to Indiana.

BECOME A MAP MAKER

To get an even better idea of your ancestor's neighborhood, use the BLM-GLO results to create a geographical representation. Graphing paper makes it easy to do this, but you can also use a blank piece of paper and ruler.

STEP 1. Start by drawing a square on the paper. The square represents the section in which your ancestor owned land; in Aaron Hendrickson's case, it's Section 35.

Divided your square into quarters. Label the top right of your square "NE" (Northeast), the top left "NW" (Northwest), the bottom right "SE" (Southeast), and the bottom left "SW" (Southwest).

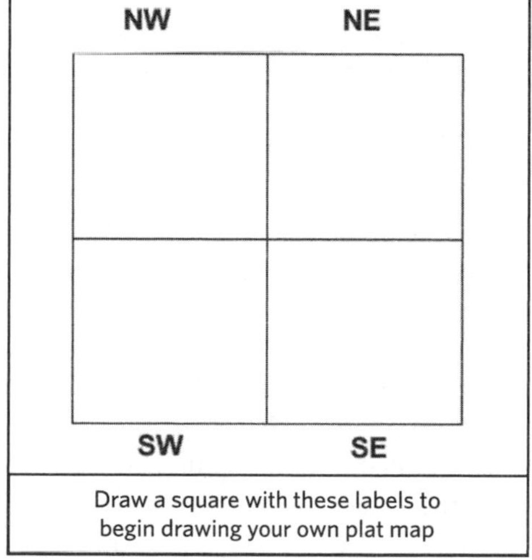

Draw a square with these labels to begin drawing your own plat map

STEP 2. Click on the land description for each person who owned land in the ancestral section and write down the details of their land description.

Using the information, fill in the section map. Be sure to write down the names of all the landowners in the same area as their land—you never know what name is going to turn up in your family tree.

Not sure how to translate something like "E½SW¼" and add it to the map?

The description sounds more complex than it really is. For example, if someone owns the E½ SW¼, all this means is: The land is located in the **SW quarter of the section** (SW¼). The particular plot in question takes up the **East half** (E½) of that quarter section.

Because I wanted to explore a little more, I returned to the search form and changed the section number from 35 to 34 (the section immediately west). There were three more patents for Hendricksons and Moores. And in Section 27 (just north of 34), every single patent belonged to someone related to Aaron either by blood or marriage.

Two hours after I began my search, I had plotted the ownership of nine sections. In all, I'd found forty-three land patents belonging to four different branches of my family. Without plotting the surrounding sections, I would never have realized the number of extended family members living in the area. To the right is a hand-drawn depiction of a portion of my findings.

As they say, a picture is worth a thousand words, and the picture that emerged from my simple maps depicted how my family intertwined through both time and space.

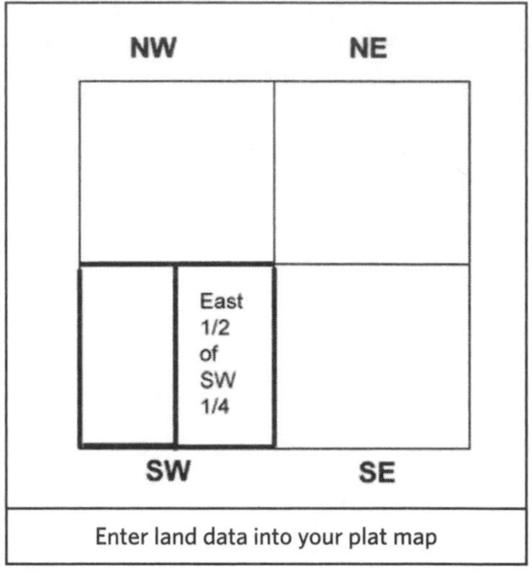

Enter land data into your plat map

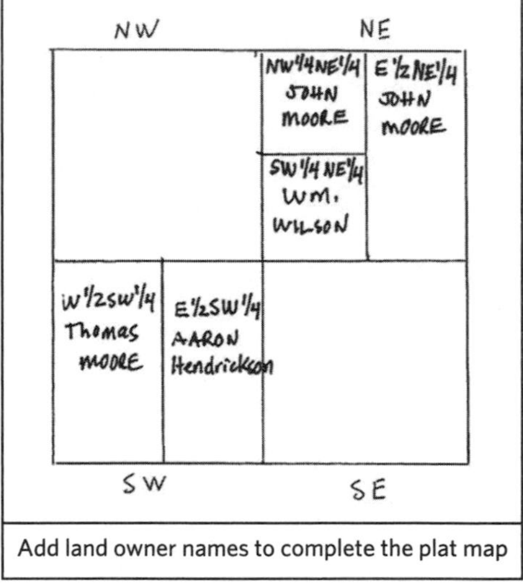

Add land owner names to complete the plat map

GOOGLE EARTH

Google Earth is an amazing, free program that will help you with your land research. Unlike other Google programs, Google Earth must be downloaded and installed on your computer. Do this for free following the instructions at <earth.google.com>. To help you get started and learn more about Google Earth, view the tutorials at any time by clicking the Learn link on the Google Earth Home page.

While you can use Google Earth to view your home and places you shop or visit, you can also use it like a flying time machine that can view historic boundaries and even pinpoint the location of an ancestor's original land patent.

Google Earth Controls

The first thing you'll notice on launching the software is a Tips panel. If you don't want to see tips when you first launch, uncheck the Show tips at start-up box.

Next, you'll see the main panel is filled with a 3-D rendering of planet Earth, while panels on the left are split between Search, Places, and Layers.

Across the top of the screen is a row of icons; place your mouse over each to read a description. It's from these icons that you'll be able to do things like show historical imagery, add place marks, and switch to Google Maps.

Finally, navigation controls are located on the upper right side of the screen. By default, they're very faint, but put your mouse on them to bring them to life.

Here's how to use the controls:

The top ring lets you look around. It's almost like standing in one place and turning 360 degrees. Click the N (North) to return the image to its upright position, with north back on the top.

The two views of the Washington Monument show how you can create a different vantage point using the controls on the upper circle.

Google Earth navigation controls, ©2011 Google

The circle in the center of navigation (the one with the Hand icon) lets you move your position on the map, using the directional arrows. So instead of rotating from a single position as you did above, the controls on this circle let you move from one place to another.

Use the navigation controls to change your vantage point, ©2011 Google

The Orange Man icon is used to view things at street level. Just drag it anywhere on the screen to enter Street View.

The bottom slider bar is a Zoom control, allowing you to get closer or farther away from the image. You'll notice that the closer you get to the ground, the more Google will tilt the screen. Instead of viewing from above, you'll almost be viewing from ground level.

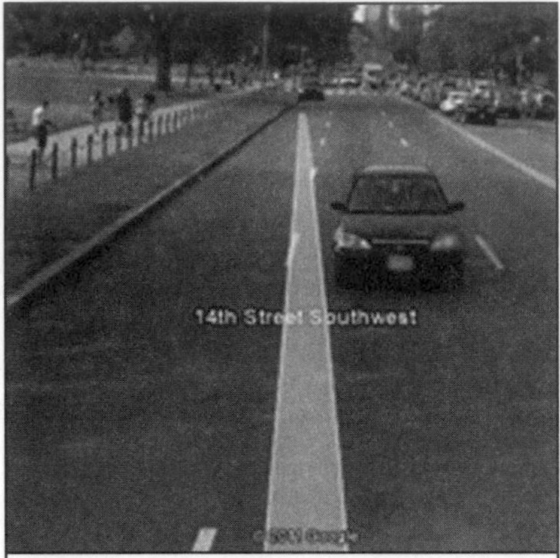

Drag the Orange Man icon for a street-level view
©2011 Google

Using the Search Panel

Use the Search Panel Fly To tab to find places of interest. Just type in the name of the place you want to see and off you'll go.

You can search for the name of a country, state, city, village, an address, GPS coordinates, zip code, and landmarks. Turn on the 3-D Buildings option in the Layers panel for a realistic 3-D view.

Use the Find Businesses tab to locate a business, and the Directions tab to navigate from one place to the next. Using Directions, Google will map out your journey, turn by turn.

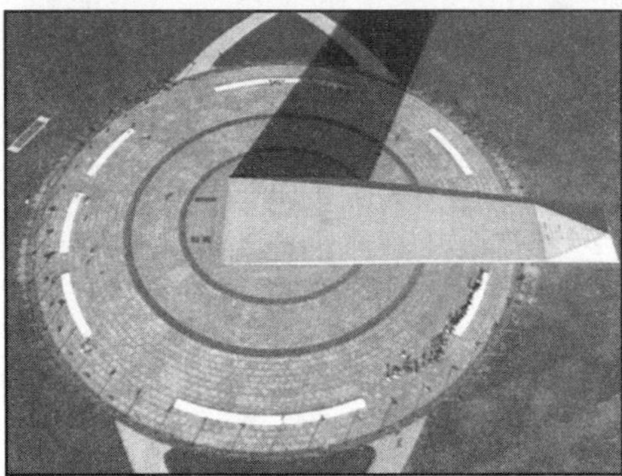

Get a closer look using the Zoom control
© 2011 Google

Using the Places Panel

The Places panel serves much the same purpose as the Bookmarks/Favorites feature in your internet browser. Here you can save and organize your placemarks and files. Double click on the name of any place listed in the Places panel and Earth will fly there.

As you add historical data, such as an overlay of historical county boundary lines, the name of the data will appear in the Places panel. Check and uncheck boxes to toggle them on and off.

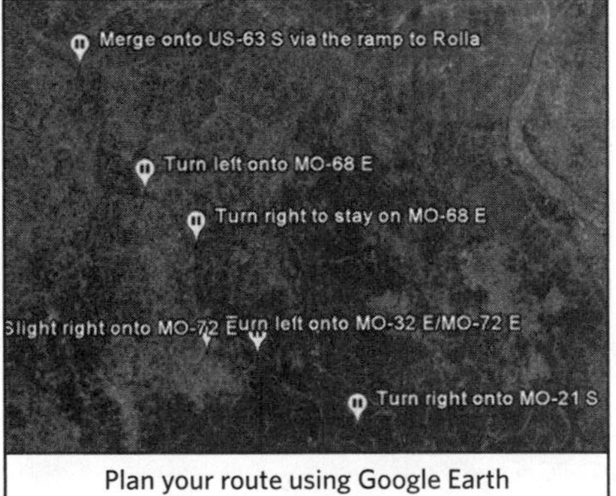

Plan your route using Google Earth
©2011 Google

The Layers Panel

This panel contains a tremendous amount of built-in data that could assist your genealogy research or simply serve as an afternoon of fascinating discovery.

Layers adds a variety of user-specified information as an overlay to Earth. For example, you can click the Shipwreck box to view wreck locations. Or toggle on a current weather report, view roads, label place names, see borders, and examine user-added photographs.

Open any Layer category by clicking the plus sign, close it by clicking the minus sign. Click the Earth Gallery button to view a collection that includes views of ancient Rome, selections from Rumsey Historical Maps, and NASA imagery.

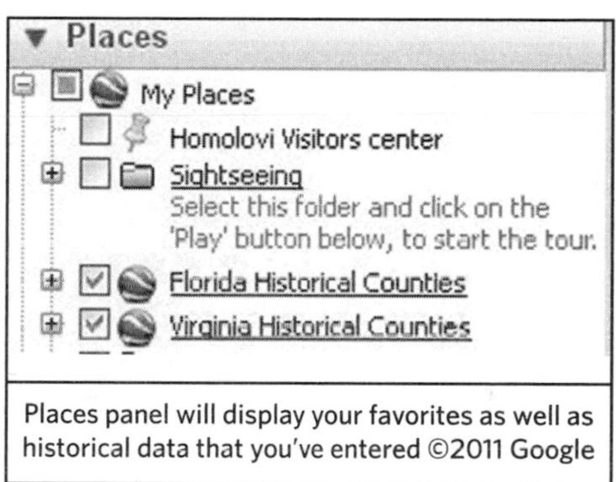

Places panel will display your favorites as well as historical data that you've entered ©2011 Google

Google Earth and Genealogy

One of the coolest features of Earth is the ability to visit your ancestor's home or farm. Anytime you find a specific address for an ancestor, you can type it into Google Earth to view the location. One place to find these specific addresses is the 1920 and 1930 federal census (discussed in chapter nine).

As you can see on this 1920 Chicago census, the Powell family lived at 2106 West Harrison. Type this address into the Search panel and fly directly to the address.

Once there, you can zoom in and even drag and drop the Orange Man icon to get a street-level view of the family home. Don't be surprised if instead of a house or apartment building, you're now looking at an office building or strip mall. You also may find there are no structures at the location—the buildings have been torn down.

If you want, you can mark this location using the Push Pin icon, located on the row of icons running across the screen. After you've placed the pin, a box will pop

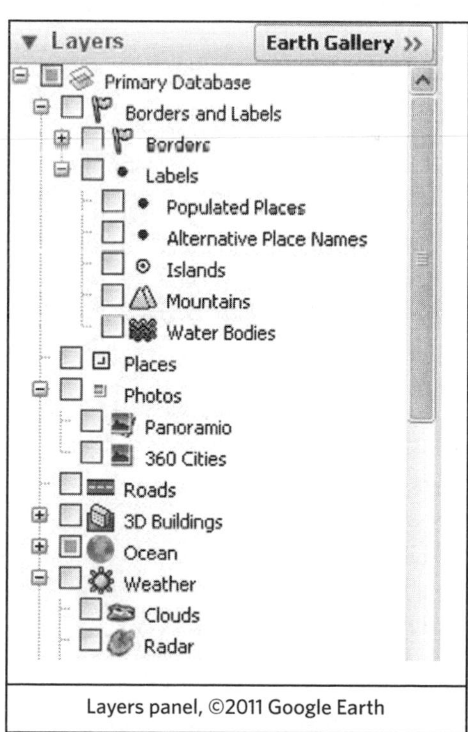

Layers panel, ©2011 Google Earth

up, allowing you to name the place mark and add descriptive information. Use the Street View icon to grab a snapshot of the location as it exists today.

You may enter a historical address that Google doesn't recognize. This doesn't necessarily mean you have the wrong address. It's possible that the street name has changed. I'll explain how to check for this a little later.

W. HARRISON STREET

2104	3	3	Brooks, Joseph E
			—— Anna
			—— Doris
2106	4	4	Powell, H. Creighton
			—— Edith
			—— Ruth
			—— Wendell
			—— Grace
			—— Miriam
2108	5	5	De Costa, Albert
			—— Ray
			—— Helen
			—— Charles
			—— Evelyn
			—— Lillian
2112	6	6	Sebald, Lena

1920 federal census, Chicago, Illinois

Fly Google Earth to West Harrison Street, Chicago ©2011 Google

Find Historical Views

Depending on the years that data is available for a specific place, you may be able to view an historical image of the location as it would have looked in your ancestor's time. On the top row of icons is a Show Historical Imagery icon represented by a clock. Click the Clock icon to open a slide bar timeline that lets you view the area using images from a previous era.

Use the plus and minus signs to zoom in and out on the timeline slider. Click the back and forward arrows to move through time, and the Wrench icon to set options of how fast to play the time sequence. As you can see, the imagery for this particular Chicago neighborhood begins in 1999 and runs to 2010.

Google Earth and the Bureau of Land Management

Earlier in the chapter you learned how to find an official record of your ancestor's land at the Bureau of Land Management-GLO website. Now you're going to use that same information to plot the land on Google Earth.

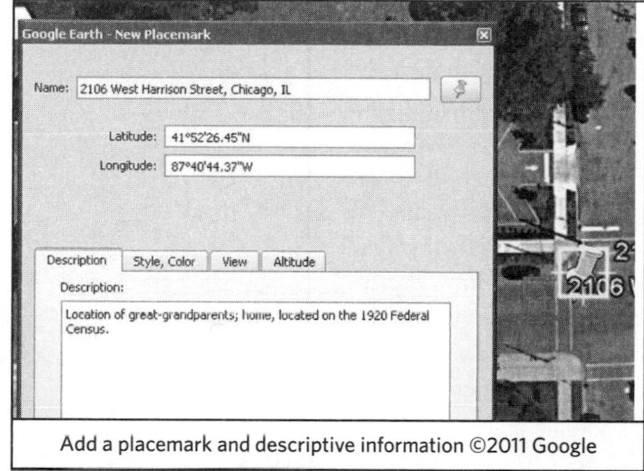

Add a placemark and descriptive information ©2011 Google

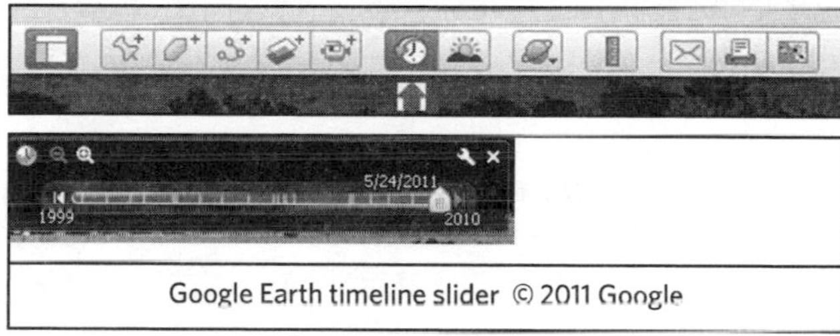

Google Earth timeline slider © 2011 Google

STEP 1. On the BLM site <www.glorecords.blm.gov>, record the township, range, and section information of your ancestor's patent along with the state, principal meridian, township, range, and section.

STEP 2. Now go to a new website—Earthpoint (Tools for Google Earth) <www.earthpoint.us>. In the left column, under USA Utilities, click on the Township & Range link. Part way down the page, you'll see a section called Convert Township, Range, and Section to Latitude and Longitude. Click the Search By Description link. Using the drop-down boxes, fill in the information you copied from the BLM-GLO site.

When you click the Fly To On Google Earth button, Earth Point will pop up a box asking you to download a Google Earth KLM file. Save the file, remembering where it was saved on your computer.

STEP 3. On Google Earth, click the File menu, then Open. Open the KLM file, and Google will fly to the coordinates saved in that file. What you'll see when you arrive at your ancestor's land is a large rectangle bordered in orange and a smaller rectangle bordered in purple.

Using the section-dividing technique you learned earlier in this chapter, you can easily see the area owned by your ancestor.

STEP 4. To mark your ancestor's land, select the Polygon tool in the top icon bar. With this tool, click each corner of the purple rectangle outlining your ancestor's land. By default, Earth will fill in that section with solid white, but you'll want to actually see the land, not a white square, so you'll need to change the default.

When you click the Polygon tool, a dialogue box will appear, which you can fill in with the name of this place and any description. Click the Style/Color tab in this box and change the Lines to a color that's easy to see—like lime green. Next change the Area from "filled and outlined" to just "outlined." This way your land will be outlined, but you will still be able to see what's there today.

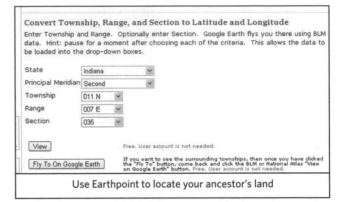

Convert Township, Range, and Section to Latitude and Longitude

Enter Township and Range. Optionally enter Section. Google Earth flys you there using BLM data. Hint: pause for a moment after choosing each of the criteria. This allows the data to be loaded into the drop-down boxes.

State	Indiana
Principal Meridian	Second
Township	011 N
Range	007 E
Section	035

View — Free. User account is not needed.

Fly To On Google Earth — If you want to see the surrounding townships, then once you have clicked the "Fly To" button, come back and click the BLM or National Atlas "View on Google Earth" button. Free. User account is not needed.

Use Earthpoint to locate your ancestor's land

Rumsey Historical Maps

A great genealogy tool in Google Earth is Rumsey Historical Map, found in the Layers panel under the Gallery heading.

Fly to your desired location and then select the Rumsey layer box. If any historic maps are available for the area, a Rumsey icon will appear on Earth. If you don't see any, zoom out, remembering that there may not be an historical map for your location.

Select the Rumsey Historical Maps in the Layer Menu, Google Earth, ©2011 Google

If you do see an icon, hold your mouse over it to view the map's date, then click the map thumbnail to overlay it on Earth.

In the case of the Chicago address, there is a map created in 1857, before the Great Chicago Fire. The map encompasses the area of West Harrison. You can now zoom in to see what homes or businesses were in the area.

When you layer a Rumsey Historical Map over the present-day map, you will be able to see where new roads have been added and where street names have changed. If you have an historical address that isn't recognized by Google Earth, seek out an historical map of the area and see if you can find the street name on that map. Using the Overlay view, you'll be able to find the present-day street name and get a view of the address.

Rumsey Historical Map of Chicago 1857, David Rumsey Map Collection, <www.davidrumsey.com>

UNDERSTANDING SHIFTING BOUNDARIES

Disappearing counties and changing boundary lines have long been a challenge for genealogy researchers. A marriage, birth, or land transaction you thought was in one county might have taken place just across a county line or during a period when county lines were moving.

Confusion continues when one state was carved from another, or several states were created from a territory. For example, if your family lived in Fincastle, Virginia, did you know that in 1776 Fincastle became the counties of Kentucky, Washington, and Montgomery? And that in 1780, Kentucky County became Fayette, Jefferson, and Lincoln counties; then in 1792, Kentucky County became the state of Kentucky? It's hard to keep up.

If you don't have a timeline of changing boundary lines, it's almost impossible to track down where you'll find the records. Fortunately, you can find a resource similar to this at the Atlas of Historical County Boundaries <publications.newberry.org/ahcbp>.

The Atlas was developed as a "resource for people seeking records of past events, and people trying to analyze, interpret, and display county-based historical data like returns of elections and censuses, and for people working on state and local history projects."

Not only can you view changing boundary lines for each state on interactive maps, you can download a boundary timeline for every single county. Plus (and this is truly cool!) you can import the data into Google Earth and use the timeline slider to view changes in territory, state, and county boundaries over time.

Let's check out the boundary changes in the state of Illinois.

STEP 1. Open the Atlas Home page <publications.newberry.org/ahcbp> and select a state by clicking it on the map. In this example I've selected Illinois.

STEP 2. Clicking the state takes you to the state's page, which contains a menu of options, including launching an interactive map, an historical commentary, and an index of county chronologies. Below the image of the state, you'll find an explanation of each menu option.

STEP 3. Click View Interactive Map to launch the program. In the upper left corner, you'll find a notation of the available dates for viewing. Dates range from the creation of the first county (or unsuccessful county proposal) through December 31, 2000.

Select the date you want displayed from the pull-down menu in the upper right corner. Note the legend indicating that historical lines are in black, while modern boundaries are in brown and white. This example shows Illinois's boundaries in 1795. You can see that they went through Michigan, Wisconsin, Indiana, and Ohio.

STEP 4. View the county boundaries from another point in history by changing the date in the pull-down menu, then click the Refresh Map button. Changing the Illinois date to 1812 produced a far different boundary map.

For more options (like Print, Pan, Zoom), use the tools running vertically along the left side of the page.

STEP 5. Use the Back button on your browser to return to the Illinois state page. Click View Individual County Chronologies from the State Page menu options. This link takes you to a page containing detailed information about each county (proposed, extinct, present, historical). Many counties have confusing and convoluted histories, and this is where you'll find exact information.

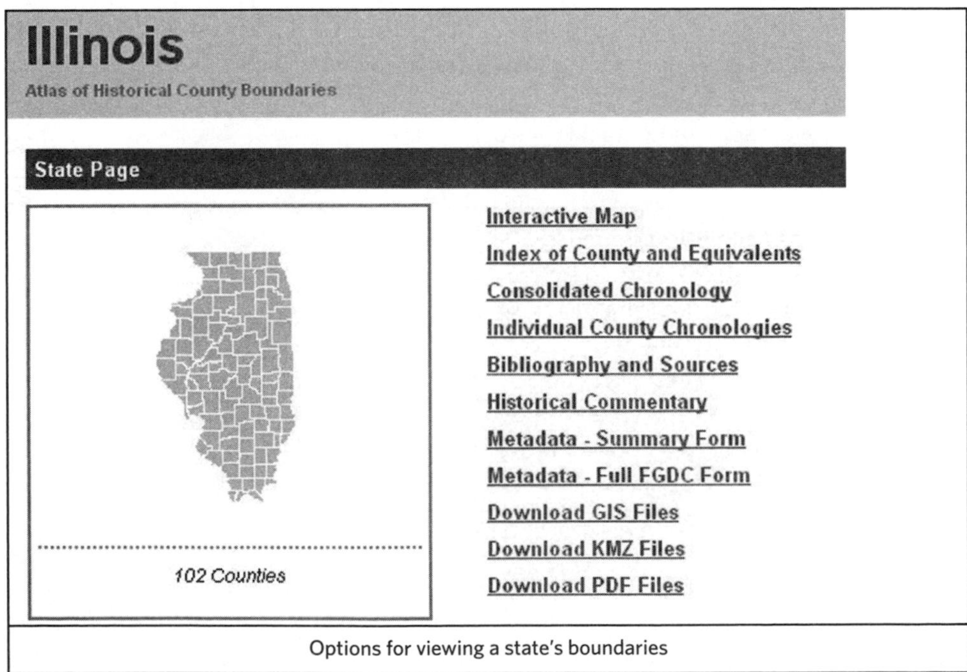

Options for viewing a state's boundaries

Boundaries for 1795 Illinois
©2011 Google ©2011 INEGI

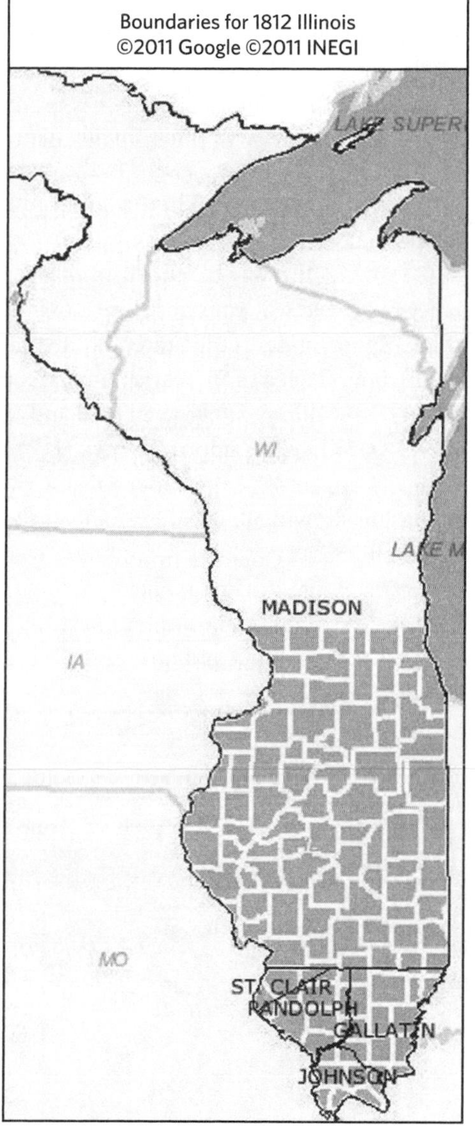

Boundaries for 1812 Illinois
©2011 Google ©2011 INEGI

For example, look at the history of modern day Christian County, Illinois. It was formed from Montgomery and Sangamon counties in 1839 and originally named Dane County. The name was changed to Christian in February 1840, and in February 1851, a piece of Christian County was annexed by Shelby County.

Google Earth and Atlas of Historical County Boundaries

The great news is you can export information from the Atlas of Historical County Boundaries to Google Earth.

STEP 1. Select your desired state from the Atlas Home page (in this case, Florida).

STEP 2. From the State Page options, click Download KMZ Files. This will download a zipped (.zip) file onto your computer. Unzip the file using your computer's zipping software (typically you can simply double click the file and it will generate an unzipped copy). The unzipped file will be named in this format: FL_Historical_Counties.kmz. See the image at right to see what the file icon will look like.

File icon for KMZ file ©2011 Google, ©2011 INEGI

STEP 3. Open Google Earth. On the menu bar, Click File > Open, and navigate to where you saved the state's KMZ file on your computer.

The KMZ file will be added to the Temporary Places panel on the left of your screen. Google Earth will automatically navigate to the state and display the historical county boundaries as an overlay on aerial photography. In these two images, you can see Florida's development between 1763 and 1826.

STEP 4. When you import historical data into Google Earth, a timeline slider will automatically appear. Use the slider to view the boundaries at a specific date or to launch an animation showing the changes. Adjust the animation speed by clicking the Wrench icon on the slider bar.

Experiment with importing data from two states where your family lived (like Virginia and Florida), then set the animation speed to slow. This way you have a visual reference of what was formed first and how each state's counties developed in reference to the other.

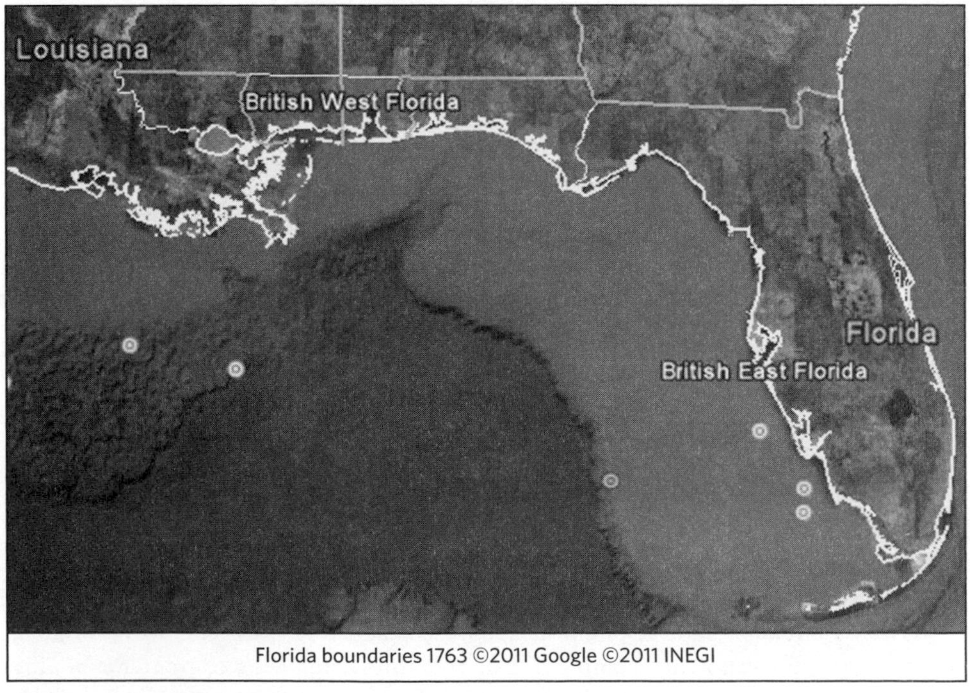

Florida boundaries 1763 ©2011 Google ©2011 INEGI

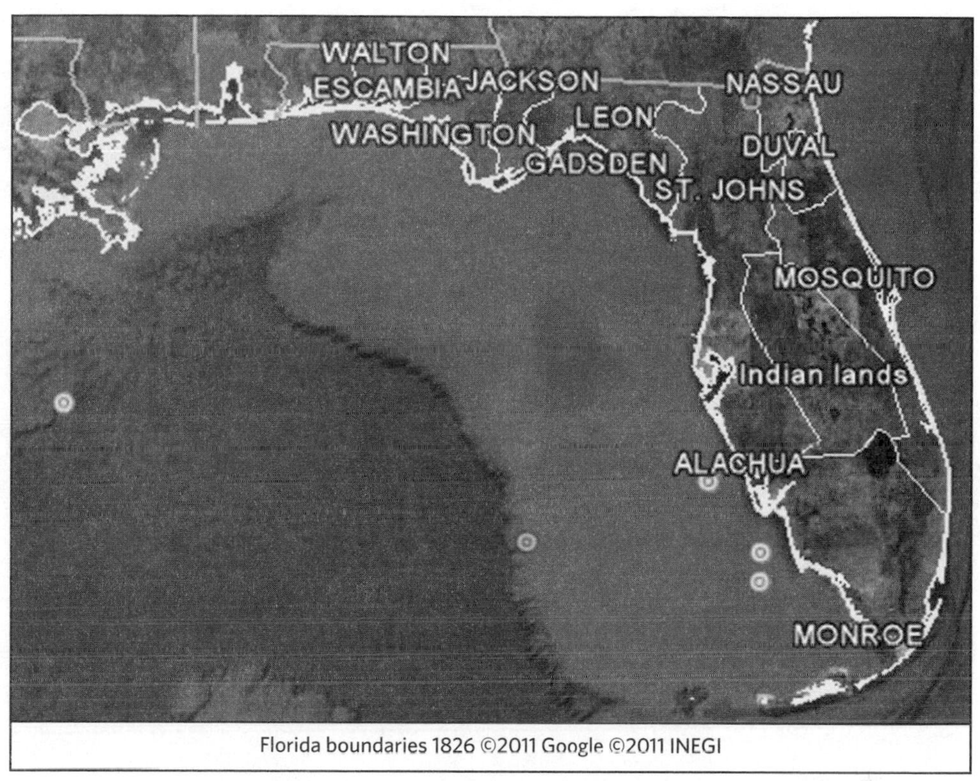

Florida boundaries 1826 ©2011 Google ©2011 INEGI

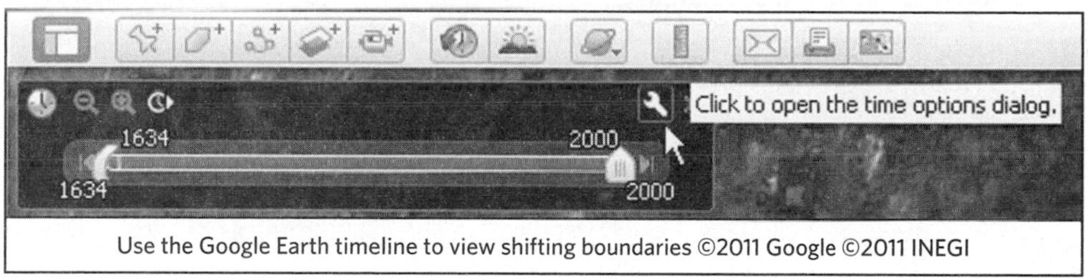

Use the Google Earth timeline to view shifting boundaries ©2011 Google ©2011 INEGI

The Census

Census records are among the most valuable documents for genealogical research. That's because they can provide the missing link that connects one generation to the next.

Census data also helps genealogists document migrations, infer family relationships, and track groups of neighbors who moved together.

Children's birthplaces and ages offer insight into the places a family lived and for how long. The value of real estate reflected prestige and social standing, as did the ability to read and write.

Every genealogist quickly learns to carefully record every item about his ancestor's family listed on a census page. If he is wise, he'll also note details about the neighbors within several dwellings on either side.

You learn, sometimes the hard way, that the reason a wife's maiden name sounds so familiar is because her family lived two farms away from your family's farm ten years earlier.

The Constitution specifies that a census be taken every ten years, and the results determine the apportionment of congressional districts. Little did the founders realize that the census would become the genealogist's best friend.

The first federal census was taken in 1790 and was simply a count of how many people lived in the United States. Because of privacy laws, census information is not released to the public for a period of seventy-two years. The 1930 census was released in 2002, and the 1940 census in 2012. The 1950 census cannot be released until 2022.

The questions asked on the census evolved over time. Before 1850, only heads of household were named; everyone else was a number. From 1850 forward, however, each member of the household was listed by name. For that reason, 1850 is the crown jewel of the nineteenth-century censuses and the one that often leads to research breakthroughs to earlier censuses.

KEY CHANGES IN THE FEDERAL CENSUS

1790: Name of the head of each household, number of free white males and females (by broad age groups), number of slaves.

1800 AND 1810: Same as 1790, but narrower age grouping.

1820: Addition of "how many people not naturalized" (to help determine the number of immigrants).

1830: Slaves were counted in age groups; asked if anyone in the household was deaf, dumb, or blind.

1840: Questions about industry (agriculture, mining, etc.) and insanity added.

1850: Names and ages of everyone in the household recorded. Included not just family members, but servants, in-laws, laborers, boarders, and friends. Value of real estate, married within the year, pauper, or convict. Place of birth.

1860: Value of personal property.

1870: Occupations of each person, parents of foreign birth. If a person was born or married within the year, the month of the event.

1880: Documented the relationship of everyone to the head of household. Asked for place of birth of each person's parents.

1890: Most of these records were destroyed in a 1921 fire.

1900: Included the month and year of birth, documented immigration and citizenship data, foreign birth, year of immigration, years in the United States, citizenship status. House and street number if living in a city. Number of children born to the female and how many of the children are still living. Did the person rent or own their home, mortgage, house, or farm.

1910: Included survivors of Union and Confederate military service. Alien or naturalized citizen, number of weeks unemployed.

1920: Year of naturalization. Employer, salaried or wage earner.

1930: Was anyone in the household a veteran and if so, what war or expedition.

1940: Residence five years prior to the census, wages, highest educational grade attained.

CENSUS RECORDS ON FREE WEBSITES

FAMILYSEARCH.ORG <familysearch.org>

One of the larger free census collections can be found at FamilySearch.org, including the 1850 Slave and Mortality Schedules. Four of the federal census collections (1850, 1860, 1870, and 1900) include images of original records. The 1880, 1910, 1920, and 1930 census collections are indexes only. If you find your ancestor on an index, you can either order the microfilm (the number is included on the index) or try to find the image at a free or fee site online.

While the FamilySearch.org census collections are extensive, they aren't infallible. Trying every conceivable combination, I could not find my Hendrickson family on the 1930 census, although I entered the names of everyone in the household as well as the county in which they were living.

Take-away: If you can't find your family in a census, try searching for them from another website. Not all transcriptions are created equal.

CASE STUDY

ALLIED FAMILIES IN CENSUSES

The 1870 census was filled with fascinating tidbits that led me down many research paths. Do you remember back in chapter four, I referenced a finding about John Hendrickson and his son-in-law, Mike Keller, going to Kansas? I knew that Mike had married Martha Hendrickson, but I didn't know much more about him. So I went looking on the 1870 census, and what I found opened up so many questions for me!

First, I found Mike living in Jackson County, Missouri, in a Groves [transcribed as Graves] family household, along with his wife, Martha, *and* (surprise to me) James Hendrickson. James was John's son and Martha's brother. What were they doing with the Groves family—people I had never encountered in my pervious research?

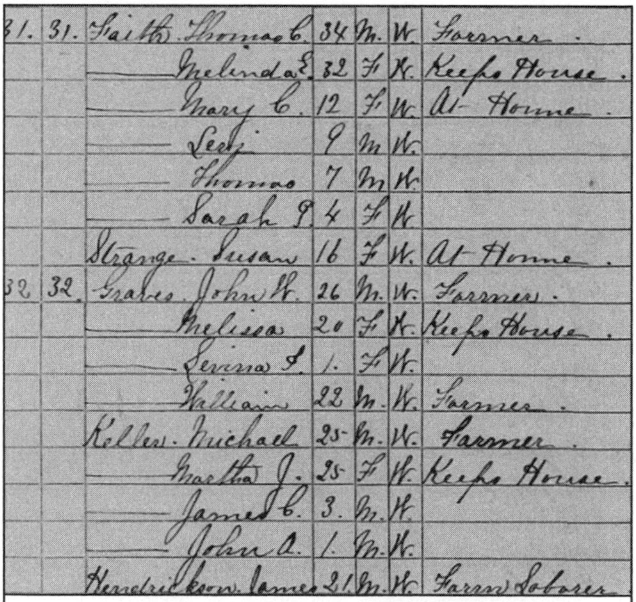

31.	31.	Faith Thomas C.	34	M.	W.	Farmer.
		Melinda E.	32	F	W.	Keeps House.
		Mary C.	12	F	W.	At Home.
		Lees	9	M	W.	
		Thomas	7	M	W.	
		Sarah [illegible]	4	F	W.	
		Strange. Susan	16	F	W.	At Home.
32	32.	Grabes John H.	26	M.	W.	Farmer.
		Melissa	20	F	W.	Keeps House.
		Serina S.	1.	F	W.	
		William	22	M.	W.	Farmer.
		Keller. Michael	25	M.	W.	Farmer.
		Martha J.	25	F	W.	Keeps House.
		James C.	3.	M.	W.	
		John A.	1.	M.	W.	
		Hendrickson. James	21	M.	W.	Farm Laborer.

1870 Cass County, Missouri, census, FamilySearch.org

I wanted to see the census image, just to find out who else was living nearby. I'm glad I did, because right next door, living in the Thomas Faith household, was sixteen-year-old Susan Strange.

Why was Susan Strange's name so familiar? Because it was the name of James Hendrickson's first wife. The 1870 census in Cass County, Missouri, was taken on July 8; James and Susan were married on July 20. Until the marriage, they were living next door to one another. As it turns out (I discovered by searching marriage records—chapter five and other census records), Susan's sister was Melinda Faith (Thomas's wife). Everything is beginning to fall into place.

But there's more. In searching FamilySearch.org for marriages, I discovered that on July 21, James's sister, Anna, married William Groves, who was living in the household with James and the Kellers. In short, James was living with his soon-to-be brother-in-law and his brother-in-law (Mike). A very tangled web of family relationships, all uncovered in a census record.

Other Free Census Websites

USGENWEB.COM <usgwarchives.net/census/>

A volunteer effort to put census indexes and images online, organized by state, county, and year. To date, the majority of the donations are of indexes rather than images.

CENSUS FINDER <censusfinder.com>

While you won't find census records on this site, you will find links to records on other sites, both free and subscription.

Census Finder is easy to navigate and is organized by census records from the United States, United Kingdom, Canada, and Native American. Using the drop-down box, choose your state, then browse through a list of available census records. As a convenience, in case you don't subscribe to Ancestry.com, is a notation on the links that go to the subscription site.

Census Finder is a good starting place if you're searching for UK or Canadian records. You'll also find links to Norwegian and Swedish records.

Statewide Massachusetts Census Records Online

1790-1890 Massachusetts Census Records at Ancestry
1790 Federal Census of the US at the U. S. Census Bureau
1840 Federal Census Pensioners
1850 Federal Census Images
1850 Federal Census Mortality Schedule Images
1855 Massachusetts State Census Records
1865 Massachusetts State Census Records
1870 Federal Census Images
1880 Federal Census - Search and View the images
1880 Federal Census Search at Family Search
1900 Federal Census Images
Massachusetts Statewide Databases of Census and Genealogy Records

Links to Massachusetts census records, Census Finder

CENSUS LINKS <censuslinks.com>
Links to thousands of free census records, both of the United States and other countries. From the Home page, navigate to the country of interest, then (in the United States) to state and then county. All links go to free records, which may be federal or state census, or census substitutes (i.e., a list of World War I residents in a county).

NAME OF SLAVE OWNER, NUMBER OF SLAVES
Transcribed by Linda Durr Rudd

- THOMAS G. ABBOTT, 7
- WILLIAM B. ABBOTT, 7
- THOMAS ADAMS, 64
- JACOB AHNER?, 2
- JAMES ARCHER, 98
- GEORGE ARMSTRONG, 15
- GEORGE ARNATT, 2

Transcription of 1860 slave schedule, Jefferson County, Mississippi, AfriGeneas

AFRICAN-AMERICAN CENSUS SCHEDULES
<www.afrigeneas.com/aacensus>
AfriGeneas, an excellent source for African-American research, has a list of links including federal census, mortality, and slave schedules. Organized by state, then county.

CENSUSDIGGINS.COM
<www.censusdiggins.com>
Not an extensive collection, but the census records that are on-site are free. If you're lucky, the records for your ancestor's county are here. Just a note—if you click the census search links at the top of the page, those links go to Ancestry.com.

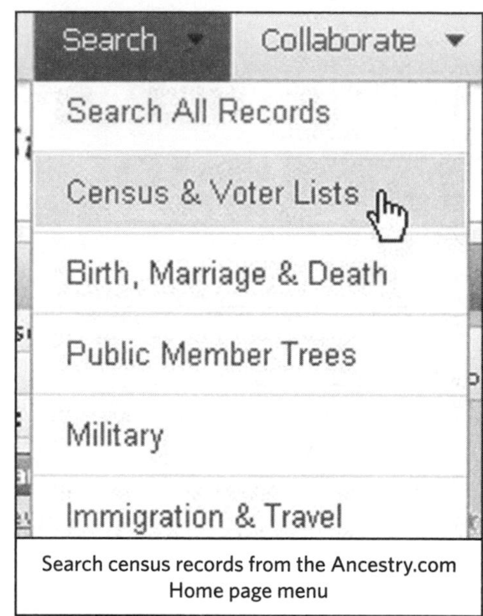

Search census records from the Ancestry.com Home page menu

CENSUS RECORDS ON SUBSCRIPTION SITES

ANCESTRY.COM <ancestry.com>
If you want to search every federal census, the mortality and slave schedules, special veteran censuses, as well as several state census records, you'll find them at Ancestry.com. From the Home page, mouse-over Search, then choose Census and Voter Lists from the pull-down menu.

Searching from the Census and Voter Lists page will search across all records. It's much easier to filter if you narrow your search to a specific census, such as the 1880 federal census, rather than running a search across all databases.

Narrow the search by selecting a census group from the Narrow by Category links.

By selecting U.S. Federal Census Collection, you can further narrow by census year.

If you're unsure in which census year you'll find an ancestor, move back up the narrowing process and select a group such as 1800s censuses.

Like any other census data collection, you may have to be creative in how you search. Just remember to use as many search combinations as needed if your initial search falls short.

Finding my great-grandfather James Hendrickson and my grandfather H. Byron was difficult. I tried searching many different combinations, but it wasn't until I added James's year of birth (1849) and the name of his wife (Ella) that the correct record appeared.

Hendrickson was spelled Hendrisson, and that's how it was transcribed. Can you see part of the problem in the census record image?

Narrow by Category

U.S. Federal Census Collection
UK Census Collection
Canadian Census Collection
1700s Censuses
1800s Censuses
1900s Censuses

Narrow your census search by category, Ancestry.com

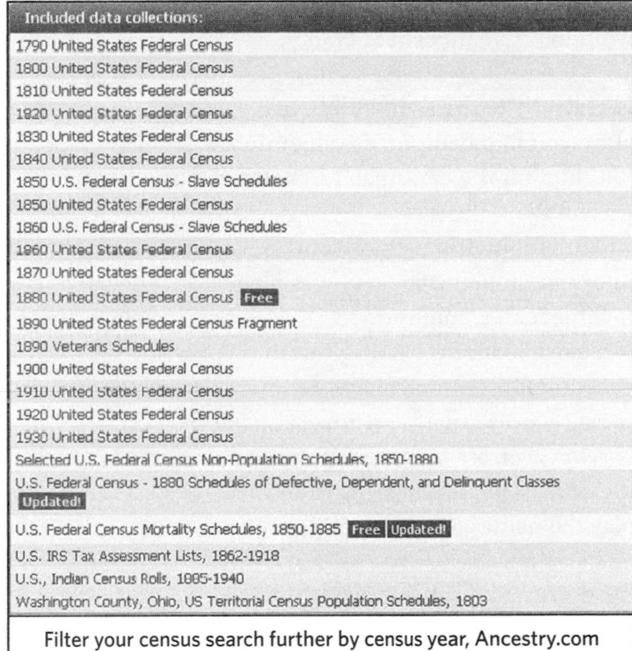

Included data collections:
1790 United States Federal Census
1800 United States Federal Census
1810 United States Federal Census
1820 United States Federal Census
1830 United States Federal Census
1840 United States Federal Census
1850 U.S. Federal Census - Slave Schedules
1850 United States Federal Census
1860 U.S. Federal Census - Slave Schedules
1860 United States Federal Census
1870 United States Federal Census
1880 United States Federal Census Free
1890 United States Federal Census Fragment
1890 Veterans Schedules
1900 United States Federal Census
1910 United States Federal Census
1920 United States Federal Census
1930 United States Federal Census
Selected U.S. Federal Census Non-Population Schedules, 1850-1880
U.S. Federal Census - 1880 Schedules of Defective, Dependent, and Delinquent Classes Updated!
U.S. Federal Census Mortality Schedules, 1850-1885 Free Updated!
U.S. IRS Tax Assessment Lists, 1862-1918
U.S., Indian Census Rolls, 1885-1940
Washington County, Ohio, US Territorial Census Population Schedules, 1803

Filter your census search further by census year, Ancestry.com

FOLD3.COM <fold3.com>

Fold3.com contains all of the twentieth-century censuses and the 1860 census. To search, type in the name of your ancestor and (optional) place where he was living. Fold3.com

1900 federal census, Ancestry.com

will serve up search results that you can then filter by adding or deleting keywords. A seven-day free trial is available to new users.

WORLDVITALRECORDS.COM <worldvitalrecords.com>
Known for a diversity of U.S. and world records, WorldVitalRecords.com has the entire U.S. federal census collection. Using a free three-day pass, you can explore the site, checking out census and other vital records. Both monthly and annual subscription plans are available.

Although smaller than Ancestry.com, WorldVitalRecords.com has thousands of diverse databases. You can search specific databases, like the census, or do a broad search across all databases. The latter may yield clues in a small and lesser-known collection you wouldn't have thought to search.

CENSUS RESEARCH TIPS

Have you found an ancestor mentioned in a newspaper article or obituary, but you can't find him on the census, even though he was a resident of the county when the census was taken?

Although some people were occasionally missed by enumerators, it's possible that the information in the obituary was incorrect. When people are grieving, it's not uncommon to forget dates, confuse facts, or even report an incorrect length of time the deceased lived in a particular city.

Look for another source to double-check the accuracy of the information, such as court records or city directories.

However, assuming the obituary was correct, it's possible your family was included in the census, but is playing hard to get. And locating them may just be a case of learning to play the name game. These tips will help you.

Be Aware of Misspellings

The enumerator could have misspelled the surname so badly you simply don't recognize it. In my own family, I've found Knox listed as Nox, and Hendrickson as Hendriksen, Henderson, Hendricks, and Hendrixson.

Although every genealogist has been cautioned about spelling variations, check every conceivable spelling of your name. For example, a Mitcham surname may have been recorded as Machun, Meekin, Mecham, Meekin, Maikin, Machen, or even Meachon. Also throw in some wildcard searches such as Mi***am or M*tcham.

Expand your search to include phonetic spellings, particularly for the first letter(s) in the name. For instance, Goggin might have been spelled Ghoggin. Or if your name begins with the letter H, the H may have been dropped and a vowel used in its place, i.e., Hager, Yaeger, Yager, Ager.

Old Handwriting Is Hard to Read

When you search census records online, you are searching transcriptions of the data, not the raw data itself. It's possible the person who transcribed the names misinterpreted the enumerator's handwriting. Penmanship has evolved over the last two hundred years. When reading old documents, what looks like an "f" to one person may look like an "s" to another. Try multiple spellings and, whenever possible, check images of the original document to verify the spelling in the census return.

You may also find numbers transcribed incorrectly. On a recent search at Ancestry.com, the person's age was listed as 78 instead of 18—all because the transcriptionist read the one as a seven.

Search Nicknames and Abbreviations

It's possible your family member was listed with an incorrect first name, or he could be listed by a middle name or nickname instead of the surname. My grandfather was shown on a census as H. Byron, although his name was Herschel. If you find someone on the census with your surname but a different first name, don't discount him—he may be yours.

You may also have difficulty locating an ancestor on the census because he was listed by his initial, not his first name, i.e., W. H. Jones. In cases like this, you won't find him if you put his first name into the search box. Instead, you'll need to search using surname, place of residence, and approximate date of birth (if known).

Also, try common nicknames—Peg for Margaret, Bob for Robert, Bill for William—but also research non-name-related nicknames your ancestor may have had such as Red if he was a redhead. Enumerators weren't required to collect legal names. They simply recorded what the family told them. If your ancestor never answered to his legal name, he's not likely to have listed it for the enumerator.

Check Relationships

Just because a person is listed on the census as a son or daughter, it doesn't mean that was the true relationship. The child could have been a stepchild or an adopted child.

On the 1920 census, it seems logical to assume that the woman listed as being married to my great-grandfather was the mother of the three children listed in the household. She was—but only to one of the three; she was the stepmother of the remaining two children.

Check Other Households

If you're certain the family lived in a particular city at the time the census was taken, try to track down the listings for neighbors or other family members. You never know—it's possible your family was living in another household.

My great-grandfather was a schoolteacher, and until he was married, he was living in someone else's home. If your ancestor wasn't married and/or he traveled for business, he may have lived with other people.

Secondly, your ancestor may have been a servant, living in the home of the employer. Or third, you may find your family member in a boarding house or a poorhouse, along with a dozen other people.

Broaden Your Search Location

Lastly, don't confine your search to where you think your ancestor should be. Expand your research into the census for neighboring townships. Or, if your family lived close to a county line, check both counties. It's possible a county line changed from one census to the next. A great resource for researching the history of county lines is the Atlas of Historical County Boundaries <publications.newberry.org/ahcbp>. See chapter eight for a detailed explanation

WHAT THE CENSUS CAN TELL YOU

Clues to Marriage and Birth Records

When the census lists the age of the mother and father as well as the number of years they've been married, you'll have a ballpark idea of when they were married. Once you know that, you can begin searching for a marriage record.

Or, if the oldest child was born in Ohio, but the next four in Iowa, Ohio should be your starting point for finding both marriage and birth records.

The census will also give you a clue about children who may have already left home. Because women married by about twenty years of age, if you find a forty-five-year-old woman on a census with only two young children at home, it's likely you'll find more children on an earlier census.

Immigration

Beginning in 1900, the census asks for year of immigration. Using this date, you'll have a starting point for searching passenger lists or border crossings. Don't be derailed if you see a male ancestor traveling alone, because it wasn't uncommon for the husband to immigrate in advance of the wife and children.

In addition, compare the years married on the census with the year of immigration to discover whether the couple was married before or after their arrival in the United States. If after, you'll need to look for the wife's immigration records under her maiden name.

If you follow a married couple over several census years, you may see the immigration year changing. If you can't find someone in immigration records based on information in a census, check another census to see if a different year is listed.

Specific Addresses

Use Google Earth (chapter eight) to fly to your ancestor's address. The street and house number are listed along the left edge of a census (if your ancestor was a city-dweller). Don't be surprised (especially if your family lived in an old neighborhood) to find that the house is gone, replaced by a parking lot, store, or office building.

Socio-Economic Make Up of a Neighborhood

Did your family live in neighborhood of families who came to the United States pre-Revolution, or were they one of thousands of newcomers? Census records for a 1920 Chicago neighborhood, for instance, shows the area was filled with immigrants.

After the census began asking the value of personal property or real estate, you'll also learn the economic strata into which the family fit. For example, the 1930 census shows the value of Elizabeth Custer's (widow of George Armstrong Custer) Park Avenue home at $18,200—a $231,921.97 value today.

Next, run down a list of occupations; in a rural area you'll find mostly farmers. In urban areas you'll likely find tradesmen, especially in middle-class neighborhoods.

FIXING A FADED CENSUS IMAGE

When you search the census, you inevitably will encounter a census with unreadable handwriting or one so faded it's almost impossible to read.

Is there any way this census image can be rescued? If you have a digital copy of the image (like a screenshot or download of a census record you found on Ancestry.com), you can try these steps, using your image-editing software or one of the online services mentioned in chapter six.

1. Invert the image. Inverting changes the image from black print on a white background to white print on a black background. This simple maneuver may do the trick.
2. If inverting doesn't help, play with the color settings. In some cases, pushing red into the photo helps.
3. Adjust brightness and contrast. If you can pull a little of the brightness out of the image or add contrast it may be easier to read.

When working on a faded image, be sure you're editing a copy of the original, not the original. This way you can experiment without worrying that you're damaging an original digital file.

SPECIAL CENSUSES

VETERANS SCHEDULES

Not sure your ancestor served in the military? Fortunately there were two special schedules taken of veterans. In 1840, a veterans schedule was taken of Revolutionary

War pension-holders. You can search this schedule for free <www.usgennet.org/usa/topic/colonial/census/1840/>.

A second special census was taken in 1890 of Union veterans and widows of veterans. This schedule can be searched on FamilySearch.org and Ancestry.com. In some cases this can be used as a substitute for the missing 1890 federal census, but unfortunately only a portion of these schedules survived. Of note, you may find a Confederate veteran listed on this census. Information included:

- name
- rank
- company
- regiment
- date of enlistment and discharge
- length of service

To learn more about military records, see chapter ten.

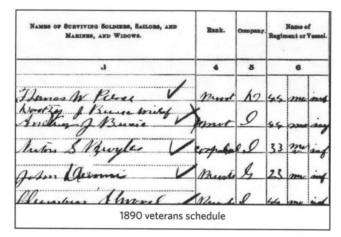

1890 veterans schedule

AGRICULTURAL SCHEDULES

Taken in 1850, 1860, 1870, and 1880, this census counted farms producing more than $100 worth of products, or more than $500 on farms larger than three acres by 1870. If you find your ancestor was listed as a farmer on a federal census between 1850 and 1880, look for him on an agricultural schedule. These schedules include information about livestock (i.e., number of horses, cows, swine, mules, oxen, sheep) and the number of bushels by crop.

Agricultural schedules can be searched on Ancestry.com. Some of the schedules have been transcribed and are posted on various websites, such as Jones County, Iowa <iowa-jones.org/agri/agri.htm>. Do a web search for *agricultural schedule* plus the county and state name to see if you can find a transcription for your county. These records are on microfilm, available either at the National Archives or (in some cases) through the Family History Library.

SLAVE SCHEDULES

In 1850 and 1860, slaves were enumerated separately from the rest of the population. Most slave schedules provide the name of the slave owner, with slaves listed by age, sex, and color, not always by name. You can search the 1850 and 1860 slave schedules on FamilySearch.org <familysearch.org> and Ancestry.com <ancestry.com>. See appendix C for more ideas for researching African-American ancestors.

NAMES OF SLAVE OWNERS.	Number of Slaves.	DESCRIPTION. Age.	Sex.	Color	Fugitives from the State.	Number manumitted.	Deaf & dumb, blind, insane, or idiotic.	No. of Slave houses.
1	2	3	4	5	6	7	8	9
John C. Carter Sr. owner	1	70	m	B.				
of Pike County, Mo	1	60	f	B.				
	1	37	f	B.				
	1	35	m	B.				
	1	33	f	B.				

Sample slave schedule, Ancestry.com

MORTALITY SCHEDULES

Mortality schedules list information about deaths occurring one year prior to the census. These schedules were taken between 1850 and 1880, with a special one taken in 1885 for New Mexico, Colorado, Florida, Nebraska, and the Dakotas.

Cause of death is included on these schedules and disease names have changed over time, so you may not understand them. One of the most common diseases you'll find is consumption—another name for tuberculosis. Find a list of old disease names on this RootsWeb site: <www.rootsweb.ancestry.com/~ohcuyah2/oddsends/disease.html>.

Note: It's a little chilling to scan down the page of an 1850 mortality schedule and see a long list of twenty-somethings who died of cholera. However, this will give you a clue about the times in which your family lived. In 1850, the United States was in the midst of a cholera epidemic. In New York City alone, cholera killed more than five thousand people. Cholera was also a major killer along the Oregon Trail. If your ancestor started the journey but you can't find him in Oregon, he may have been among those who died along the way.

Read an excellent article about life and death on the Oregon Trail by the Oregon-California Trails Association <www.octa-trails.org/learn/people_places/articles_life_death.php>.

DEFECTIVE, DEPENDENT, AND DELINQUENT SCHEDULES

The 1880 census supplemental report enumerated people who were:

- insane
- idiots
- deaf-mutes
- blind
- paupers and indigent persons
- homeless children
- prisoners

Schedules exist for only some states. Existing schedules can be accessed at Ancestry.com and on microfilm at the National Archives and the Family History Library.

STATE CENSUS

Some states counted their citizens in the years between federal census (usually at the five-year mark) or prior to statehood as a territorial census. Generally, these records are not well documented and may only include a handful of counties.

Ancestry.com has some state and territorial censuses online, including as early as the 1796 California Spanish Missions census. You can also find some state censuses transcribed and posted on websites; do a general web search for your state or territory to see if you can find it online.

CENSUS SUBSTITUTES

It never fails to happen. You're hot on the trail of an ancestor, and you desperately need to find them in the 1890 census. Except the 1890 census doesn't exist. What next?

There are three solid substitutes that might help in your search when you can't find what you want in a census:

1. City Directories: These contain alphabetical listings of people in a specific place with names, addresses, and occupations. Some places also published directories for organizations like churches, schools, or veterans groups. Ancestry.com has some city directories and Cyndi's List identifies sites with either transcriptions, images, or information about city directories <cyndislist.com/city-directories>.

2. Tax Lists: County clerks (and town clerks in New England) maintain local tax records. The Family History Library has some tax records, particularly for areas where they're needed as substitutes for land and census records. FamilySearch.org has tax lists for Ohio and Texas. Do a general web search to see if you can find other tax records online. A good place to begin is the USGenWeb Archives.

3. Maps: Plat maps show property boundaries and the property owner's name. If your ancestor was a city-dweller, he may be listed on a Sanborn Fire Insurance Map that covered twelve thousand cities. A sampling of Sanborn maps can be found on the David Rumsey Map Collection website <davidrumsey.com>. Federal land conveyance information is held by the Bureau of Land Management (chapter eight).

USING CENSUS TRENDS TO FURTHER YOUR RESEARCH

In broad terms, the federal census reflects where Americans live and how we make a living. It tracked the westward expansion and then the massing of the population into the cities. It noted the decline of the small farm and the rise of industry. The census takes a community's pulse, then uses those statistics to calculate the health of the population and economy. These general statistics can give genealogists a great snapshot of daily life, and

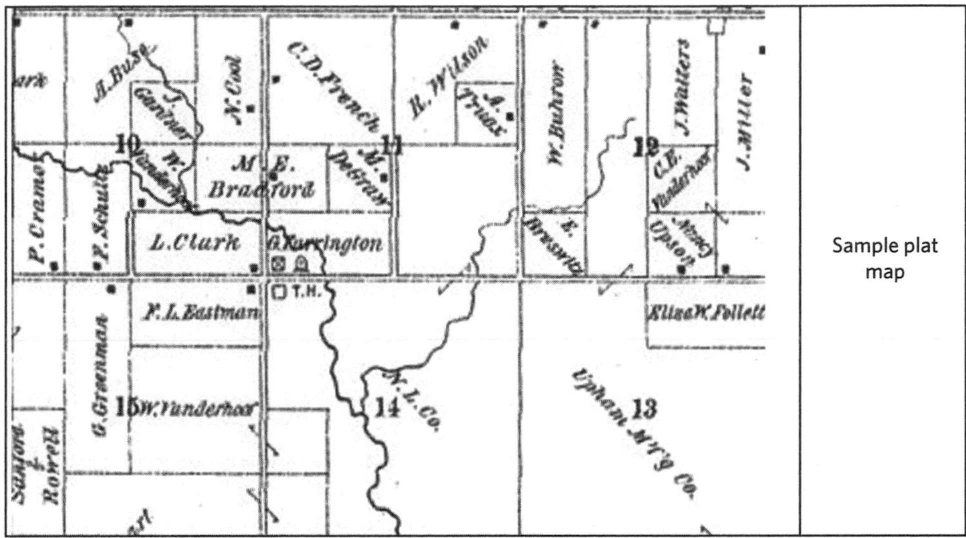

Sample plat map

fortunately, much of the census statistics have been compiled and published on the internet. Two great sources are the Historical Census Browser and the U.S. Census Bureau.

HISTORICAL CENSUS BROWSER <fisher.lib.virginia.edu/census>
This website allows you to create a series of tables using preselected categories for the census years 1790 through 1960. The categories vary with each census year, but may include agriculture, churches, education and literacy, population, manufacturing, race and place of birth, taxation, property.

Within each of the categories, several variables may be selected, like number of acres of unimproved woodland, number of Lutheran churches, or total annual agricultural wages paid. Once all of the categories are selected, a table is created for each "value," organized by state. For example, you can create a table for the 1790 census, comparing the number of white males under sixteen years of age in each state.

You can also request a new table be created for one or more individual states. These tables are divided by county.

You can create comparison tables in an almost endless number of ways. To utilize the number genealogically, you may want to compare the literacy rates of all of the states your ancestors lived in during one of the census years, then compare it to the national numbers to get a feel for the norm. Or, if you had family living in several counties in a particular state, compare the data in each of those counties. For instance, if there were five thousand people in a county and only twenty of them could read and write; and you know, based on your own census research, that your ancestor was one of them, what could you infer from this and how would it further your research?

Arkansas				
County	TOTAL INDIAN FEMALES Map It!	FARMS OF 3-9 ACRES Map It!	TRUE VALUE OF PERSONAL PROPERTY Map It!	SLAVEHOLDERS HOLDING 20-29 SLAVES Map It!
Arkansas STATE TOTALS	24	1,823	147,246,393	586
ARKANSAS	0	30	5,639,712	21
ASHLEY	0	24	4,229,611	29
BENTON	10	60	1,332,090	0
BRADLEY	0	43	3,483,633	20
CALHOUN	0	3	1,137,638	9
CARROLL	0	39	1,545,333	1

Historical Census Browser

U.S. CENSUS BUREAU <census.gov>

Although you can't access information on individual citizens from the Census Bureau (except in rare instances), you can access tables of previously compiled statistics. The Census Bureau has an extensive collection of data about America's foreign-born population, as well as general tables of population and housing density.

Use the Census.gov search engine <census.gov> to search on *historical census data*.

CASE STUDY

TRICKY PRE-1850 CENSUS RESEARCH

Before 1850, the only person listed on a census was the head of household. No one else was named. Other residents in the home are noted as tally marks in age groups separated by gender.

To follow your family back in time, pre-1850, you'll have to put on your deductive reasoning cap and see if the numbers make sense.

Here's an approach to the "no-name" census.

STEP 1. Start with the 1850 census. The 1850 census shows John Snow* was living in Jackson County, Missouri, with his wife, Francis, and children Sarah, Stephen, James, and Charles. Per the census, everyone in the family was born in North Carolina and ages (with estimated birth dates) are:

John	57	b. 1793
Francis	56	b. 1794
Sarah	21	b. 1829
Stephen	20	b. 1830
James	16	b. 1834
Charles	14	b. 1836

*Snow was misread as Show and transcribed as such.

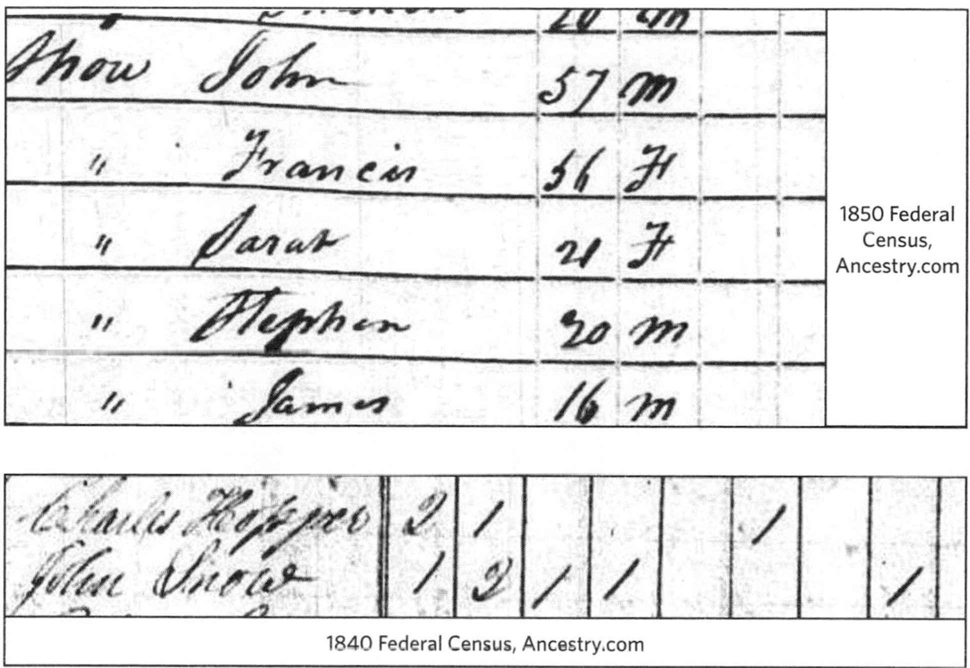

1850 Federal Census, Ancestry.com

1840 Federal Census, Ancestry.com

STEP 2. Look for the family on the 1840 census. Searching the 1840 Jackson County census, we find one John Snow with the following white males and females in the household, and an assumption of who they might be in parentheses:

1840		
MALES		
Under age 5	1	(Charles)
5-10	2	(James and UNKNOWN A)
10-15	1	(Stephen)
15-20	1	(UNKNOWN B)
50-60	1	(John)
FEMALE		
10-15	1	(Sarah)
20-30	1	(UNKNOWN C)
40-50	1	(Francis)

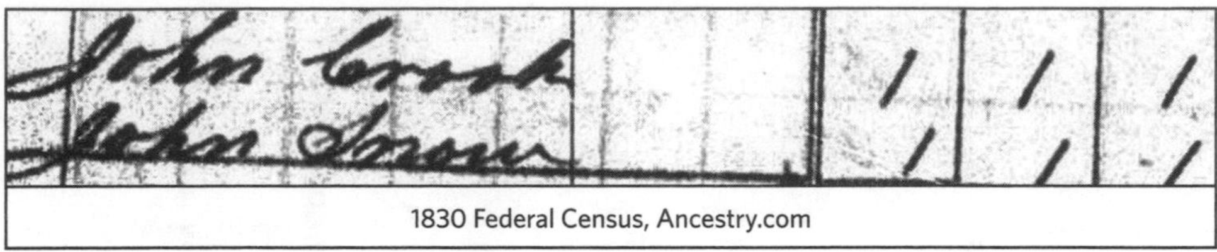

1830 Federal Census, Ancestry.com

Three of the children on the 1840 census are not listed with the family in 1850: one male between five and ten years old, one male between fifteen and twenty, and one female between twenty and thirty.

It makes sense because by 1850, the missing five to ten year old male could be in his late teens or twenty and out of the house; it is the same with the male aged fifteen to twenty and the female age twenty to thirty. Consider, too, some of these people may be farmhands living with the family, but not family members.

STEP 3. Look for the family on the 1830 census. If we go back to 1830, the family is no longer in Missouri. We know this because the 1850 census tells us all of the children were born in North Carolina, and James and Charles were born after 1830. A search finds them in Surry County, North Carolina. Here the census records show the following people, with assumptions that the UNKNOWNS in 1840 were the same UNKNOWNS in 1830.

1830		
MALES		
Under age 5	1	(UNKNOWN A)
5-10	1	(Stephen)
10-15	1	(UNKNOWN B)
40-50	1	(John)
FEMALES		
Under age 5	1	(Sarah)
5-10	1	(?)
10-15	1	(UNKNOWN C)
30-39	1	(Francis)

You can see why the 1850 census is so valuable, because trying to match people of a certain age with a specific family before then is challenging.

One other tip when using the pre-1850 census is to skim down the list of other people who lived around your ancestor. On both the 1830 and 1840 census, I found other Snow family members as well as people in the Easley family. The Easley and Snow families were related by marriage and traveled together from North Carolina to Missouri.

10

Military Records

As with most genealogy research, the best place to begin your search for military records is at home. If you're searching for twentieth-century records, you may already have your dad's or grandfather's discharge papers, awards, or first-hand accounts of military life from them or a sibling who was in the service.

You also may have heard stories of ancestors who served in the military. My grandmother told me stories of how her grandfather (my second-great-grandfather) was wounded at the Battle of Shiloh during the Civil War. Maybe you have stories of ancestors in the Revolutionary War.

Maybe you have a photo of an ancestor in civilian clothes but wearing some kind of insignia, medal, or pin. If you can enlarge the photo by looking at a digital scan of it, you might be able to tell if the insignia is military.

Gather as much information as possible from home sources so your searches can be focused and well-informed. You have a better chance of finding the records you seek if you know when and where your ancestors served. If your search turns up little or nothing, you can seek out clues on the internet.

SEEKING EVIDENCE OF MILITARY SERVICE

Gravestones

An official military tombstone (pictured here) is inscribed with the legal name, years of birth and death, and branch of service; additional information might be place of birth (state), name of conflict, and decorations, i.e., Purple Heart. There may also be a religious symbol (Christian cross, Star of David); a tombstone of a Medal of Honor recipient bears the symbol of the medal.

The U.S. Department of Veterans Affairs site <gravelocator.cem.va.gov> allows you to search all VA national cemeteries across the country. Its database also includes information about veterans buried in private cemeteries if the information has been provided to the VA. You can search Civil War burial sites on the Civil War Soldiers and Sailors System website <www.itd.nps.gov/cwss/cemeteries.htm>.

Military service inscriptions aren't limited to official tombstones provided by the government. Private tombstones in civilian cemeteries can bear useful inscriptions, too. If you don't find your ancestor on the VA's site, search Find A Grave <findagrave.com>.

Obituaries

Similar to tombstones, obituaries can include military service information such as branch of service or place of deployment. Like most obituaries, those of service members might include:

- place of birth
- date of birth

Tombstone, Medal of Honor recipient, Fort Rosecrans National Cemetery

Military service can be noted on a tombstone such as this one found in Lone Jack, Missouri.

- names of parents
- names of siblings
- name of spouse
- names of children
- where died
- cause of death
- where buried

See chapter five for a complete list of sites to search for obituaries.

County Histories

If your family were pioneers, they might be included in a county history. And the clues about your soldier ancestor might provide a fascinating look into his life. Search Google Books <books.google.com> for histories of your ancestors' counties.

For example, one of these tombstone images notes that Calvin Dimmitt was a member of the 7th Tennessee MTD (mounted) Infantry.

A glowing biography of Dimmitt in a county history tells that he was born in Tippecanoe County, Indiana, and in 1862 enlisted in the 65th Illinois (called the Second Scotch Regiment), Company E, where he served eighteen months before reenlisting in the 7th Tennessee. The biography also mentions an 1860 marriage to Nancy Markham, a native of East Tennessee.

The biography contains enough information to easily track down military information. But there's more to the story than meets the eye. See the case study at the end of the chapter for the remainder of this tale!

Census

Military service information is available in four federal censuses:

1. The 1840 census shows surviving Revolutionary War pensioners or their widows.
2. The 1890 special veterans census of Union veterans or widows (only a partial census remains) includes:

- name of surviving service member and widow
- rank
- regiment
- enlistment date
- discharge date
- length of service
- address
- disability

This veterans schedule is often used as a substitute for the missing 1890 federal census.

3. The 1910 federal census asks if the respondent was a survivor of the Union or Confederate Army or Navy.

4. The 1930 federal census shows military service in any major war through World War I.

See chapter nine for details on searching census records.

Newspapers

You may find a mention of your ancestor's military service in a newspaper article.

Medals Given Army Officers For Service in Korean War

Awards of the bronze star medal for services in Korea to four army officers from Portland recently were announced from military sources.

Lt. Col. Garey M. Wells, 1410 S. W. Park avenue, received the bronze star with oak leaf cluster for meritorious service while he was a military advisor to Korean national police. He is now attending the provost marshal general's school at Camp Gordon, Ga.

First Lt. Thomas F. Pritchard, 3224 S. E. Alder street, received the bronze star for meritorious service as a member of headquarters, 3d infantry division.

Capt. Joseph M. Brooks, ex-employe of the Union Pacific railroad at Portland, received the medal for meritorious service as intelligence officer of the 3d infantry division.

Capt. Edgar W. Whitlock, 1535 N. E. 24th avenue, received the medal for outstanding performance of duty with the 1st cavalry division's 15th medical battalion.

SAW TAKES FINGERS

Dade W. McKay, 68, 5427 S. E. Schiller street, a carpenter, Friday suffered the loss of several fingers in an electric power saw on a job at S. E. 59th avenue and Kelly street.

13 April 1952, *The Oregonian*, page 34, GenealogyBank.com

Church Newsletters

During a major conflict, like World War II, it's likely you'll find your ancestor mentioned in a church newsletter. The newsletter could have an excerpt from a letter the soldier wrote home, a request from a service member to hear from members of the congregation, news of a serious wound, or a brief note to the minister about daily life.

Unless the church has an online archive of historic newsletters, you'll probably have to contact the church directly (e-mail, phone, or regular mail) to see if copies are available.

FINDING EIGHTEENTH- AND NINETEENTH-CENTURY SOLDIERS

America was born during a war, and the young nation fought many bloody conflicts within its first 125 years.

The National Archives houses compiled military service records from the Revolutionary War through the Philippine Insurrection (1899–1902). Conflicts that took place during this time period are:

- Revolutionary War, 1775–1782
- War of 1812, 1812–1815
- Mexican-American War, 1846–1848• Civil War, 1861–1865
- Spanish-American War, 1898
- Philippine Insurrection, 1899–1902

These records are written on a card and contained in a jacket and include basic information about the soldier and his service. Information the service card may contain includes:

- name
- rank
- unit
- age
- pay information
- hospital notes
- state
- physical description

You may find a card that has a long list of numbers; these numbers correspond to a number stamped on the back of each service record card within the jacket.

Compiled service records (pre-World War II) may be ordered online directly from the National Archives <archives.gov/veterans/military-service-records/pre-ww-1-records.html> or by submitting Form NATF 86, which can download from this same web page, completed and mailed in.

However, to order the records, you must know that they exist. Fortunately, you can search for these records online.

J | 3 P. H. B. Inf. Md.

Otis Johnson

Pvt., Co. H, 3 Reg't Potomac Home Brigade, Maryland Inf.

Age 16 years.

Appears on Co. Muster-out Roll, dated

Baltimore, Md. May 29, 1865.

Muster-out to date May 29, 1865.

Last paid to Aug. 31, 1864.

Clothing account:

Last settled ...., 186 ; drawn since $........ 100

Due soldier $........ 100 ; due U. S. $ 7 24/100

Am't for cloth'g in kind or money adv'd $........ 100

Due U. S. for arms, equipments, &c., $........ 100

Bounty paid $........ 100 ; due $ 100 100

Remarks: Due Govt. for Ordnance 80 cts & Q.M. Stores $3.41.

Book mark:

Hunter
Copyist.

(661)

Service card, Civil War Compiled Records, Fold3.com

REVOLUTIONARY WAR AND CIVIL WAR RECORDS

The Revolutionary War spanned eight long years, from 1775 to 1783. Friction between the colonists and Great Britain started with the Stamp Act of 1765 and reached a boiling point with the Intolerable Acts of 1774.

While the battles of Lexington and Concord birthed the war, the 1781 siege at Yorktown ended it, although the official negotiations weren't complete until the Treaty of Paris in 1783. According to legend, the British drummers and fifers, upon marching out from Yorktown, played the tune "The World Turn'd Upside Down."

The Revolutionary War took place across a broad expanse of the continent, with campaigns from the Northeast down into the Carolinas and Georgia. Was your ancestor among the patriots?

From 1861 to 1865, Americans fought one another, not so much over slavery as over state's rights. Did one state have the right to govern itself and, in doing so, dissolve its membership in the Union?

To answer the question, more than three million men went to war and more than 600,000 of them never returned home.

Advances in weaponry raised the mortality rate higher than any previous war. This was the bloodiest conflict in all of America's history, with more than ten thousand battles fought across the continent. At Cold Harbor, Virginia, seven thousand men fell in twenty minutes. Antietam saw 23,000 casualties, and Gettysburg claimed 51,000.

The end came in April 1865, with Robert E. Lee surrendering the Army of Northern Virginia to Ulysses S. Grant.

If your ancestor was of fighting age (and ages of soldiers varied from teenagers to old men), it's likely you'll find a record of his service. Because there were two governments in operation at the same time, records aren't as centralized as they might have been with a unified fighting force. Finding records for your Confederate ancestor may be a challenge because much of the South's vital records and military records were destroyed during the war.

Subscription sites

ANCESTRY.COM <ancestry.com>

This site contains a variety of military records. These include World War I and World War II draft registration cards, an index to Confederate and Union compiled service records, and registers of enlistments in the U.S. Regular Army 1798–1914. Search the latter and you'll find a 2nd Lieutenant named Ulysses S. Grant, who, in 1846, was camped on the Rio Grande opposite the Mexican town of Matamoros during the Mexican-American War. The site also contains the special military schedules from the 1840, 1890, 1910, and 1930 federal censuses.

FOLD3 <fold3.com>

This site specializes in U.S. military records and provides access to compiled service records for the Revolutionary War, War of 1812 (Lake Erie), and the Civil War (Union and Confederate), with more databases being added as they are digitized.

AMERICAN CIVIL WAR RESEARCH DATABASE <www.civilwardata.com>

This is a comprehensive, fully searchable source of soldier and regimental data. For an annual fee of twenty-five dollars (or a seven-day pass for ten dollars), you can search through more than four million records for both Union and Confederate personnel.

The site's dynamic links will take you into several layers of information, ranging from the names of other men who enlisted from the same hometown, regiments with the highest desertion rates, an analysis of death by cause, and names of those who died in any given battle.

Locating your ancestor is as easy as entering a surname and launching a search. Be sure to follow search tips, though, because many records identify soldiers only by an initial for a first name. In addition, many soldiers joined a neighboring state's military unit, so you may not find them if you specify the state where they lived. After you locate an ancestor, you can click on the name to read the individual's history, including dates of enlistment, age at enlistment, and rank achieved, along with source citations. Because a large amount of information in the database is from state rosters, you'll find data that might not be on another site.

As a bonus for researchers, you can follow the link to your ancestor's place of residence (if known) and see a name of every other soldier in town.

If you know what regiment your solider served in, use the Regiment Lookup screen to dive into battles fought, regimental assignments, and a graphical view of the unit's combat experience. From the Casualty Analysis screen you can view the dates and places where soldiers were killed, wounded, captured, or reported missing, along with the names of the individual soldiers in each of those categories.

If you're interested in understanding how the losses in your ancestor's regiment compared with other regiments, use the Regimental Dynamics screen to sort statistics by several options, including the percentage of men who were killed, wounded, disabled, or captured. Sorting can also be done by unit type, state, and length of enlistment. For example, in sorting Union regiments by percentage of deserters, you'll see that of the 257 men in the 154 PA Infantry, nearly 44 percent went over the hill. These statistics lead, of course, to questions about the ability of the officer corps, camp conditions, or recruiting techniques.

Although you can probably find your ancestor in other free databases, the dynamic links on this site can give you a much more detailed view into what was going on in any given regiment.

Free sites

CIVIL WAR SOLDIERS AND SAILORS SYSTEM (CWSS) <www.itd.nps.gov/cwss>

While you can't find compiled service records on this free site, CWSS does contain an index of more than six million Union and Confederate soldiers. After you find your ancestor, you can also read a history of his regiment and browse a list of all other soldiers with whom he served.

James Longstreet (First_Last)

Regiment Name General and Staff Officers, Men, Staff Departments, C.S.A.

Side Confederate

Company ?

Soldier's Rank_In ? lieut. Col.

Soldier's Rank_Out ? Lieut. General

Alternate Name ?

Notes

Film Number M818 roll 15

Civil War Soldiers and Sailors System

CYNDI'S LIST <cyndislist.com/us/civil-war> <cyndislist.com/us/american-revolution>

You'll find plenty of links to websites full of specific information on both the Civil War and the American Revolution.

DAUGHTERS OF THE AMERICAN REVOLUTION (DAR) <dar.org>

This site is a great jumping-off place for Revolutionary ancestors, even if you have no interest in applying for DAR membership. It contains a database of "patriots" already accepted by the DAR as having served the country from 1774 to 1783. Not all patriots were soldiers; some supplied the Army, others were at the Boston Tea Party, signed the Declaration of Independence, were gunsmiths for the Army, or lent money to the Colonies.

You can also order copies of the lineage information submitted by DAR members. If someone has already proven your lineup to the early twentieth century, you won't have to provide as much information.

FAMILYSEARCH.ORG <familysearch.org>

FamilySearch.org has some federal and state records from the Revolutionary War and the Civil War available for searching.

ONLINE INSTITUTE FOR ADVANCED LOYALIST STUDIES <royalprovincial.com>

Is it possible your ancestor remained true to the crown during the Revolution? John Adams believed that one-third of the colonists remained loyal to the British crown. More recent estimates put the number at 15 to 20 percent. Following the Revolution, many loyalists either returned to England or settled in other British territories such as Canada. You can search for loyalist ancestors at the On-Line Institute for Advanced Loyalists Studies or these sites:

- Loyalist <redcoat.me.uk/loyalists.htm>
- Black Loyalists <americanrevolution.org/blackloyalists.html>

There are also several excellent books on loyalists, among them *Liberty's Exiles: American Loyalists in the Revolutionary World* by Maya Jasanoff (Knopf).

Remember, too, that your patriot ancestor might have served in a state militia, and as such won't appear on the rolls of the Continental Army. Do a search for *Revolutionary War* and the name of your state to see if there's website that contains a list of state militia.

Assuming your military ancestors lived long enough to apply for a pension, your next best step is tracking him down in pension files.

Pensions

From the Revolutionary War onward, service members were paid for their service with either a pension or a bounty land warrant. Both of these records can be family history gold mines.

A pension file (or widow's pension) can tell you when and where the veteran was born, his state of health, disabilities relating to military service, names of children, dates of battles, name of commanding officer, neighbors or friends who vouch for him, and any property he may own. If the soldier was unmarried, you may also find a pension request from his mother.

Bounty land warrants were free land given to veterans of the Revolutionary War, War of 1812, and the Mexican War. After the veteran's application was approved, he was issued a warrant that could be exchanged for land.

The "free" land was located in the frontier areas of the time. For many, it was a powerful inducement to enlist. Not only did the bounty land policy help increase enlistments, it was also part of a strategy to place veterans and their families in areas where they could be relied upon to protect settlers from Indians.

Pension files and bounty land information can be ordered from the National Archives <eservices.archives.gov/orderonline>; pension files may be found on fold3.com <fold3.com>.

Fold3.com has a few different ways of searching the system, but for this search I'm using the Advanced Search option, which is found in the pull-down box by Search. Using the Advanced option, you can specify which collection you wish to search.

In this search, my pension options for Civil War service were the Widows Pension database, or the records of Civil War and Later Veterans Pension Index. The Widows files can contain several different items, such as an affidavit from people saying the widow is who she says she is; it could be a request for an increase in the pension; it can also list the names and ages of children.

I selected the Widows Pension records, hoping to find information on any of the Knox family. The search was done by entering *Knox* as the last name, selecting *Missouri* as the place, and then in the pull-down box choosing the name of the database.

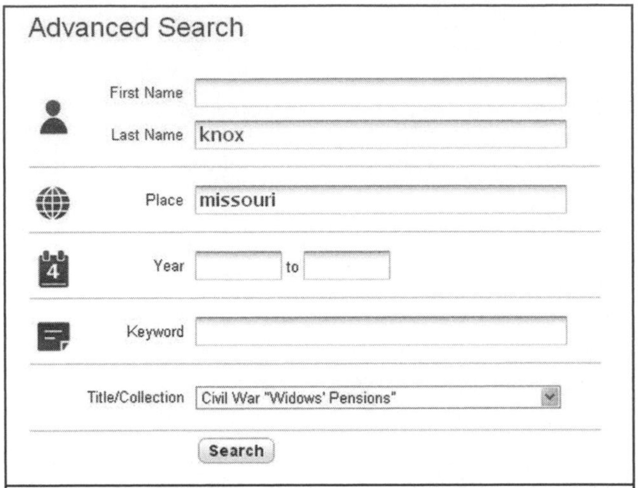

Fold3.com advanced search option

If your search returns too many results, add relevant words in the Keyword search box; if too few, remove keywords.

The fold3.com records are taken from the National Archives microfilms, with both a name index and images from the original files. The handwritten records (like this shown) may have been presented by the veteran, someone who vouched for him, a widow, or children. Both Revolutionary War pension and Civil War widows pension files are available on fold3.com.

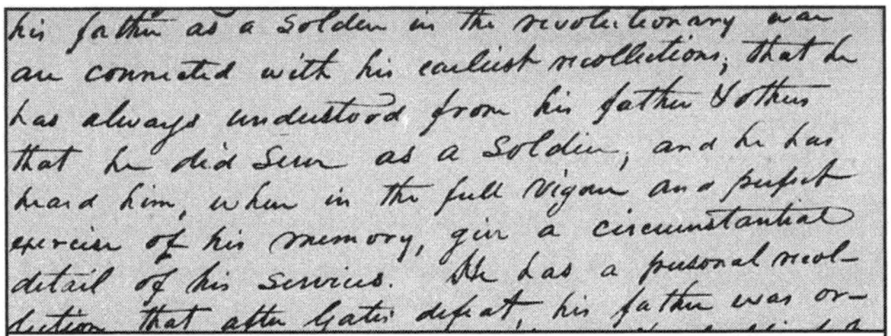

his father as a Soldier in the revolutionary war are connected with his earliest recollections; that he has always understood from his father & others that he did Serve as a Soldier, and he has heard him, when in the full vigour and perfect exercise of his memory, give a circumstantial detail of his services. He has a personal recollection that after Gates' defeat, his father was or-

This file reads in part that the son of the veteran remembers from his "earliest recollections" that his father served in the Revolutionary War. Further, following Gates's defeat, his father was ordered to forage the surrounding countryside for supplies left by the enemy. Fold3.com

Some libraries have a subscription to HeritageQuest Online, which includes a Revolutionary War database of pensions and bounty land. If the library subscribes, you can access these databases for free.

Because HeritageQuest Online only carries a portion of the information in a pension file, if you find your ancestor, you will want to order the entire file from the National Archives.

If you don't want to use a subscription site, FamilySearch.org has a free online index to Civil War pensions. The cards give the soldier's name, unit, the application number,

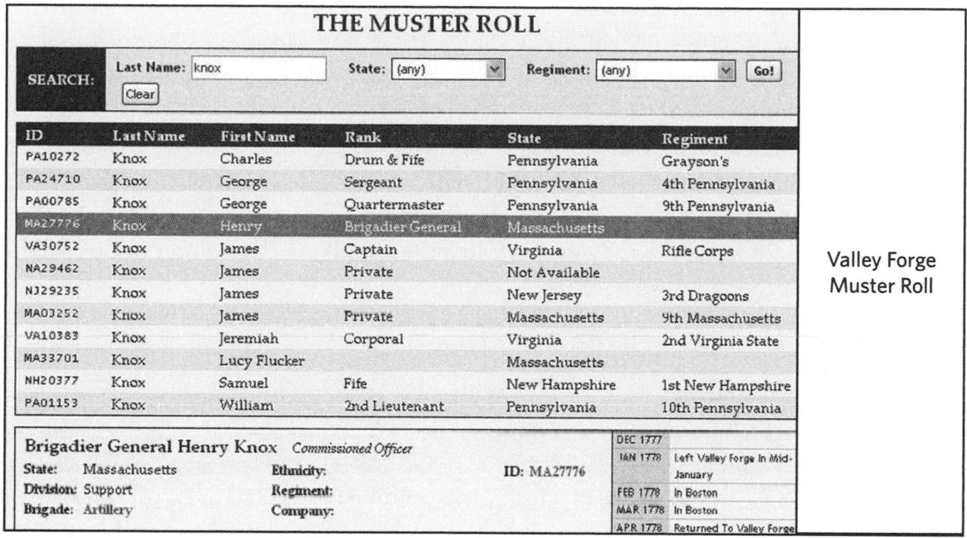

THE MUSTER ROLL

SEARCH: Last Name: knox State: (any) Regiment: (any) Go! Clear

ID	Last Name	First Name	Rank	State	Regiment
PA10272	Knox	Charles	Drum & Fife	Pennsylvania	Grayson's
PA24710	Knox	George	Sergeant	Pennsylvania	4th Pennsylvania
PA00785	Knox	George	Quartermaster	Pennsylvania	9th Pennsylvania
MA27776	Knox	Henry	Brigadier General	Massachusetts	
VA30752	Knox	James	Captain	Virginia	Rifle Corps
NA29462	Knox	James	Private	Not Available	
NJ29235	Knox	James	Private	New Jersey	3rd Dragoons
MA03252	Knox	James	Private	Massachusetts	9th Massachusetts
VA10383	Knox	Jeremiah	Corporal	Virginia	2nd Virginia State
MA33701	Knox	Lucy Flucker		Massachusetts	
NH20377	Knox	Samuel	Fife	New Hampshire	1st New Hampshire
PA01153	Knox	William	2nd Lieutenant	Pennsylvania	10th Pennsylvania

Brigadier General Henry Knox *Commissioned Officer*

State: Massachusetts Ethnicity: ID: MA27776

Division: Support Regiment:

Brigade: Artillery Company:

DEC 1777	
JAN 1778	Left Valley Forge In Mid-January
FEB 1778	In Boston
MAR 1778	In Boston
APR 1778	Returned To Valley Forge

Valley Forge Muster Roll

the certificate number, and the state from which the soldier served. Occasionally you may find rank, date, and place of death.

Delving into pension records may present you with a surprise or two. You may find an application from both a wife and a mother—with the mother swearing her son was never married. Now that's something to investigate.

Revolutionary and Civil War Resources

- Liberty! The American Revolution <pbs.org/ktca/liberty>
- Revolutionary War <historycentral.com/Revolt/index.html>
- Revolutionary War Timeline <ushistory.org/declaration/revwartimeline.htm>
- Revolutionary War Battles <en.wikipedia.org/wiki/List_of_American_Revolutionary_War_battles>
- Revolutionary War People <library.thinkquest.org/TQ0312848/people.htm>
- Civil War <civilwar.com>
- Civil War Battles <sonofthesouth.net/leefoundation/civil-war-battles.htm>
- Civil War Home Page <civil-war.net>
- Timeline of the Civil War <memory.loc.gov/ammem/cwphtml/tl1861.html>
- Civil War Photographs <memory.loc.gov/ammem/cwphtml/cwphome.html>
- Valley Forge Muster Roll <valleyforgemusterroll.org>

WAR OF 1812 RECORDS

If your ancestor was born as late as 1790, he would have been too young for the Revolutionary War, yet he would have been too old for the Civil War. It's possible, though, that he fought in the War of 1812. And, while many genealogists concentrate on records from the Revolutionary or Civil wars, there is an increasingly large number of War of 1812 records online.

For many Americans, the War of 1812 (known as America's Forgotten War) remains an enigma. Tucked between two wars fueled by independence and slavery, the War of 1812 was sparked more by special interests than national zeal.

- New Englanders, who were making a fortune supplying the British in their fight with Napoleon, remained neutral.
- Native Americans saw the war as a clear-cut case of land-hungry frontiersmen trying to eat up the entire continent.
- Expansionists dreamed of adding Canada and Florida to the national coffers. Here were the first faint rumblings of Manifest Destiny.
- Opponents called it "Mr. Madison's War."
- The War Hawk Congress called it a battle for national pride and freedom on the high seas.

The most clearly defined origin of the war traces its roots back to the 1807 shelling of the USS *Chesapeake* by the British ship *Leopard*, and the impressment of four of her sailors.

Had Thomas Jefferson declared war then, it's likely the majority of Americans would have rallied behind him. Instead, he clamped an embargo on American goods.

As the years passed, sentiments shifted and loyalties divided. Post-Revolutionary War America had no standing army, and the thought of going back to war against Britain seemed a wearisome task to the new country.

An 1812 article in the *Evening Post* branded the call for war as "humbugging on a large scale."

British agents in Canada were active in encouraging Native Americans to continue their attacks along the frontier. But, for America's small Navy, the issues were clearer: Between 1803 and 1812, British captains impressed more than five thousand America sailors.

In addition, merchant ships and merchant cargoes were seized for allegedly violating the British blockade of Europe. Finally, the war became a contest about American financial interests unwillingly trapped in a European conflict.

War was finally declared in 1812, and lasted until 1814. The Battle of New Orleans catapulted Andrew Jackson to national prominence and the presidency.

During this war, Francis Scott Key wrote what would become our national anthem, and the USS *Constitution* sailed into history as "Old Ironsides."

Most significantly, this marked the last time British troops would fight on American soil.

The biggest losers were the Native Americans whose lands were served up to pioneers on a platter. The biggest winner was Canada, who secured its status as a British colony and put an end to dreams of a continent dominated by the United States of America.

War of 1812 Resources

THE WAR OF 1812 WEBSITE <militaryheritage.com/1812.htm>

If you've ever wondered what it was like on the "other side," this Canadian-slanted website is the one to visit. Its information is primarily about Canadian and British soldiers and policies. Links include personal stories of the war as told through soldiers' letters home which chronicle the horrors of battle, as well as life in an Army camp.

Articles include a full account of the Chesapeake-Leopard Affair, the summary of major battles, and eyewitness accounts. You'll also find period newspaper articles that debate the pros and cons of the war.

For an inkling of how Canadians felt about the American invasion of their country, one verse of the period song "The Bold Canadian" is

The Yankees did invade us,
To kill and to destroy,
And to distress our country,
Our peace for to annoy,
Our countrymen were filled
With sorrow, grief and woe,
To think that they should fall
By such an unnatural foe.

THE OHIO HISTORICAL SOCIETY WAR OF 1812 ROSTER OF OHIO SOLDIERS
<ohiohistory.org/resource/database/rosters.html>

Ohio was the center of some of the strongest pro-war sentiment. In all, more than 25,000 Ohioans served in the Army. This site offers a searchable index of the full text of the roster from the Adjutant General records.

When searching for a soldier's name, the results page will return hits ranked in the order of their relevance to your query. When you click on a hit, you'll see the actual roster page, which includes the name of the soldier's company, the county of origin (if known), as well as the name and rank of everyone in the company.

THE LIBRARY OF VIRGINIA INDEX TO WAR OF 1812 PAY ROLLS AND MUSTER ROLLS
<bit.ly/rvhbjN>

This searchable database is an index of forty thousand names in "Pay Rolls of Militia Entitled to Land Bounty Under the Act of Congress of Sept. 28, 1850" (Richmond, 1851).

Database of Illinois War of 1812 Veterans			
NAME	RANK	COMPANY	PLACE OF ENLISTMENT
JOHNSON, JAMES	PVT	S WHITESIDES	ST CLAIR CO
JOHNSON, MALCOM	PVT	CHAMBERS	
Search for your Illinois War of 1812 Veteran			

ILLINOIS WAR OF 1812 VETERANS DATABASE <ilsos.gov/GenealogyMWeb/1812frm.html>
This searchable database contains the names of Illinois militiamen listed on the War of 1812 muster rolls included in the ninth volume of the "Report of the Adjutant General of the State of Illinois" (1902).

To search the database, use the last name, first name format. Searches are not case sensitive. If your vet shows up in the database, his rank, company, and place of enlistment (if known) will be listed.

FAMILY HISTORY LIBRARY U.S. MILITARY RECORDS RESEARCH OUTLINE
<familysearch.org/sg/Military.html>
Although not an online searchable index, this outline offers excellent tips on U.S. military research. The guide includes references to the 1812 records held by the National Archives and state agencies, as well as the addresses to write for records.

PRESERVE THE PENSIONS, WAR OF 1812 <fgs.org/1812>
The Federation of Genealogical Societies, the National Archives, and the genealogy community have banded together to digitize War of 1812 pension records. Digitized images from the project are viewable for free at fold3.com.

THE USGENWEB ARCHIVES PENSION PROJECT <usgwarchives.org/pensions>
This site is posting pension transcriptions for all wars prior to 1900. These documents include bounty land files.

STAR-SPANGLED 200 <starspangled200.org>
The official site for Maryland's War of 1812 Bicentennial Commission. This is a great site for finding the events that commemorate the two hundredth anniversary of the opening shots of the war.

WORLD WAR I

According to the National Archives, during World War I there were "three registrations. The first, on June 5, 1917, was for all men between the ages of 21 and 31. The second, on June 5, 1918, registered those who attained age 21 after June 5, 1917. (A supplemental

Last Name	First Names	Birth	Ethnic GRP	Birth Site or Other Info	City/County	State
James	Jack	15 Sep 1893	B	Rock Bluff FL	Gadsden	FL
James	Jack	30 May 1881	B	works in Yazoo City MS	Humphreys	MS
James	Jack	30 May 1882	B	relat. lives Cruger MS	Humphreys	MS
James	Jack	7 Feb 1877	B	lives in Vicksburg MS	Washington	MS
James	Jack	7 Feb 1877	B	relat. lives Belzonia MS	Washington	MS
James	Jack	1 May 1892	B	Houston TX	Menard	TX

World War I Draft Registration search results, RootsWeb.com

registration was held on August 24, 1918, for those becoming 21 years old after June 5, 1918. This was included in the second registration.) The third registration was held on September 12, 1918, for men age 18 through 45."

This means basically every U.S. male completed a draft registration card. Cards can include valuable information for your genealogy research, with full name, date and place of birth, race, citizenship, occupation, personal description, and signature.

More than twenty-four million cards exist for all states, as well as Alaska, Hawaii, Washington, D.C., and Puerto Rico. (Alaska and Hawaii didn't become states until 1959.)

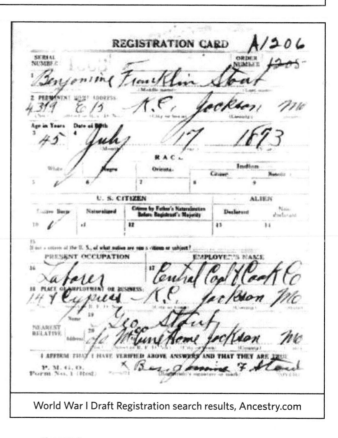

World War I Draft Registration search results, Ancestry.com

World War I draft registration cards are available on the subscription site Ancestry.com as well as for free RootsWeb at <rootsweb.ancestry.com/~rwguide/WWIdraft.html>.

While the RootsWeb database contains basic information, at Ancestry.com you can view the actual card and complete information.

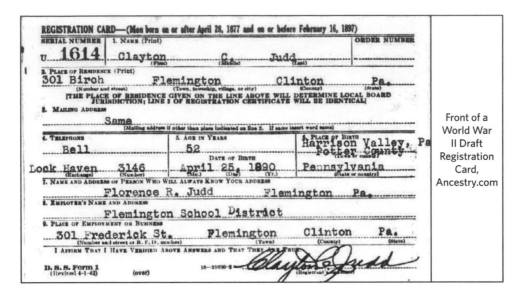

REGISTRATION CARD—(Men born on or after April 28, 1877 and on or before February 16, 1897)

SERIAL NUMBER U 1614 | 1. NAME (Print) Clayton (First) C. (Middle) Judd (Last) | ORDER NUMBER

2. PLACE OF RESIDENCE (Print)
301 Birch (Number and street) Flemington (Town, township, village, or city) Clinton (County) Pa. (State)
[THE PLACE OF RESIDENCE GIVEN ON THE LINE ABOVE WILL DETERMINE LOCAL BOARD JURISDICTION; LINE 2 OF REGISTRATION CERTIFICATE WILL BE IDENTICAL]

3. MAILING ADDRESS
Same
(Mailing address if other than place indicated on line 2. If same insert word same)

4. TELEPHONE Bell Lock Haven (Exchange) 3146 (Number) | 5. AGE IN YEARS 52 DATE OF BIRTH April (Mo.) 25, (Day) 1890 (Yr.) | 6. PLACE OF BIRTH Harrison Valley, Pa Potter County (Town or county) Pennsylvania (State or country)

7. NAME AND ADDRESS OF PERSON WHO WILL ALWAYS KNOW YOUR ADDRESS
Florence R. Judd Flemington Pa.

8. EMPLOYER'S NAME AND ADDRESS
Flemington School District

9. PLACE OF EMPLOYMENT OR BUSINESS
301 Frederick St. (Number and street or R. F. D. number) Flemington (Town) Clinton (County) Pa. (State)

I AFFIRM THAT I HAVE VERIFIED ABOVE ANSWERS AND THAT THEY ARE TRUE.

D. S. S. Form 1 (Revised 4-1-42) (over) 16—21630-2 Clayton C. Judd (Registrant's signature)

Front of a World War II Draft Registration Card, Ancestry.com

WORLD WAR II

Because of privacy laws, only the so-called "old man's registration" is available for World War II draftees. Officially called the Fourth Registration, it only registered men born on or between 28 April 1877 and 16 February 1897. These men would have been between forty-five and sixty-four years old at the time of the 1942 registration.

Draft card information included name, age, birth date, birth place, residence, name of employer, physical description, and the name and address of a person who would always know the registrant's whereabouts.

The "old man's registration" database is available at Ancestry.com and on microfilm at the National Archives and Family History Library. The same card index and images are available for free at FamilySearch.org.

World War II enlistments are also available at Ancestry.com. This database contains information on about 8.3 million men and women who enlisted in the U.S. Army during World War II. If your ancestor does not appear in this database (my dad isn't there), it doesn't mean he didn't serve. The database isn't complete.

Do you remember the Access to Archival Databases (AAD) <aad.archives.gov/aad> from chapter four? From here, you can search more than nine million World War II enlistment records as well as information about prisoners of war.

If your twentieth-century military ancestor died while serving overseas, the American Battle Monuments Commission <abmc.gov> maintains a searchable database of those lost at sea, interred overseas, or missing in action.

Be aware that some Americans were buried in the country in which they fell, but were later reinterred in a U.S. cemetery.

View Record	SERIAL NUMBER	NAME	SERVICE CODE	STATE OF RESIDENCE	AREA	STATUS	DETAINING POWER	CAMP
	O&716896	SADLER GEORGE W	ARMY	Virginia	European Theatre: Holland	Returned to Military Control, Liberated or Repatriated	GERMANY	Undefined Code

World War II data, prisoner of war, Access to Archival Database

View Record	MILITARY SERVICE	COUNTRY OF CASUALTY	TYPE OF CASUALTY	NAME	SOCIAL SECURITY OR SERVICE #	DATE OF DEATH or DATE DECLARED DEAD (MM/DD/YYYY)	HOME OF RECORD CITY	HOME OF RECORD STATE CODE
	DN [Department of the Navy]	Republic of Vietnam (South Vietnam)	Hostile - Died While Missing	HOOVER WILLIAM CLIFTON	4841380	06/10/1965	SAN DIEGO	California

Search of Vietnam War deaths, Access to Archival Database

Other twentieth-century searchable databases at AAD include Korea and Vietnam dead, wounded, and prisoners of war.

If you want to learn more about World War I and II history in maps, posters, and images, search the American Memory Collection at the Library of Congress <memory.loc.gov/ammem/index.html>.

SPIES AMONG US

Because of the nature of their work, it's possible you had an ancestor who was a spy, but you just didn't know it. Ohio members of Capt. Thomas Hinkson's Mounted Spies are clearly listed in *Roster of Ohio Soldiers in the War of 1812* (find it on Google Books <books.google.com>). Of interest, one of those spies was William Spencer, an itinerant Methodist Minister. What a perfect profession to allow him access across the countryside.

If your ancestor was Rose Greenhow, Belle Boyd, or George Scott—a runaway slave who spied for the Union—you won't find them in a database of Civil War soldiers.

If you're certain your ancestor served during a major conflict, but they're nowhere to be found, do a little Google sleuthing to see if his name shows up in connection with any known spies.

Still can't find him? It's possible he enlisted under one name, deserted, and then re-enlisted under another name.

In 1889, Congress passed an act that removed from military records the charge of desertion for a wide variety of circumstances. Because of this, more veterans became eligible for pensions.

CASE STUDY

WHAT CAN MILITARY RECORDS REVEAL?

Let's investigate the military clues we discovered about Calvin Dimmit in the county history mentioned earlier in the chapter. If you recall, the history says that he was born in Tippecanoe County, Indiana, and in 1862 enlisted in the 65th Illinois (called the Second Scotch Regiment), Company E, where he served eighteen months before reenlisting in the 7th Mounted Infantry in Tennessee. The biography also mentions an 1860 marriage to Nancy Markham, a native of East Tennessee. His obituary (which we studied in chapter four) corroborates this information. We can use these clues to learn more about Calvin's military service.

STEP 1. I started by investigating the 65th Illinois on the Civil War Soldiers and Sailors System site <itd.nps.gov/cwss>. From the Home page, I clicked Search Regiments, then chose the search parameters of *Union*, *Illinois*, and *65*.

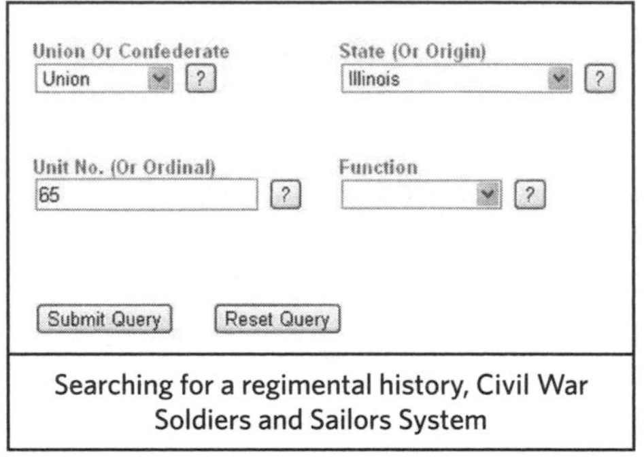

Searching for a regimental history, Civil War Soldiers and Sailors System

On this site, I learned that the 65th Illinois took part in the siege of Harper's Ferry, surrendered on September 15, 1862, and were paroled on September 16, 1862. Because Dimmitt's regiment surrendered, he would have been a prisoner of war, albeit for a brief period (twenty-four hours). The history on the site also says that after the parole, the regiment was in Chicago until April 1863. Later that same year, they were in Tennessee.

While I didn't find online information on Dimmitt's prisoner-of-war status, I did learn that the prisoner exchange program was implemented early in 1862, but broke down by the summer of 1863. An interesting equivalency table was established; for example, one general equaled forty-six privates, while one colonel could be exchanged for fifteen privates.

If your ancestor was a prisoner at the infamous Andersonville Prison in Georgia, you should be able to find him at Ancestry.com or the Civil War Soldiers and Sailors System (CWSS) <www.itd.nps.gov/cwss/andSearchp.cfm>. CWSS also has a database of Confederate prisoners at Fort McHenry.

In addition to Andersonville, Ancestry.com's Civil War Prisoner of War Records, 1861–1865, contains Confederate soldiers in a variety of prisons as well as those captured at Vicksburg, Mississippi.

Information about Civil War prisons is sprinkled across the internet, including:

Libby Prison <mdgorman.com/Prisons/Libby/libby_prison.htm>

Civil War Prisoner Search Engines <ancestorhunt.com/genealogical_prison_records.htm>

Civil War Prisons <censusdiggins.com/civil_war_prisons.html>

One other possible source of Civil War POW information is the Google News Archives (chapter seven); you might find an article like this 1863 *New York Times* list of soldiers in the Richmond, Virginia, prison who had died since December 1, 1862 <www.nytimes.com/1863/01/16/news/prisoners-richmond-list-wounded-who-have-died-since-dec-1-military-prison.html>.

On this left of the Union line, a courageous stand by John S. Casement's brigade, containing the 65th Illinois, the "Second Scotch Regiment" commanded by Colonel William Stewart of Chicago, and Israel N. Stiles's brigade, containing the 112th Illinois, a Henry County regiment commanded by Colonel Thomas Henderson of Toulon, saved the breach from being widened. During the conflict at this spot, over 200 Confederates fell in front of the 65th, and the colors of the 15th Mississippi were captured by the Illinois regiment. The 112th was to merit special attention in the battle reports. Inserted into the break caused by Strickland's defection, it fought a dismal but rewarding struggle with Cheatham's men before the latter retreated.[16]

Illinois in the Civil War, Google Books

STEP 2. Don't stop with just one source in your research. I wanted to find books that might contain information about the 65th Illinois, so I did a Google Book search <books.google.com> and found *Illinois in the Civil War*, which included a description of the regiment's bravery at the 1864 Battle of Franklin, Tennessee.

STEP 3. Now that I know more about where the 65th Illinois fought and served, it's time to see if I can find official records that prove Calvin Dimmitt was a part of this regiment. Because this was a state regiment, I started my search at the Illinois State Archives <ilsos.gov/genealogy>. Interestingly, the Illinois State Archives don't show Dimmitt as being in any Illinois regiment at all.

I expanded my search to the Internet Archives <archive.org/stream/reportofadjutant04illi1#page/360/mode/1up> and found him listed in a report of the Adjutant General of the State of Illinois!

By returning to Google and searching *"roster "65th Illinois""*, I also found a very helpful website that had the rosters of the 65th. Calvin Dimmitt is listed as a deserter.

Interestingly, neither Ancestry.com nor fold3.com had any record of Dimmitt's Civil War enlistment in Illinois.

STEP 4. The biography also says Dimmitt served in the 7th Mounted Infantry in Tennessee. I searched the records on the Civil War Soldiers and Sailors System and found Dimmitt listed as serving in Company H of the 7th TN MTD (Tennessee Mounted Infantry).

STEP 5. To learn more about this regiment, I conducted a Google search using the search term *7th Tennessee mounted infantry* and found that this regiment was formed

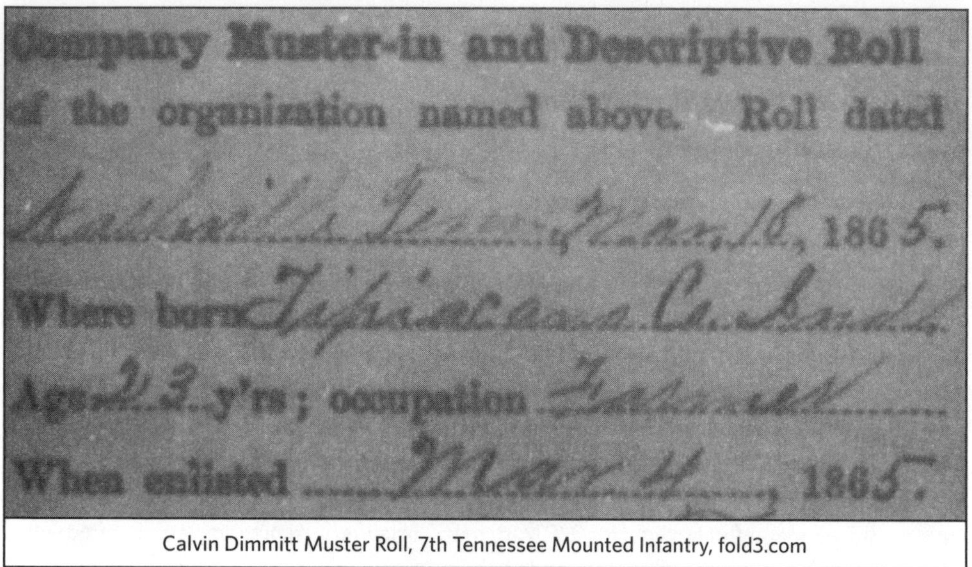

Company Muster-in and Descriptive Roll
of the organization named above. Roll dated
Nashville Tenn Mar. 16, 1865.
Where born Tippecanoe Co. Ind.
Age 23 y'rs; occupation Farmer
When enlisted Mar 4, 1865.

Calvin Dimmitt Muster Roll, 7th Tennessee Mounted Infantry, fold3.com

in Tennessee in August 1864. However, in searching the records at fold3.com, there is no volunteer enlistment of Dimmitt until March 1865.

Was Dimmitt still with the 65th Illinois in the fall of 1863? I don't know. We know he came to Tennessee at some point, but the details are sketchy about when he deserted the 65th Illinois.

STEP 6. According to the biography, Dimmitt's wife seems to be the connection to Tennessee. She is listed as a native of Eastern Tennessee. I searched for Dimmitt's 1860 marriage to Nancy Markham (Marcum) by doing a Google search for *""Calvin Dimmitt" "Nancy Markham""*. The first result was the listing of early Tennessee marriages. Guess what? Calvin and Nancy weren't married in 1860; the marriage didn't take place until the summer of 1864 <freepages.genealogy.rootsweb.ancestry.com/~themeltingpot/marcum/marmar1.html>.

So now the question is, did Calvin go to Tennessee with the Illinois regiment, meet Nancy Markham, desert the 65th, get married, and rejoin the Tennessee regiment? So many clues and so much more to discover.

Finding Local Resources Online

Sometimes local or regional organizations are the best resources for your genealogy research. The good news is most organizations now have websites, and some of them have even posted data online. However, many of these larger organizations may have valuable research libraries that contain information, such as local newspapers, county histories, and historical papers, you simply can't find online. These groups probably don't participate in an interlibrary loan program.

Because of the wealth of information sitting in local repositories, offline sources need to be a part of your online search. While you may not find the records online, you can find contact information so you'll know whom to go to for assistance.

Types of local organizations to include in your research:

- local or state genealogy societies
- historical societies
- special-interest foundations (like Germanna.org)
- churches
- fraternal organizations
- courthouses

- libraries
- regional research facilities
- small-town newspapers
- occupational organizations

WHAT CAN YOU FIND?

Local organizations can be a wealth of information. Records and resources you may find include:

- transcripts of local records
- historical newspapers (even from very small towns)
- county histories
- naturalization papers
- township histories
- cemetery records
- city directories
- industry records (e.g, railroad records)
- information on patriotic, fraternal, and veterans organizations
- baptismal and marriage records
- wills, probate records, and land transactions.

Do a general internet search for your state name and historical society to see what your state's society offers. You can also use this strategy to find county-level historical and genealogical societies. Don't limit your search to where you live.

COUNTY HISTORIES

County histories are one of the greatest genealogy resources you can find, though they can be difficult to track down online. These accounts provide fascinating glimpses of an area's early days. They often included information on flora, fauna, geology, industry, local history, prominent citizen biographies, photographs, and mentions of early settlers. And many were written around the turn of the twentieth century, which, in some cases, meant early settlers or their children were still living. (Don't forget you may be able to find a county history at Google Books <books.google.com>.)

The *History of Albemarle County, Virginia*, published in 1901, lists Revolutionary War-era volunteers, county military organizations, magistrates, attorneys, sheriffs, jailors, immigrants to other states, and representatives to the House of Burgesses.

Even if your family isn't mentioned by name in the published history, you'll still learn much about their community and neighbors. And it's possible that a collateral family is mentioned, or a family that your ancestors married into, or people who served as a witness on a will or land record.

Look for county histories in:

- a local library
- a FamilySearch Center (the Church of Jesus Christ of Latter-day Saints)
- a used bookstore
- an online used book site like AbeBook <abebooks.com>
- a genealogy society library
- Google Books (chapter seven)

If you can't find a county history, look for a volume of vital records, like those published in the 1930s by local chapters of the Daughters of the American Revolution (DAR).

One of the DAR books, *Vital Historical Records, Jackson County Missouri*, contains:

- history of county churches
- lists of church members with dates of joining the church
- where local churches met
- family burial grounds
- cemeteries and cemetery histories
- tombstone transcriptions

LOCAL SOCIETIES

Local societies are specific to a city, town, or county, and have access to all kinds of local records. If you live hundreds of miles from your ancestral hometown, joining the society where your family lived should be at the top of your to-do list.

Because of their easy access to records, local societies are where you'll find information that is difficult to locate anywhere else.

Local genealogy or historical societies often generate revenue by selling transcripts of local records. Some examples of the publications:

- *Episcopal Church Records - Holy Trinity, 1872-1887* (San Diego Genealogical Society)
- *Pleasant Hill War Casualties* (Pleasant Hill Historical Society, Missouri)
- *Reconstructed 1858-1859 Lafayette City Directory* (Tippecanoe County Area Genealogical Society, Indiana)
- *Civil War Veterans Pension Claims Examinations 1896-1903* (Florida State Genealogical Society)
- *Pennsylvania Land Applications, Volume 2: New Purchase Applications—1769-1773* (Genealogical Society of Pennsylvania)

The Lycoming County (Pennsylvania) Genealogical Society <lycominglineage.org/store.htm> sells more than twenty publications, including local histories and funeral and burial records.

The Surry County (North Carolina) Genealogical Association <surrygenealogy.wordpress.com> offers publications of local history (including biographies) as well as area churches.

Joining a society in the area where your family lived will also give you the possibility for long-distance research and networking with possible cousins. Many societies have members who will either do free look-ups in local records or delve into your family research for a minimal hourly fee. Some volunteers will—out of genealogical kindness—go to the courthouse and copy records for free, asking you to pay only for copy costs and postage.

Sometimes, if a society knows you're searching for information on a specific surname, they'll contact you if information surfaces. One genealogist actually received an original deed from a society because members knew the deed was part of the family research being done by a long-distance member. (If you get so lucky as to encounter this, I suggest keeping a copy and returning the original documents.)

Although membership benefits vary from society to society, it's likely you'll receive a monthly, bimonthly, or quarterly newsletter, as well as the right to post free queries in the newsletter or on the society's website.

The newsletter itself often contains records that society members have transcribed and may include a reference to your family. For example, the Kansas City, Missouri-based Heart of America Genealogical Society newsletter once contained transcriptions of local church records, including a history of the church that included members' names and the date of their church membership, contributed by the society's first president, Leo Jane Shore.

Depending on a society's size and resources, it may sponsor special interest groups (SIGs), such as a computer or genealogy software group, or groups that research topics specific to geographic areas.

Larger societies may have their own meeting place or library. The San Diego Genealogical Society <casdgs.org> has its own library that contains thousands of volumes and subscriptions to the most popular family tree magazines and newsletters.

Other society benefits can include discounts to workshops, classes, or genealogy-related tours, such as a trip to a large genealogy library or the Family History Library in Salt Lake City.

If you join a society where you live (which I recommend), be sure to take advantage of the monthly meetings. Typically, monthly meetings are on a specific topic, presented by a local or regional speaker.

Large societies may have an annual meeting with a nationally known speaker who gives a half-day or full-day seminar.

STATE GENEALOGY SOCIETIES

State organizations often publish a quarterly magazine containing transcripts of statewide records in addition to a bimonthly newsletter with queries, book reviews, and articles of general genealogical interest. Their events may include an annual conference.

Like local societies, state organizations publish hard-to-find records. Members of the Maryland Genealogical Society <www.mdgensoc.org> receive the *Maryland Genealogical Society Journal*, published three times a year. The *Journal* features information concerning Maryland genealogy research, case presentations, family pedigrees, technology guides, and Bible transcriptions, as well as other material focusing on Maryland research.

Some state societies maintain a variety of searchable online databases; the Missouri State Genealogical Association <www.mosga.org> has posted all the surnames mentioned in its quarterly journal from 1981 to 2008 on its website.

The Florida State Genealogical Society <www.flsgs.org/index.php> uses its website to post all of the ongoing or completed genealogy projects at the state or county level.

Many state societies issue pioneer, early settler, or "first families" certificates. Requirements vary, but most often require applicants to prove direct descent from people who settled in an area prior to statehood or a significant date, like the formation of a county. Pioneer certificates can be a fun way to show off your heritage, and they also make great gifts for other family members.

Membership in a state society can also give you access to researchers-for-hire, particularly those who specialize in that particular state. Rates vary, but it's not unusual to find someone who will search local records for as little as ten or fifteen dollars an hour. For the total fee of forty dollars, I hired an Iowa researcher who copied census, land, and marriage records, as well as checked cemetery and probate files. You can also find county- or town-level researchers through your local society.

REGIONAL AND NATIONAL GROUPS

Regional genealogy societies may span several state lines. The best known regional society is the New England Historic Genealogical Society <www.americanancestors.org>, founded in 1845. The NEHGS research center, located in downtown Boston, houses more than 200,000 books, 100,000 microforms, and more than two million manuscripts and family papers.

No matter how long you've been climbing your family tree, there's always something new to learn. And it's easy to add to your research bag of tricks thanks to efforts by two of the best-known national societies—the Federation of Genealogical Societies (FGS) <fgs.org> and the National Genealogical Society (NGS) <ngsgenealogy.org>.

NGS, founded in 1903, helps members hone their research skills through many routes: an online and home study course, creation of standards for sound genealogical research, and publication of a quarterly journal that includes genealogies, case studies, and articles on new methodologies.

NGS also sponsors an annual conference open to members and nonmembers alike. This multi-day event is hosted in various cities and features top names in the field. If you want an in-depth learning experience, you'll find it at an NGS conference. Recent seminar topics ranged from learning how to draw land plats to untangling Louisiana French records.

FGS is actually an umbrella organization for genealogy societies. FGS benefits are received through your local society, if it's a member. Benefits include a subscription to the *Forum*, a quarterly publication with feature articles, book reviews, and an ethnic/international column.

Like NGS, FGS also hosts an annual conference for genealogists at all levels of experience.

HOW TO FIND A SOCIETY

Societies that belong to the Federation of Genealogical Societies are listed in an online database <www.fgs.org/societyhall/index.php> that can be searched by society name, city, state, or zip code.

If you think an area has a society, but it isn't listed in the FGS database, go to any internet search engine and type in a term like *Jefferson County Tennessee genealogy society* or *Hiawatha Kansas Genealogy*. If you hit a brick wall, contact a local historical society—they often work in conjunction with the local genealogy society.

SPECIAL INTEREST GROUPS

A final group of societies that you might want to explore are specific to a surname, country of origin, military service, ethnic or religious background, or line of descent (lineage society). While local and state societies cover a fairly broad area of research, these special societies have more of a laser-beam focus.

Some surname associations focus on researching all instances of a surname (like a one-name study), while others are interested in learning everything possible about the descendants of a specific ancestor. If you're stuck in your research regarding a specific surname, joining a surname society or association can provide you with a network of other researchers who may have already climbed over your brick wall.

Other societies have been established for people whose family migrated or emigrated together. For example, I belong to the Muttenz Descendants <muttenzdescendants.org>, an association of people who tie their history to 120 emigrants from Muttenz, Switzerland, in the eighteenth century. The association members collect and share historical and genealogical information about their families.

The Czechoslovak Genealogical Society International <cgsi.org> is a resource for families of Czech, Bohemian, Moravian, Slovak, German, Hungarian, Jewish, Rusyn, and Silesian origin.

The benefits of joining special-interest groups are primarily educational; they may be the best resource for learning about any peculiar naming conventions, the main areas of immigration, or any geographic name changes.

Conduct a general internet search for special interest societies. See chapter five for a listing of heritage societies you may want to join.

If you want to join a surname society or family association, look through alphabetical listings at Cyndi's List <cyndislist.com/surnames.htm>. The same site also has links to ethnic, religious, and military societies <cyndislist.com/soc-gen.htm>.

HISTORICAL SOCIETIES

Although historical societies weren't established with genealogy as their primary goal, many of them house treasure troves of genealogical information, at both the state and local levels.

For example, the Minnesota Historical Society <mnhs.org/index.htm> holds state and federal census records; naturalization papers; information on patriotic, fraternal, and veterans organizations; township histories; cemetery records; and city directories. In addition, the library holds the records of the Great Northern and Northern Pacific Railroads.

Similarly, the Montana Historical Society <mhs.mt.gov> houses the papers of the Society of Montana Pioneers, which include a 1907 survey of the routes people took to reach Montana. The society also owns original homesteading diaries.

On the local level, city or town historical societies often house papers, diaries, or belongings of early pioneer families or prominent citizens. They are also an excellent source for photographs and maps. The San Diego History Center <www.sandiegohistory.org> owns more than two million photos, some dating back to 1860, and more than two thousand maps, including the Sanborn Fire Insurance series.

If you can't visit an historical society in person, some societies will do a quick look-up for free (usually limited to thirty minutes), charge a minimal hourly fee, or refer you to a local researcher who is familiar with the society's archives.

WHAT ARE YOU WAITING FOR?

With the increasing popularity of internet research, many people forget the value of genealogy societies. It's good to remember that before the rise of the internet, the majority of family tree research was done by people who learned research techniques in a local society.

If you live far from your ancestral hometown(s), get online and track down the contact information for the societies, and join. Pay particular attention to the areas where your family lived for several years because you're more likely to find references to them in local land or probate records.

Of course, I recommend joining your own hometown society. It's a great way to learn genealogy, keep up on the latest techniques, network with other family tree enthusiasts, and get involved in volunteer projects that may just help a stranger—like you!

GIVING BACK

Giving back to the genealogy community can be both fun and fulfilling. You may not be able to wield a chainsaw through an overgrown cemetery, but there are other ways to help a stranger in need when you are a society member.

One way is by transcribing original documents or doing look-ups. The Durham-Orange Genealogical Society of North Carolina <ncgenweb.us/dogsnc/lookups> lists on its website the names of people willing to do look-ups and the books these volunteers own.

You can also assist your local society by volunteering to help on a committee; most societies need help in transcribing cemetery records or contributing to a monthly newsletter or quarterly journal. You can also volunteer with fundraising events like book sales, society trips, or family history fairs. If you have web experience, you could also get involved in maintaining your society's website, answering e-mails, posting queries, or coordinating press coverage of society events.

Tracing Immigrant and American Indian Ancestors

Think of America before habitation. Vast and empty, waiting for our ancestors to appear. And appear they did.

Some walked across the Bering Strait and became our American Indian ancestors, others left Europe, sailing out of Bremen, Southampton, Liverpool, and Cherbourg. Still others came unwillingly—millions kidnapped from Africa, victims of the slave trade.

We are a nation of immigrants. And whether your family tales are of the Irish in Boston, the Indian princess, the Eastern European Jew who escaped the pogroms (mob attacks, often against Jews living in Eastern Europe and Russia, during the late eighteenth and early nineteenth centuries), or the South Carolinian slave, you want to discover your first American ancestor.

Ellis Island is probably the most iconic immigration port in American history. But Europeans began migrating to America as early as the sixteenth and seventeenth centuries, with major influxes in the mid-nineteenth century. Ellis Island did not open until 1892, just in time to welcome the swell of immigrants that arrived in the first decade of the twentieth century.

To effectively search for immigration records, you need to know when your family immigrated. If you've found your ancestor on the 1880 federal census, there's no way that branch immigrated through Ellis Island. It's also helpful to have an idea of where your ancestors came from so you know which ports they likely traveled through.

FINDING THE YEAR OF IMMIGRATION

Surprisingly, you may be able to find immigration data in the federal census. Beginning in 1900 and continuing through 1930, the census required foreign-born people to indicate their year of immigration and whether they were naturalized. In 1920, they were asked for the year of naturalization.

Although this question was a boon to genealogists who seek a year of immigration as a stepping stone to a passenger list, it can cause confusion. It was very common for people to give inconsistent responses to the immigration and naturalization question. On the 1900 census, for example, Joseph Brooks gave his date of immigration as 1888; on the 1910 census he stated 1870; in 1920 he stated his immigration date as 1885 and his naturalization date as 1906.

The census will also contain information on the place of birth—another clue when searching down country of origin. Again, inconsistencies abound; one ancestor's place of birth changed through the census years, from Gibraltar to Madrid to England to Malta. When investigating records such as these, remember to check the history of a country; with Gibraltar you'll learn that it has been under the control of England since 1713. So someone born there would be English.

One other help in locating country of origin are census records indicating "mother tongue." Here, you may find a listing such as English (Irish), or country of birth as Can (English) or Can (Fr). The notation of English can indicate areas such as Ontario, while Fr would be the area of Quebec (French-speaking). While not infallible, these are clues that can help in tracking down a port or country of embarkation to the United States or Canada.

Naturalization Records

Naturalization records are another way to determine the year of immigration and the country your ancestor immigrated from. Naturalization is the process in which an immigrant becomes an American citizen. While it's a voluntary process, it is required for United States citizenship.

These records can also provide clues to finding the name of the ship and even the place of birth for the individual.

Naturalization is the process of becoming a U.S. citizen. To become a citizen, your ancestor probably filed the process of first making a declaration of intention and then petitioning to become a U.S. citizen.

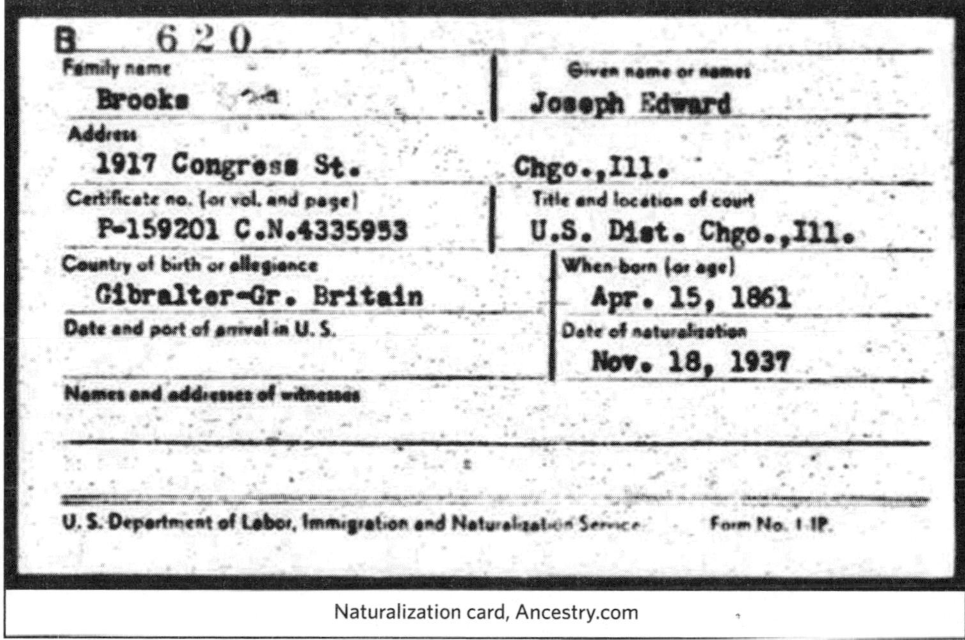
B 620
Family name: Brooke
Given name or names: Joseph Edward
Address: 1917 Congress St. Chgo.,Ill.
Certificate no. (or vol. and page): P-159201 C.N.4335953
Title and location of court: U.S. Dist. Chgo.,Ill.
Country of birth or allegiance: Gibralter-Gr. Britain
When born (or age): Apr. 15, 1861
Date and port of arrival in U. S.
Date of naturalization: Nov. 18, 1937
Names and addresses of witnesses
U. S. Department of Labor, Immigration and Naturalization Service Form No. 1 IP.

Naturalization card, Ancestry.com

In a declaration of intention, the applicant declared his intent to become a citizen and renounced his allegiance to a foreign government. Early records will typically include name, country of birth, application date, and signature. Records post-1906 were more detailed, with place of birth, port, and date of entry.

The second part of the process was undertaken after residency requirements were met and a formal application was made. Genealogical treasures can be found in the naturalization petition beginning in 1906; among the details included were a physical description, date and port of immigration, place of birth, and occupation. Beginning in 1929, a photo was also required. At the end of the process, your ancestor received an official certificate of naturalization.

Over time, members of the military were allowed to expedite part of the process; if you were an Army veteran of any war, honorably discharged, and had one year of residence, you could apply without going through the intention process. The process for military personnel changed over time, due to changes in the law.

You can search for naturalization records on fold3.com and Ancestry.com. Ancestry's database ranges from 1795 to 1972 and is an index to U.S. naturalization records for various courts.

Fold3.com has close to a dozen naturalization databases, including records from

- San Diego
- New York

- Maryland
- World War I soldiers

DETERMINING THE PORT OF ENTRY

Though Ellis Island is the most famous immigration port, immigrants entered the United States through a number of different ports. The reality is there was no central point of entry. New York saw the most immigrants, but other ports included:

ANGEL ISLAND, SAN FRANCISCO. This port opened in 1910 and processed immigrants from China.

BALTIMORE. A popular destination far before the American Revolution, Baltimore's immigration records span from about 1820 to the close of the nineteenth century. Irish and German settlers were among the first to enter via Baltimore, with the numbers increasing during the Irish Potato Famine.

BOSTON. Immigration records for Boston begin in the 1820s and run through 1943. Immigrates came to Boston from Ireland, Europe, and Eastern Europe.

CASTLE GARDEN, NEW YORK CITY (1820-1892). This was New York's primary port of arrival until the opening of Ellis Island.

CHARLESTON, SOUTH CAROLINA. Records for this port run from about 1820 to the mid-twentieth century.

GALVESTON, TEXAS. Records began in the 1840s. Check New Orleans records too, some passengers were on ships that first stopped in New Orleans.

NEW ORLEANS. This was one of the busiest of the U.S. ports from 1820 to 1952. Immigrants often traveled up the Mississippi and settled in areas along the river.

PHILADELPHIA. This city served as the port of entry for 1.3 million immigrants from 1815 to 1985. Beginning in 1873, steamships made regular runs from Europe to Philadelphia.

PORT TOWNSEND, WASHINGTON. Immigrants from China came through the Port Townsend immigration station in the late 1800s.

ST. ALBANS, VERMONT. The St. Albans records cover anyone crossing from Canada into the United States from 1895 to 1917, and from 1917–1954 cover anyone crossing east of the Montana-North Dakota line.

This list should help you rule out a number of ports for your immigrant ancestor, and it may make you aware of some previously unknown ports that you should explore.

PASSENGER LISTS

When you have an idea of when your ancestor immigrated and where he came from, you can start searching for him in ship lists to find the exact date of arrival. Details vary from ship to ship and era to era, but in addition to date of arrival, passenger lists can also provide you with:

- full name
- date of birth
- birth place
- last residence (city and country)
- occupation
- associates already in America
- intended destination in America
- traveling companions

Before 1820, immigrant documentation was haphazard at best. Ships' lists were hit or miss, and those that were kept are not completely indexed or digitized. You might find them on websites, and in libraries, historical societies, and archives. Some online databases for early passenger lists include:

PILGRIM SHIP LISTS EARLY 1600S <packrat-pro.com/ships/shiplist.htm>
This site contains passenger lists for more than 250 ships. More than 7,100 families are documented in the database, which is organized by passenger names, ship names, and ship dates.

PALATINE SHIPS TO NEW YORK, 1710 <genesearch.com/genealogy-records/newyorkpalatines1710.html>
This site contains reconstructed passenger lists for twelve ships that carried nearly 3,200 Palatine (German) immigrants from London to New York in 1710.

PENNSYLVANIA GERMAN PIONEERS PASSENGER LISTS, 1727–1808 <freepages.genealogy.rootsweb.ancestry.com/~pagermanpioneers>
This site contains more than two hundred links to German passenger ships that arrived in Philadelphia between 1727–1808. Most immigrants are from the southwest Pfalz region of Germany.

Other online passenger lists databases include:
IMMIGRANT SHIPS TRANSCRIBERS GUILD (ISTG) <immigrantships.net>
ISTG is an organization of volunteers who transcribe passenger lists. The site contains more than eleven thousand individual passenger manifests that can be searched for free.

NATIONAL ARCHIVES IRISH FAMINE IMMIGRANTS, 1846–1851 <aad.archives.gov/aad/series-list.jsp?cat=SB302&bc=sb>
The National Archives has posted a searchable database of passenger records of ships that arrived at the port of New York during the Irish Famine (1841–1851). These records include name, age, native country, port of embarkation, and arrival date.

Castle Garden

Located on the tip of Manhattan, Castle Garden was the first official immigrant station, processing eleven million immigrants from 1820 to 1892. If you've always heard that your family came here via Ellis Island, but can't find them, check Castle Garden.

Castle Garden's ship and immigration records have been transcribed and are part of an online database that you can search for free at <castlegarden.org>. You cannot view images of the original manifests on the database as you can do at Ellis Island.

1. From the Home page, click the Search link. Next fill in as much information as you can in the search box. If you don't get the results you'd hoped for, either add or delete search filters.
2. Your search will return a list of hits. In this case, there was only one result that fit my search criteria.
3. Click the surname of the person whose record you want to view. The resulting screen contains all of the information available about this passenger. As you can see, the potential exists for locating family in the "old country" (i.e., name and address of relative left behind), but in the case of this record, that information was not provided.

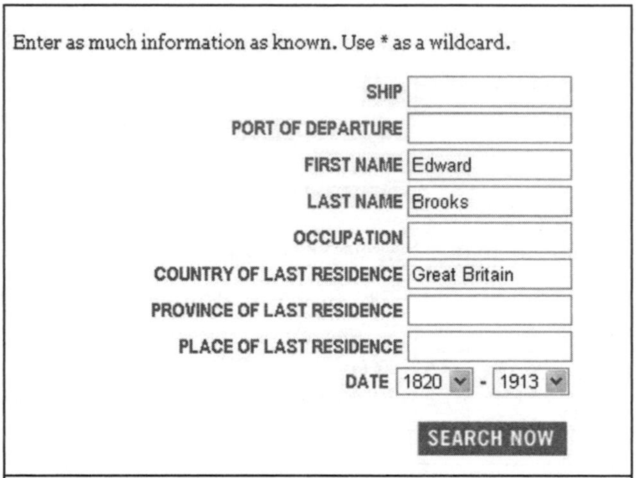

Enter as much information as known. Use * as a wildcard.

SHIP
PORT OF DEPARTURE
FIRST NAME Edward
LAST NAME Brooks
OCCUPATION
COUNTRY OF LAST RESIDENCE Great Britain
PROVINCE OF LAST RESIDENCE
PLACE OF LAST RESIDENCE
DATE 1820 - 1913
SEARCH NOW

Simple search of the Castle Garden database, CastleGarden.org

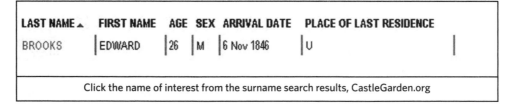

LAST NAME ▲	FIRST NAME	AGE	SEX	ARRIVAL DATE	PLACE OF LAST RESIDENCE
BROOKS	EDWARD	26	M	6 Nov 1846	U

Click the name of interest from the surname search results, CastleGarden.org

Ellis Island

The passenger lists from Ellis Island have been added to <ellisisland.org>. This free database contains transcripts for more than twenty-two million passengers, immigrants, and crew members arriving in New York between 1892 and 1924. These transcripts will tell you:

EDWARD BROOKS			
FIRST NAME	EDWARD	RELATIVE LEFT BEHIND	
LAST NAME	BROOKS	NAME OF RELATIVE LEFT BEHIND	
OCCUPATION	FARMER	ADDRESS OF RELATIVE LEFT BEHIND	
AGE	26	TICKET	
SEX	Male	PAID BY	Self
LITERACY	Unknown	IN THE US BEFORE	Unknown
SHIP	DEVONSHIRE	IN THE US WHEN	
ARRIVED	6 Nov 1846	IN THE US WHERE	
COUNTRY	GREAT BRITAIN	GOING TO SOMEONE IN THE US	Unknown
PORT OF DEPARTURE	LIVERPOOL	RELATIONSHIP TO THAT SOMEONE IN THE US	
PLACE OF LAST RESIDENCE	U	NAME OF RELATIVE IN THE US	
PROVINCE OF LAST RESIDENCE	UNKNOWN		
CITY OR VILLAGE OF DESTINATION	UNITED STATES	ADDRESS OF RELATIVE IN THE US	
PLAN	Unknown	CITY OF RELATIVE IN THE US	
PASSAGE	Unknown	COUNTRY OF BIRTH	GREAT BRITAIN
MONEY		PLACE OF BIRTH	

Immigrant ancestor's details, CastleGarden.org

- immigrant's given name
- immigrant's surname
- ethnicity
- last residence (town and country)
- date of arrival
- age at arrival
- gender
- marital status
- ship of travel
- port of departure
- line number on manifest

Search for your immigrant ancestor by name or by ship's name, and print a copy of the ship's manifest. The site also contains ship photos and free genealogy forms, including a Passenger Arrival Log.

THIS SHEET IS FOR STEERAGE PASSENGERS.

STATES IMMIGRATION OFFICER AT PORT OF ARRIVAL.

to the United States Immigration Officer by the Commanding Officer of any vessel having such passengers on boa

Arriving at Port of NEW YORK 2 MAY 1909

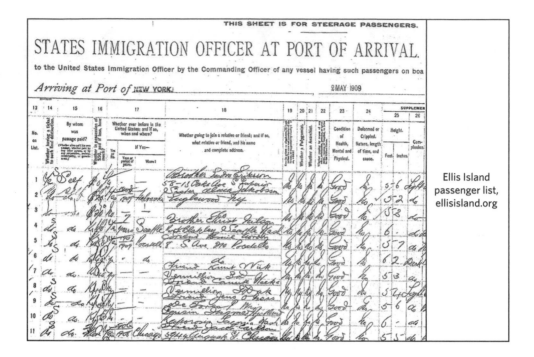

Ellis Island passenger list, ellisisland.org

SEARCHING ANCESTRY.COM'S IMMIGRATION RECORDS

With more than 100 million names from more than one hundred U.S. and foreign ports, Ancestry.com <ancestry.com> has the largest online collection of immigration records.

Not only can you search for arrivals to America here, you'll find databases containing immigrants to Canada, the UK, and Australia. If your ancestor was in Canada or Mexico, search the Border Crossing databases.

Ancestry.com's Immigration & Travel databases have six categories:

1. Passenger Lists
2. Citizenship & Naturalization Records
3. Border Crossings & Passports
4. Crew Lists
5. Immigration & Emigration Books
6. Ship Pictures & Descriptions

The type of information contained in each database is different; some have images, others indexes, while still others have original records. The entire Immigration & Travel collection can be searched at the same time or each database can be searched separately.

A typical immigration search might go something like this:

1. Log on to <ancestry.com>. Place your mouse over Search on the top menu. When the pull-down menu appears, select Immigration & Travel.

In this search, I'm looking for information on a William Brooks, date of birth about 1833. I don't have a year of immigration, but was told that his port of arrival was Baltimore. From the Passenger Lists category, I selected the database of Baltimore Passenger Lists 1820–1957.

Name
First & Middle Name(s): william
Last Name: brooks

Event
Lived In — Location
Arrival — Day, Month, Year, Location
Departure — Year, Location

More
Keyword: 1833
e.g. pilot or "Flying Tigers"

A search on Ancestry.com for an immigrant ancestor

In reading the information about this database, I learned that it contains names of people who entered the United States at other ports or border crossings (Port Huron, Michigan; Tampa, Florida; Portal, North Dakota, etc.) but who were living in Baltimore.

2. I began the search by entering the name *William Brooks* and date of birth *1833*. I could have browsed the database by date of entry, but I thought that kind of search would be more time-consuming than valuable. However, if your ancestor arrived very early, i.e., 1820, there were only eight ships in September of that year, so the number of people to search through would be minimal.
3. If you're not having much luck with a name search, try adding a keyword or two as a filter. Or, if you're getting too many hits, you may want to specify "exact," which forces Ancestry.com to only return hits with the exact spelling that you indicated.

You can also limit your search results by including birth place, residence, place of arrival and departure, and place of origin.

4. Keep in mind that this particular database doesn't have a section for birth date, but you can add it in the keywords section.
5. I found William in the results, although his name on the record was listed as Wm.

If your search for Robert or William or John doesn't return results, try searching for an abbreviated version of the name.

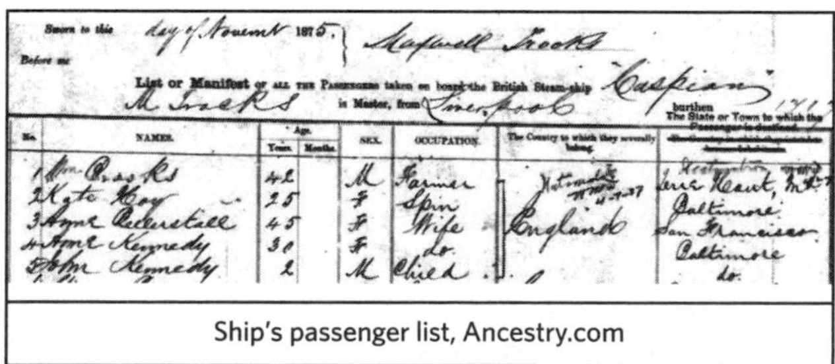
List or Manifest of all the Passengers taken on board the British Steamship Caspian

Ship's passenger list, Ancestry.com

After you've found your ancestor, click to view the actual record. In this case, we can see the departure date, age, port of departure, occupation, and final destination within the United States, and name of the ship (*Caspian*).

6. A Google image search for *1875 ship Caspian* turned up a website with a photo, manifest for 1872, and a description of the ship <freepages.genealogy.rootsweb.ancestry.com/~brett/payne/payne_journapp1.html>.

TIP

Don't be confused by an unexpected "country of origin" on a passenger list. The country listed may be where your ancestor boarded the ship (the ship's country of origin), not your ancestor's country of origin (where he was born).

ANCESTORS FROM CANADA

It's not unusual to find ancestors who originally immigrated to Canada and then came to the United States. Although there isn't an abundance of records online, the Library and Archives Canada does maintain a website with genealogical resources, including immigration <collectionscanada.gc.ca/genealogy/022-908-e.html>.

Prior to April 1908, people could move freely across the border from the United States into Canada; no record of immigration exists for those individuals.

You can, however, search the 1881 and 1891 Canadian censuses (for free). These records will give a place of birth; that means if your ancestor originally immigrated to Canada and was there for either the 1881 or 1891 censuses before coming to the United States, you can find his place of birth <collectionscanada.gc.ca/lac-bac/search-recherche/anc.php?Language=eng>.

To learn more about your Canadian ancestors, begin investigating the official sites such as the Archives of Ontario or the Archives of Quebec (Bibliothèque et Archives nationales du Québec).

Ancestry.com also has databases of Canadian immigrants, passenger lists, and Canadian census records starting in 1851.

PASSPORT RECORDS

Prior to 1941, U.S. citizens were not required to have passports for travel abroad, except for a few brief periods around the time of the Civil War and World War I.

If you're looking for early passport records, your search will take you to the National Archives or microfilms through the Family History Library.

Passport applications, particularly those of the early twentieth century, contained an abundance of information, including a physical description, name, date and place of birth, residence, occupation, and (sometimes) where traveling.

Ancestry.com has a collection of passport applications, ranging from 1795 to 1925. If you want a post-1925 application, you'll need to write the Passport Office at the Department of State, 1425 K Street NW, Washington, DC 20520. If the applicant is still alive, you'll need to get a permission letter from her; if deceased, you'll need to provide a copy of a death certificate and a letter stating your relationship to the deceased.

This 1906 passport application of William F. Cody (Buffalo Bill) tells us that he was 6'1", had a high forehead, brown eyes, straight nose, medium mouth, square chin, gray hair, florid complexion, and an oval face. Almost as good as a photo!

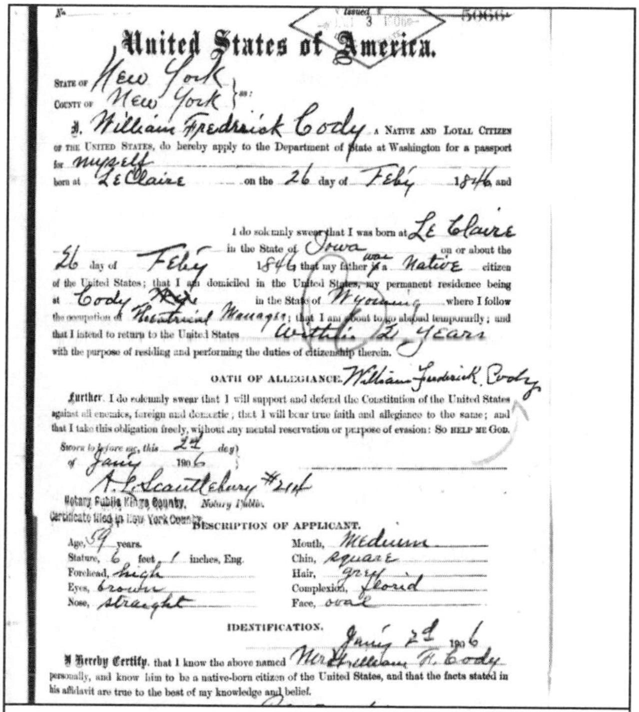
United States of America.

State of New York
County of New York } ss:

I, William Fredrick Cody, a Native and Loyal Citizen of the United States, do hereby apply to the Department of State at Washington for a passport for myself born at Le Claire on the 26 day of Feby 1846 and

I do solemnly swear that I was born at Le Claire in the State of Iowa on or about the 26 day of Feby 1846 that my father was a Native citizen of the United States; that I am domiciled in the United States, my permanent residence being at Cody Wyo in the State of Wyoming where I follow the occupation of Theatrical Manager; that I am about to go abroad temporarily; and that I intend to return to the United States within 2 years with the purpose of residing and performing the duties of citizenship therein.

Oath of Allegiance. William Fredrick Cody

Further, I do solemnly swear that I will support and defend the Constitution of the United States against all enemies, foreign and domestic; that I will bear true faith and allegiance to the same; and that I take this obligation freely, without any mental reservation or purpose of evasion: So help me God.

Sworn to before me, this 24 day of Jany 1906

A. L. Scantlebury #214
Notary Public Kings County, Notary Public.
Certificate filed in New York County

Description of Applicant.

Age, 59 years. Mouth, Medium
Stature, 6 feet, 1 inches, Eng. Chin, square
Forehead, high Hair, grey
Eyes, brown Complexion, florid
Nose, straight Face, oval

Identification. Jany 24 1906

I hereby Certify, that I know the above named Mr. William F. Cody personally, and know him to be a native-born citizen of the United States, and that the facts stated in his affidavit are true to the best of my knowledge and belief.

Buffalo Bill Cody's passport application, Ancestry.com

THE UNWILLING AND UNWANTED

If you're searching for Jewish or African-American ancestors online, you're in luck; your search may be challenging, but you'll find plenty of websites to aid in the journey.

Jewish Ancestors

The first large wave of Jewish immigration was in 1860, when 200,000 German Jews came to the United States. Another two million arrived between 1882 and 1914, primarily from Eastern Europe as a result of Russian pogroms. Because of the complexity of Jewish research, specialist Schelly Talalay Dardashti offers a seven-step strategy for tracing Jewish roots in appendix B. Here are some useful sites for researching Jewish ancestry:

AVOTAYNU <avotaynu.com>

Avotaynu: The International Review of Jewish Genealogy started in 1985 as a quarterly newsletter about Jewish genealogical issues. Also subscribe to the site's free e-newsletter, "Nu? What's New?" to stay up to date on books and resources.

THE BEIT HATFUTSOT: MUSEUM OF THE JEWISH PEOPLE <bh.org.il>

This Israeli museum keeps track of Jewish roots from cultures around the globe. The Douglas E. Goldman Genealogy Center has an extensive computerized database of more than 850,000 names. For five dollars, the staff will search the database for you and send you the results. You can upload your own family tree to the database for free.

CONSOLIDATED JEWISH SURNAME INDEX <avotaynu.com/csi/csi-home.html>
Avotaynu's gateway to information, about 699,084 surnames, mostly Jewish, that appear in forty-two online databases.

CYNDI'S LIST—JEWISH <cyndislist.com/jewish>
This page links to more than 240 sites, books, audiotapes, web rings, and much more.

DOROTREE <dorotree.com>
Dorot is the Hebrew word for roots. This site offers a GEDCOM program that also types and prints out in Hebrew and you don't need a Hebrew-language operating system to use the program, which makes it convenient for those who wish to share their heritage with relatives in Israel, or those who have ancestors best represented with Hebrew characters, the same characters used for Yiddish. This website offers a free demo and more web links.

FAMILYSEARCH JEWISH FAMILY HISTORY RESOURCES
<familysearch.org/eng/home/welcome/site_resources.asp?whichResourcePage=Jewish>
This is a guide to researching Jewish roots and finding records in the Family History Library.

GENEALOGY RESOURCES ON THE INTERNET: JEWISH MAILING LISTS
<rootsweb.ancestry.com/~jfuller/gen_mail_jewish.html>
Connect with other researchers via e-mail.

JEWISHGEN <jewishgen.org>
This is the all-encompassing site for Jewish genealogy. Features include a directory of Jewish Genealogical Societies, Yizkor (memory) books project, Shtetl Seeker, and the Family Finder with surnames and town names. Upload your own family tree for free, in GEDCOM format, to be included in the Family Tree of the Jewish People.

JEWISH WEB INDEX <jewishwebindex.com>
A compendium of links for Jewish genealogical research.

JUDAISM 101: JEWISH NAMES <jewfaq.org/jnames.htm>
Dispelling surname myths and explaining given-name practices.

ONE-STEP WEB PAGES BY STEPHEN P. MORSE <stevemorse.org>
Tools on this site help you search a variety of Holocaust- and Eastern European-related websites, convert Jewish calendar dates, translate Hebrew writing, and more.

TRACING THE TRIBE <tracingthetribe.blogspot.com>
Schelly Talalay Dardashti's blog is a must-read for news and resources about tracing Jewish ancestors.

African-American Ancestors

It's been estimated that between 1619 and 1819 more than twelve million Africans were brought to America against their will. The trans-Atlantic slave trade grew out of a strong demand for labor, particularly in the southern states where a large labor force was needed to produce crops of cotton and tobacco.

By the time of the 1790 federal census, slaves comprised almost half of South Carolina's total population of 249,073. And by the 1820s, slaves constituted a majority of the Palmetto state's population.

Researching slave ancestors requires the same techniques used to climb any family tree—but in this instance you'll need to trace your line back to the 1870 census, the first federal census following the abolition of slavery. What names did your family use and where did they settle?

Kenyatta D. Berry, a noted African-American researcher, offers valuable tips on researching not only your slave ancestor but the ancestry of the slaveholder's family. See appendix C.

An excellent resource for researching African-American ancestors is the four-week course, Finding African-American Ancestors in Newspapers, offered through Family Tree University <familytreeuniversity.com>. This course will walk you through newspaper research and give you the skills to seek out and utilize information found in African-American newspapers.

As you begin your journey toward unraveling your heritage, look to the following websites to provide you with even more clues, records, and data in which to find your family.

AFRIGENEAS <afrigeneas.com>
Here you'll find slave records collections, a surname database, and death and marriage records.

AFRIQUEST <afriquest.com>
This site features user-submitted genealogy finds and stories.

AFRO-LOUISIANA HISTORY AND GENEALOGY 1719–1820 <ibiblio.org/laslave>
This is a database of 100,000 Louisiana slaves.

DIGITAL LIBRARY ON AMERICAN SLAVERY <library.uncg.edu/slavery>
More than 150,000 individuals, including 80,000 slaves, are named in the thousands of documents in this library.

DOCUMENTING THE AMERICAN SOUTH <docsouth.unc.edu>
A free resource for researchers with African-American roots or others with Southern roots.

LOWCOUNTRY AFRICANA <www.lowcountryafricana.net>
Documenting African-American heritage in the historic rice-growing areas of South Carolina, Georgia, and extreme northeastern Florida.

USF AFRICANA HERITAGE PROJECT <www.africanaheritage.com>
Search Bible records, slave narratives, wills, church records, and plantation journals. The virtual library has how-to articles.

TRACING AMERICAN INDIANS

A note before we begin: In genealogy terms, a person is native to the country he is born in. To avoid confusion, we'll use the term American Indian to refer to the people who populated the United States before European settlers arrived. Tracing American Indian roots will take you into new territory, away from familiar research habits. No longer will the federal census be the backbone of your investigation. And, although you may still find clues in land and military records, you'll be delving into regional files, federal "rolls," and a culture still deeply rooted in oral tradition.

American Indian history—conflict, the reservation system, non-inclusion on early censuses, and forced migrations—makes tracing your native roots a challenge. These five steps can help kick-start your search.

1. START WITH YOUR OWN FAMILY. Like Alex Haley's search for his African-American roots, your search may have been inspired by snippets of an oral tradition or family legend. You may have heard someone mention an Indian princess or perhaps just a rumor of Indian blood.

(Stories of an Indian princess in the family tree have become urban legend. This isn't to say your family doesn't have American Indian blood—just a caveat to be aware that a princess is a common claim.)

Sit down and talk with your family. Go through family papers, Bibles, and letters, looking for birth, death, and marriage records. Clues about American Indian ancestry can sur-

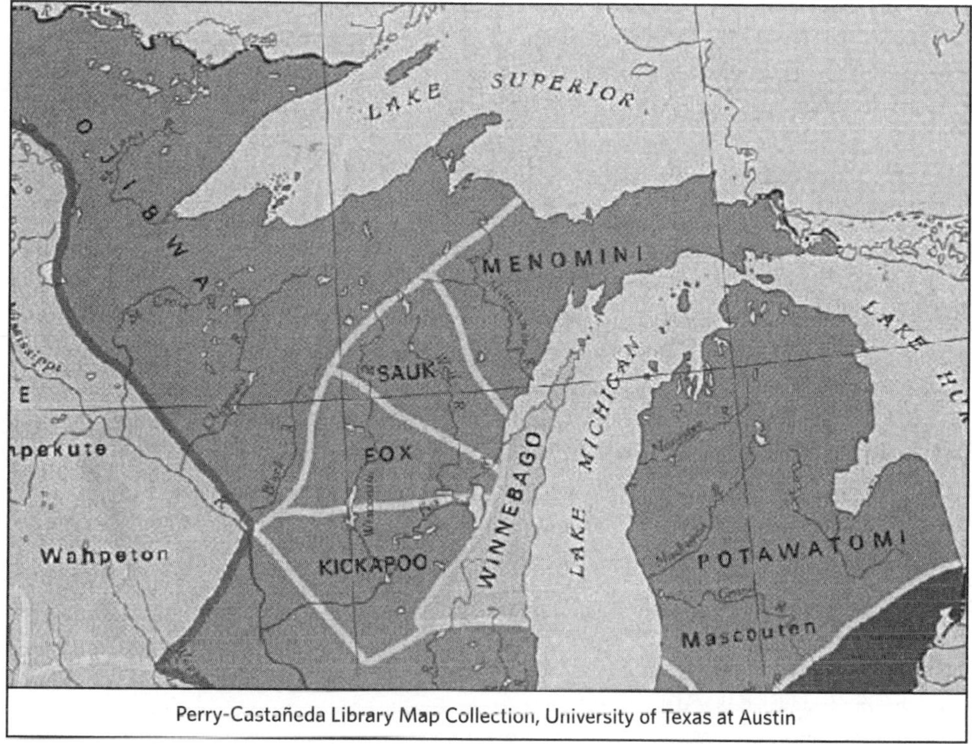

Perry-Castañeda Library Map Collection, University of Texas at Austin

face from the most unexpected sources; a name you vaguely remember hearing as a child may be your first link to a shadowy past. Or an old tombstone may contain a reference to an Indian name or place.

The most important mystery to unravel is the name of your ancestor's tribe. Hopefully, you'll find that information buried in family records, vital statistics, letters, or diaries. If not, you'll need to expand your research into tribal histories and migration patterns.

2. FIND YOUR ANCESTOR'S TRIBE. Begin your search for your ancestor's tribe by locating the tribes that lived within the same area as your ancestor and during the same period in time. Start your search here:

- American Indian tribes by geographic area
  <davemcgary.com/native-americans-heritage.htm>
- Early Tribes, Eastern United States
  <lib.utexas.edu/maps/united_states/early_indian_east.jpg>
- Early Tribes, Western United States
  <lib.utexas.edu/maps/united_states/early_indian_west.jpg>

To find your ancestor's tribe, you need to know enough about tribal history and migration to recognize an error in assumption. For example, if someone in the family tells you that your native connection is a Cherokee tribe living in Michigan, you'll recognize the improbability. The Cherokee migrated through many states, but Michigan wasn't one of them.

Did your ancestors live in the area around Lake Michigan or Lake Superior? If so, you'll be searching Chippewa or Ojibwa roots.

If your family hails from present-day New Mexico, your first search will probably be narrowed to Southwest tribes like the Navajo, Hopi, or Apache.

3. LEARN TRIBAL CULTURE AND HISTORY. After you have located your tribe, go to Google and do a search on phrases such as *Ojibwa history* or *Ojibwa culture* or *Ojibwa genealogy*. This will help you find websites devoted to information about your tribe.

You will also find links to many tribal sites at Native Web <nativeweb.org>. The knowledge you gain from these websites can greatly inform your genealogical research. For example:

- Over a 150-year time span, the Cherokee lived in the Carolinas, Georgia, Arkansas, and Oklahoma.
- If your family belonged to one of the Iroquois linguistic groups, you'll learn enough about the culture to know it was matrilineal—descended through the female line. Children were not recognized in the paternal line of descent.
- In the Ojibwa tribe, women controlled their homes and the family's property and made all decisions within the home.
- Hopi women owned the property, and their husbands worked to benefit the wife's family.

4. KNOW WHAT RECORDS ARE AVAILABLE. Most genealogists depend on federal and state census records to lay a basic foundation of research. However, tribal Indians were not included in early federal censuses. In fact, census records from 1790 to 1850 included only Indians living in settled areas who were taxed and did not claim a tribal affiliation. Indians on reservations or who lived a nomadic existence were not taxed, and therefore not counted.

By the time of the 1860 federal census, a category called "Indian (taxed)" was added. From 1870 to 1910, the category of "Indian" was included, but did not include reservation Indians until 1890. Because most of the 1890 census is unavailable, the first federal census you can research that contains most American Indians is the 1900 census.

Special counts were made of several tribes, with the best-known being the Dawes Rolls, listing the names of members of the Five Civilized Tribes: the Cherokee, Choctaw, Chickasaw, Seminole, and Creek tribes.

Because of the well-documented nature of the Five Civilized Tribes—so called because of their early adaptation to white culture—these records are among the easiest to find on the internet.

Search these databases for your American Indian ancestors:

ANCESTRY.COM <ancestry.com>
Ancestry.com's records include:

- U.S. Indian Census Rolls, 1885–1940
- U.S. American Indian Applications for Enrollment in Five Civilized Tribes, 1896
- U.S. American Indian Enrollment Cards for the Five Civilized Tribes, 1898–1914

NATIONAL ARCHIVES <archives.gov/research/native-americans/dawes>
You can search the Dawes Rolls on the National Archives site. The Dawes Rolls are the lists of individuals who were accepted as eligible for tribal membership in the Five Civilized Tribes (Cherokees, Creeks, Choctaws, Chickasaws, and Seminoles). Membership in one of the tribes entitled the registrant to free land. More than 100,000 names appear on the rolls, spanning 1898–1914.

ROOTSWEB <userdb.rootsweb.ancestry.com/nativeamerican>
The RootsWeb's American Indian database contains more than seventeen thousand surnames. See appendix A for more American Indian resources.

5. UTILIZE ONLINE COMMUNITIES. After you've located your tribe, you can join in discussions at the nearly two hundred e-mail lists dedicated to American Indian research. Each list pertains to specific topics, and everyone on the list shares similar research goals.

You'll find a list of Native Roots mailing lists on these websites: <rootsweb.com/~jfuller/gen_mail_natam.html> and <lists.rootsweb.com/index/other/Ethnic-Native>.

Share What You've Found

Back in the day (that means a year or so ago), one of the few ways genealogists could share findings was by e-mailing a GEDCOM file or posting research on a blog or website.

Today (a year later) your research may still be sitting in a file or on a blog, but getting the word out to other genealogists has become far easier, thanks to social networking.

In this chapter you're going to discover how to use social networking to share your findings and network with other researchers, even if you've never tweeted a tweet or friended a friend.

But first, about that GEDCOM.

GEDCOM, THE ONE-SIZE-FITS-ALL FILE FORMAT

Genealogy software stores data in a format that's unique to that software, which means the files can't be opened by other genealogy programs. You can quickly see the limitations this can create. If you don't have the same software program as another genealogist, you can't access that genealogist's electronic files. GEDCOM was created to solve this problem.

GEDCOM is an acronym for GEnealogical Data COMmunication. They are similar to PDFs in that GEDCOM turns the document from a software-specific format to a format that can be read by almost any Windows or Mac genealogy software. This means you can export your Family Tree Maker file as a GEDCOM, and a friend can import that same GEDCOM into her Legacy Family Tree or any other genealogical software.

You can send a GEDCOM as an e-mail attachment, burn it to CD and mail it, or upload it to a website. Keep in mind that a GEDCOM is a text file, so any images, audio, or video that you've attached in your software program won't transfer over to the GEDCOM file.

In almost all instances, a GEDCOM does a perfect job of transmitting standard data such as names, dates, and places. However, there are times when your notes may not convert seamlessly. In this case, the person receiving your GEDCOM may have to do a little editing.

Creating a GEDCOM

Each program has a unique process for creating the GEDCOM, but this overview should apply to most programs. To create a GEDCOM, open the family file then select Export from your File menu. You will probably be asked whether you want to export the entire file or only part of it.

You'll also choose whether you want to export all of the information (notes, sources, etc.) and whether you want data for living people to be suppressed.

After you've set the parameters, choose a file name and then click Save. You can now share your findings with your family or other researchers.

Opening a GEDCOM

If you receive a GEDCOM file from another researcher (or download it from the internet), save the file to your hard drive and make a note of the file's name and location. Before opening, be sure to scan the file with your antivirus software.

Next, open your genealogy software program and from the File menu, select Import. Locate the file on your computer, select it, and click the Open or OK button. If it looks like the file contains quality information, you can either save it in your own software's native format or merge it with an existing file.

GOING SOCIAL

Although Twitter, Facebook, and YouTube may seem like the playground of the young, they're rapidly becoming popular with genealogists. Where else can you instantly meet new researchers, share findings, join special interest groups, or get help from across the globe?

At their heart, social networks are like the nineteenth-century country store, except they're online. Social networks are places where people can check in during the day, say hi, share a link to an interesting news article, let everyone know about a helpful blog post, or spend an hour talking about genealogy.

Twitter

Twitter isn't just for kids. It's true, Twitter initially struck a chord with the "texting" generation because "the kids" were used to sending brief messages using lots of shorthand:

- GTG (got to go)
- SB (stand by)
- TLK2UL8R (talk to you later)
- YR (yeah right)
- BBL (be back later)

Like texting, Twitter limits your message to 140 characters (counting spaces). That may not seem like a lot, but you'd be surprised what can fit in a Tweet.

- *Please RT: Family Tree Univ Virtual Conference - register before July 15 for early bird rate (tweet, tweet!) http://p-k.me/kT #genealogy*
- *Part 1 of how to climb your French family tree - a quick (kind of!) guide to French genealogy http://p-k.me/xj #french #genealogy*
- *Tension between black and white Union soldiers on Gulf Coast #CivilWar prison http://p-k.me/sj*
- *#honoringancestors Robert Dimmitt, b @1762, Baltimore, MD. My 5th great-grandfather, died @1810, Tennessee #genealogy*
- *This time in Family Tree Finders Weekly: societies using social media, shipwrecks, and genealogy vacations http://bit.ly/jlwPjv*
- *@genealogyteach #FF @SligoGenealogy @geneabloggers @SocAustGen @genealogyteach @jencoffeelover @FGS2011 @ngsgenealogy*

As you read these, you might have noticed a couple of curiosities: the RT, the # (hashtag), the @ (at), and #FF.

The RT is shorthand for retweet. A retweet is when you pick up someone else's tweet and send it out on your own Twitter feed. It's a quick way to spread the same message to lots of different people. It's as easy as clicking the "retweet" button on a Twitter post. You can ask others to RT to spread your own Twitter posts; in this case I was asking other genealogists to retweet a notice about an early-bird discount at Family Tree University <familytreeuniversity.com>.

The # (hashtag) is a commonly used symbol on Twitter. It's a way to tag a keyword. Twitter users can search by hashtag, so if you're interested in genealogy, you can go to Twitter's search box <http://search.twitter.com/> and search *#genealogy*. You'll then get a list of all of the recent tweets that used that hashtag. Click on a user's icon to see their profile.

The @ (at) symbol is used to mention a Twitter user. So if you wanted to mention me in a tweet, you would use @genealogyteach.

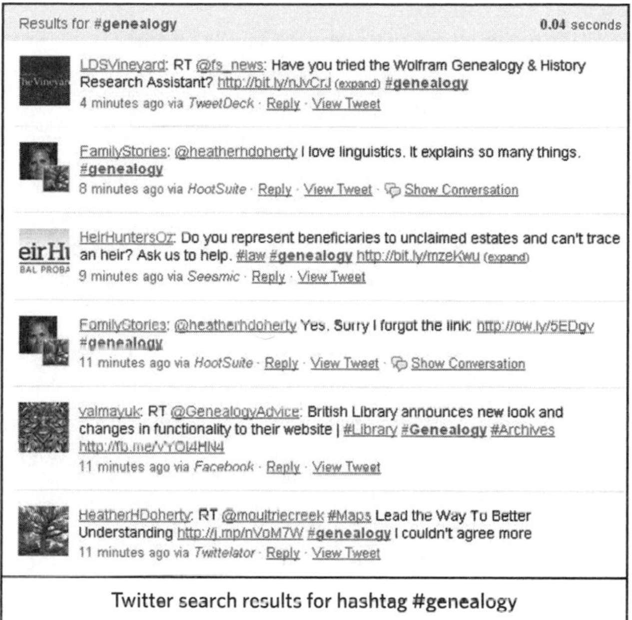

Twitter search results for hashtag #genealogy

The #FF is a hashtag that you'll often see on Fridays—that's because it's shorthand for "follow Friday." It's common for Twitter users to tweet a list of their favorite people on Fridays—in short, alerting their followers to other people who are worth following.

For genealogists, there's really no value in having thousands of followers or following thousands because it's impossible to read the posts of that many people. The real value lies in following people who post valuable tweets or following organizations you belong to or are interested in.

Some possible follows are:

- FamilyTreeU (Family Tree University)
- genealogyteach (me!)
- geneabloggers (Geneabloggers)
- rjseaver (Randy Seaver, Geneamusings)
- LisaCooke (Lisa Louise Cooke, Genealogy Gems Podcast)

Many state and local historical and genealogical societies also have Twitter accounts:

- Virginia Historical Society (vahistorical)
- Kentucky Historical Society (kyhistsoc)
- Smithsonian Civil War (smithsonianCW)
- CAancestors (California Genealogical Society)
- IlGenSoc (Illinois State Genealogical Society)

If you're researching non-U.S. genealogy, you'll find many UK, Irish, Scottish, and Jewish genealogists on Twitter.

Twitter is also a place where you'll find breaking genealogy news, links to excellent articles and blog posts, or sites to network with people researching your surname, your state, or your field of interest.

Facebook

In the summer of 2011, Facebook's user population topped 750 million, more than double the population of the United States. While Facebook began as a network for college students, it's expanded to include just about every demographic, from universities and sports teams to political parties and activists. And among the demographic are genealogists.

Here's the low-down on how Facebook (FB) works. Once you join (it's free), you can "friend" people by finding your friends or relatives (search by name or e-mail address) and then sending a friend request. If they accept the request, you're now FB friends.

Each time you post something on your wall (the wall is a way of telling people what you're doing), this post (called a status update) is automatically posted on their Facebook Home page. They can "like" what you said or comment on it.

For families with members spread across the country (or the globe), Facebook is an easy way to keep in touch, share family news, chat in real time, or share photos. You can even find free apps just for the genealogy crowd, including Family Village (a game like FarmVille), Mundia (search Ancestry.com's public trees), and Live Roots.

Don't want everyone knowing what you're up to? You can use the FB privacy settings to determine who sees what.

While many genealogists confine their "friends" to real friends and family, Facebook also has something called Pages (formerly called Fan Pages). Pages are a place for people of similar interests to congregate. For example, there may be a Page for your alma mater or your local bookseller.

There are also genealogy-related Pages that you can "like," including:

- Allen County (Indiana) Public Library (home of PERSI) <facebook.com/AllenCountyLibrary>
- Association for Gravestone Studies <facebook.com/gravestonestudies>
- *Family Tree Magazine* <facebook.com/familytreemagazine>
- Find A Grave <facebook.com/pages/Find-A-Grave/56406323679>
- Fold3.com <facebook.com/footnotepage>
- Olive Tree Genealogy <www.facebook.com/pages/Olive-Tree-Genealogy/16127378259>

If you love Facebook, think about starting a surname Page or a Group. To start a Group, log in to your Facebook account and click Home at the top of the page, then click Groups on the left, then Create a Group at the top. You can now invite anyone else to join the group.

Want to limit who can access the Group? Not a problem; it's easy to set up a private Group. With a private Group, you'll need to OK membership. When anyone posts within the Group, their posts are *not* seen on their friends' walls; posts to private group walls can only be seen by other group members.

Are you interested in sharing ancestral photos with Facebook friends? You can create albums for ancestor photos, cemeteries, and even records you've digitized. Post them to your Facebook ancestor album, then click the Share button to post them to your profile or send to friends. You can even tag images with names.

YOUR SOCIAL PROFILE

As you visit social sites, you'll quickly get a feel for which ones are a good fit for you and which ones aren't. On the sites you like, you'll need to set up your profile.

If you're very private, you may not want to post any information about yourself. But we do recommend sharing enough information so other researchers have some idea of the surnames you're searching. We don't recommend including anything personal, such as an address or phone number. In addition, you may not want to include a date of birth.

Your social profile will only go so far in attracting the attention of other researchers. To interact you'll need to begin posting to Facebook or Twitter.

Etiquette here is the same as it would be in person. Use the sites to make new friends, share goals, accomplishments, tips, and successful techniques.

After all, it's about sharing.

Social Bookmarking

When you find a genealogy website you like, you can create a Bookmark or Favorite in your browser. Social bookmarks work the same way, but instead of sitting on your computer, they're online at bookmarking sites where other people can see them.

Why would you want to use a social bookmarking site?

So much of genealogy is about sharing what you've found. When you create online bookmarks, you're telling other people, "Hey! This is a really good genealogy site and worth visiting." Social bookmarking sites are all about sharing sites you like.

Some of the most popular social bookmarking sites are:

- Digg <digg.com>
- StumbleUpon <stumbleupon.com>
- Reddit <reddit.com>
- Yahoo! Bookmarks <bookmarks.yahoo.com/welcome>
- Google Bookmarks <google.com/bookmarks>
- Delicious <www.delicious.com/>
- Fark <fark.com>

You'll have to create free accounts at these sites to use them. You've probably seen bookmarking icons, but may not have known what they're for. The most common place you'll see them is on a blog. At the end of the blog post, or somewhere in the sidebar, you'll

Samples of social bookmarking icons found on blogs

often see a block of social bookmark icons. If you like the blog post, you can click the icon, and the site will be saved to your bookmarking account.

The block of icons will vary depending on which site you're on, but they all work the same way. You click an icon, the site is saved to your social bookmarks, and other people see that you like the post. People viewing your bookmarks can click them to visit the sites. Social bookmarking is simply one person telling another person who tells another person to go look at this site.

YouTube

Even if you don't want to make videos, you may want to watch them—particularly genealogy tutorial videos. You may not consider YouTube <youtube.com> a social networking site, but it can be. If you want to make videos, YouTube allows you to create a free account, a free channel (kind of like your own TV station), and upload videos.

Your videos could be:

- family reunions
- family trips
- cemetery videos
- historic site videos
- genealogy tutorials

If you're not into creating videos, search YouTube to find genealogy resources like *Family Tree Magazine*'s how-to videos <youtube.com/user/familytreemagazine>

or the National Archives videos on federal records <youtube.com/user/usnationalarchives>.

Maybe you'd like to make videos but want them to be private. That's not a problem because YouTube's settings allow you to keep your video unlisted, viewable only by people to whom you've given a link.

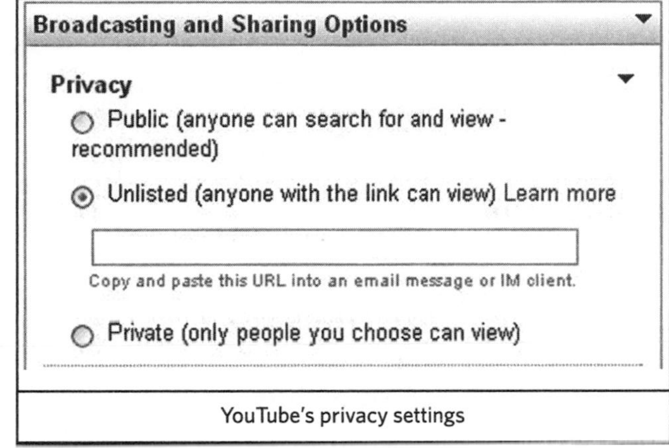

YouTube's privacy settings

NEWSLETTERS

Another way to share your research findings is a family newsletter. These newsletters can have many different goals:

1. Sharing research findings with family
2. Trading family recipes, legends, stories
3. Just keeping in touch
4. Sharing old family photos

A newsletter can bring a family closer as well as introduce cousins who've never met in person. Your idea of what a newsletter should be may be very loosely defined; you may want to write up something only when you've made a major research breakthrough. Or you may want to publish on a quarterly schedule, reaching out to other family for contributions. If the latter, a little planning now will save you headaches later.

Things to consider:

- How often do you want to publish?
- How long will the newsletter be?
- Will you be the sole writer, or will you ask for contributions from other family members?
- Will the newsletter have a specific focus?
- How much time and effort are you willing to invest?
- Will you include ongoing columns on specific topics?
- What format will you use for the newsletter?

If you're the sole writer, editor, publisher, and chief bottle washer, and you're uncertain of the time commitment, you may want to publish sporadically. If the family enthusiastically pitches in, quarterly may be your best bet.

When you're starting out, it's tempting to write about everything you know in the very first issue. However, you don't want to run out of steam with issue number one and then have nothing else to say. Advance planning makes it easier to balance each issue with an interesting variety of topics.

If you don't want to be the sole contributor, e-mail your family members and let them know that you'd like their help. If they volunteer, give them a deadline.

Newsletter Topics

Here are a few ideas to get you started:

VITAL STATISTICS. Include the birth, marriage, and death dates of a few ancestors in each issue. This data gives family members an opportunity to check their own records and correspond about any discrepancies.

CULTURAL/RELIGIOUS HERITAGE. Does your family have an interesting cultural or religious heritage, like Acadian, Palatine, or Huguenots? If you've researched this background, share what you've learned. Your family will be thrilled to learn about their cultural heritage.

FAMILY RECIPES. Every family has favorite recipes. In mine, it's Grandma's apple dumplings and Mom's potato salad.

I REMEMBER GRANDMA. Ask family members to share their memories of one specific ancestor. You'll be surprised how each person's memories differ. In my family, one cousin remembers Grandma's homemade blackberry lemonade, while my sister remembers her hollyhocks.

SINGLE-TOPIC ISSUES. Consider dedicating an entire issue to a single topic, like "Our Indiana Ancestors," or "Our Civil War Ancestors." These mini-biographies are priceless additions to family histories, and help us see our ancestors as real people.

OLD DOCUMENTS. For whatever reason, my ancestors didn't save letters, military papers, diaries, or much else on paper. I think it's because they couldn't read! So of course, I'm in envy of all the families who still have these treasured mementoes. If you own old documents, transcribe them and include excerpts in your newsletter.

FAMILY HAPPENINGS. There's always something going on—marriages, new babies, graduations, deaths, promotions, engagements, or a new home.

GENEALOGY RESEARCH PROJECTS. If your newsletter goes to a group who is active in genealogy research, you can use the newsletter to share research discoveries or even to split research tasks to avoid duplicating efforts.

FAVORITE FAMILY STORY. Every family has a favorite silly story. For me, it's a toss-up between Grandpa eating dog food and my brother falling down a sewer. Forty years later, we still laugh about the sewer incident.

WHERE OUR FAMILY LIVED. Did your family come from a small village in France or a bustling German town? If someone in the family has visited the family homestead, a newsletter is a great place to share photos and stories.

WHEN WE WERE KIDS. Ask your oldest living relatives to write about their childhoods. Their remembrances will give your children a look at a society that they probably can't even imagine. If your elderly relative doesn't want to write, give them a phone call and capture the story for them.

FORUMS

Genealogy forums are one of the oldest online methods of sharing what you've found or asking for help with a research problem. Posting a query on a forum may bring you a quick, positive response, or you may have to wait a year or more before you learn anything new. But at least the query is out there and one day the right person will see it.

Using forums and posting queries are two very good reasons for you to acquire a "genealogy-only" e-mail address. (It's easy to create a free e-mail account. Try <gmail.com> or <mail.yahoo.com>.)

Some of the queries you'll see online are from ten years ago. Sadly, when you try to connect with the person who posted, you may find that the e-mail address no longer exists. With a free e-mail account dedicated only to genealogy, you can always keep the same address, no matter how many different cable or DSL providers you have. And, when that right person finds your query, they'll still be able to contact you even if its years after you made the post.

Three of my favorite forums for posting or reading queries are:

USGENWEB <usgenweb.com> Find details about this site in chapter four. Every county has a place to leave queries about ancestors who lived there.

GENFORUM <genforum.com> This forum, which is actually comprised of thousands of forums, has been in existence for many years. Here you'll find forums for virtually every surname, as well as U.S. states, countries, and topics.

Use the Forum Finder to locate your surname forum, then write your post. You'll need to register (it's free) to post on GenForum but not to read the messages. If you want to contact a forum user, click their name and you'll see their e-mail, but it will be embedded in an image. This keeps spammers from trolling through the forums and picking up e-mail addresses.

After you're in a surname forum (like the Wilson Forum), you can search within that specific forum. This will save you the time of reading through every single post on the boards.

ROOTSWEB <boards.rootsweb.com> This is the largest online community, with more than seventeen million posts on more than 161,000 boards. Use the search box to find forums by keyword or by topic.

If you get thousands of hits, use the Advanced Search to filter by message type and the time frame within which the message was posted.

BLOGS

Blogs are free, easy to set up, and the quickest way for you to share your family tree with the world. If you're interested in building a blog, but don't know how, Family Tree University <familytreeuniversity.com> offers a four-week course; at the end of four weeks your site will be up and running.

But if you want to try building on your own, two excellent free services for blog building are Wordpress <wordpress.com> and Blogger <www.google.com/blogger>. In a nutshell, Wordpress offers more flexibility (you have more control over the look and setup, but you need more tech knowledge to exercise this control), while Blogger is a little more user-friendly. However, both afford you the opportunity to quickly and easily build beautiful family tree sites to share with the world. (Wordpress and Blogger both have privacy settings if you want a family-only site that is not viewable by the rest of the world.)

Even though the websites are built using a blog platform, it doesn't mean you have to write something every day. Using a blog service just makes it easy to build a site, which you can then add to at your convenience.

The website shown here, Roseland Roots, was created by Kim Alfano in Family Tree University's four-week course on building a family website.

Roseland Roots blog, Kim Alfano, on Wordpress.com

Personal websites like these blogs are where many of us find genealogy gems. It really is easy, and if you hit a challenge, you can take a class or use YouTube to find Wordpress and Blogger tutorials.

SHARING, IT'S A GOOD THING

Some of my most valuable discoveries have been a result of information shared by other genealogists. A simple query brought me a multigenerational genealogy from a fellow researcher; Twitter friends have led me to data-rich blogs and websites; and Google searches have opened up a whole world of family-related images thanks to other genealogists posting their information online.

If you have family information that you'd like to share, start posting online, including:

- your own blog
- bulletin boards
- a county page at the USGenWeb
- on Twitter or Facebook
- forums

You never know when your act of kindness will repay you a hundredfold.

Putting It All to Work

When you began this journey, you started with charts, forms, and simple searching. With each new chapter, you gained the skills needed to excel at using the internet in genealogy research.

In this chapter, you're going to see many of these techniques used in real-life examples. But before getting to the examples, there's one last technique I'd like to share. It's a mind-mapping technique I've developed and used over many years to "see" a genealogy problem in a different light.

A typical genealogy search is linear. By that, I mean it starts at Point A and methodically works its way to Point B, Point C, and so on. A mind mapping approach is more free-flowing; it starts at Point A, but instead of moving to Point B, the clues may lead you to Point R.

I use genealogy mind mapping to simply get all of the thoughts out of my head and onto paper (or software) in a way that I can more readily see connections.

If you're not familiar with mind mapping, it's a graphical method of connecting words and ideas that relate to a central keyword or idea. In the simple mind map example image, the central idea is "cookies," and the spokes represent thoughts that relate to cookies.

In its most simple form, mind mapping is a way of graphically brainstorming. With mind mapping, you can create a picture of all the thoughts you have on a subject. It's really a form of random association.

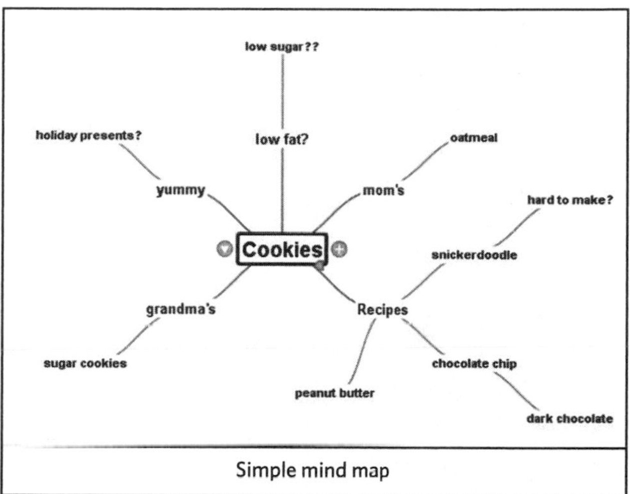

Simple mind map

Although you can certainly achieve the same outcome using other methods, such as list making (if you are more of a linear thinker), I like mind mapping because it's visual, and it helps me take all of the parts and pieces of a puzzle and begin to make sense of them.

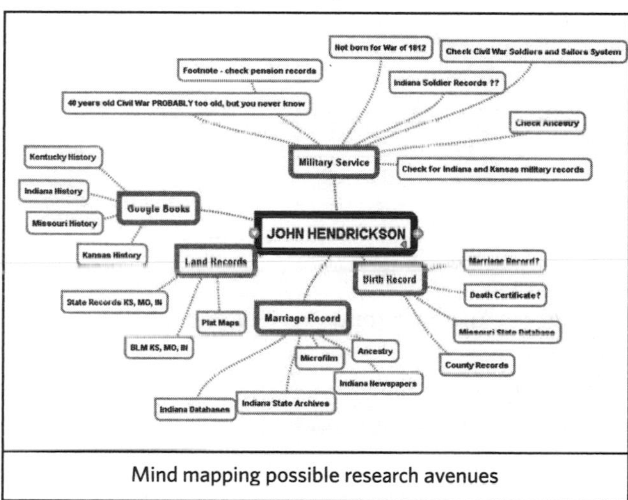

Mind mapping possible research avenues

Mind mapping for genealogy is just a technique of stating a research problem (the central hub of the spoke), then writing down all the ideas associated with it. In the example at the right, you'll see the research ideas I had when deciding what I needed to research about John Hendrickson, my great-great-grandfather, and what websites I wanted to search.

As you can see, my major areas of focus are land, marriage, birth, military, and Google Books. From each of these topics, I've created subtopics with ideas or questions I had, as well as the websites I needed to explore.

Again, you can create the same kind of list in your genealogy software, in a spreadsheet, or in a word-processing document. However, I personally like working in this fashion because a picture sticks with me more than a list.

If you'd like to try genealogy mind mapping, you can download free programs:

- The Brain <www.thebrain.com>

- MindMeister <www.mindmeister.com>
- Mindomo <www.mindomo.com>

Now on to the examples of internet research.

TECHNIQUE 1: WORKING WITH AN UNUSUAL SURNAME

In chapter three you learned how to refine searches when working with a common surname. Now let's talk about the opposite—the unusual surname. Mine is Faulkenberry, also spelled Falconbury, Falkenbery, and a half-dozen other variations.

My suggestion for your search may seem unusual, but it can bring amazing results. You're going to search the U.S. Geographic Names Information System (GNIS) <geonames.usgs.gov/pls/gnispublic>. This site can be used to find places (including historic places) in and outside of the United States.

Instead of entering a place name in the query form, enter your unusual surname to see if any places have the same name. When I entered Faulkenberry, GNIS returned four locations—three in Limestone County, Texas: Faulkenberry Creek, Faulkenberry Cemetery, and Rocky Creek (variant name).

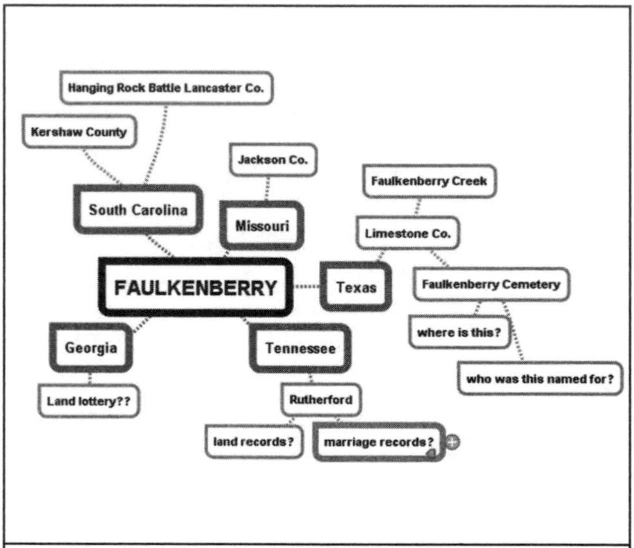

Mind mapping ideas from military and land records

Although I wasn't aware of any of the family living in Texas, I recall a note, apparently written in the 1930s, that my Aunt Mollie Belle Cave wrote about my ancestor Thomas Faulkenberry. The note said, "After moving from Tennessee to Missouri, Thomas traveled to Texas, but did not like it so he shortly returned to Missouri." I had always wondered what prompted the brief stay. I now had a place in Texas to begin searching.

The mind map here depicts research ideas based on the GNIS findings and the info from the Revolutionary War Bounty Land and Pension search in chapter eight.

TAKE-AWAY: Begin thinking outside of the "genealogy-only" box.

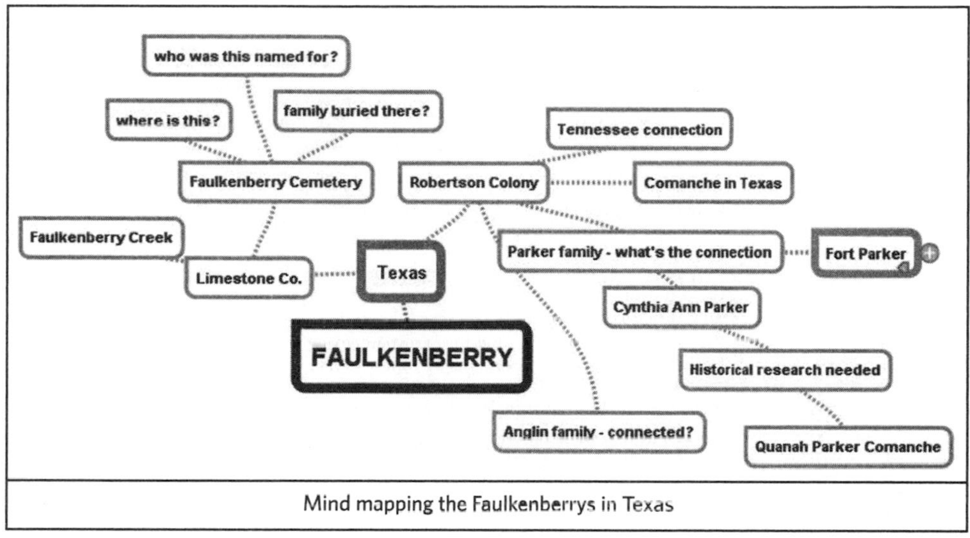

Mind mapping the Faulkenberrys in Texas

TECHNIQUE 2: YOUR "CLIP FILE" OF STATE-RELATED RESOURCES

Back in chapter one I wrote about the importance of starting your own clip file of state resources. Continuing my Texas adventure, I went to my clip file and found *The Handbook of Texas Online* <www.tshaonline.org/handbook>. The handbook contains more than 23,000 articles on Texas history and culture.

I entered Faulkenberry in the search engine. One of the four results noted that Faulkenberry Creek was probably named for David Faulkenberry, who settled in the area in 1835 as part of Sterling C. Robertson's colony.

David and Evan Faulkenberry reportedly helped repel the Indian attack on Fort Parker on May 19, 1836, but arrived too late to save Cynthia Ann Parker and four others from being taken captive.

A second entry said David came to Texas with a group from Illinois, including the Parker and Anglin families.

Following the leads in the handbook, I learned more about the Robertson Colony, including the fact that Robertson recruited settlers in Tennessee. Because I knew that "my" Faulkenberrys had been in Tennessee, I was pretty sure there was a connection. Even more to research!

I created another mind map, this one concentrating on all the questions I had about the Texas connection. As you can see, once I begin adding what I've learned, new questions appear—and possible avenues of research.

TAKE-AWAY: Develop your clip file of state (or topic) online resources.

Tip: Find content with a Creative Commons license. Learn more...

☑ Only search within **Creative Commons**-licensed content

☑ Find content to use commercially

☑ Find content to modify, adapt, or build upon

Searching Flickr for images within Creative Commons

This photo is © All Rights Reserved

View all sizes: Medium 500 • Medium 640 • Large

Flickr prevents downloading of images when all rights are reserved

TECHNIQUE 3: TRACKING DOWN IMAGES

In technique one I found Faulkenberry Cemetery on the GNIS site. I'm going to use the Google Images search to see if I can find an image of this cemetery that I can use in my genealogy reports.

From the Google Home page, I clicked on Images and then entered the search term: *Faulkenberry cemetery.* The Results page included several images, but none were copyright free, meaning I can't use them in my reports..

Next I went to Flickr <flickr.com> and used the Advanced Search option. I specified the results include only photos that fall within the Creative Commons license for commercial use. (Follow the links to learn about the various types of licenses.) For my purposes I'm searching for an Attribution, which means I can use the photo if I give credit to the image owner.

Attribution means:
You let others copy, distribute, display, and perform your copyrighted work - and derivative works based upon it - but only if they give you credit.

Noncommercial means:
You let others copy, distribute, display, and perform your work - and derivative works based upon it - but for noncommercial purposes only.

No Derivative Works means:
You let others copy, distribute, display, and perform only verbatim copies of your work, not derivative works based upon it.

Share Alike means:
You allow others to distribute derivative works only under a license identical to the license that governs your work.

The different types of Flickr's Creative Commons licenses are clearly stated

If you try to save a photo that isn't within one of the Creative Commons license types, a pop-up box will appear on the photo. Unfortunately, no Faulkenberry Cemetery images fell under a Creative Commons Attribution license, so I e-mailed image owners asking

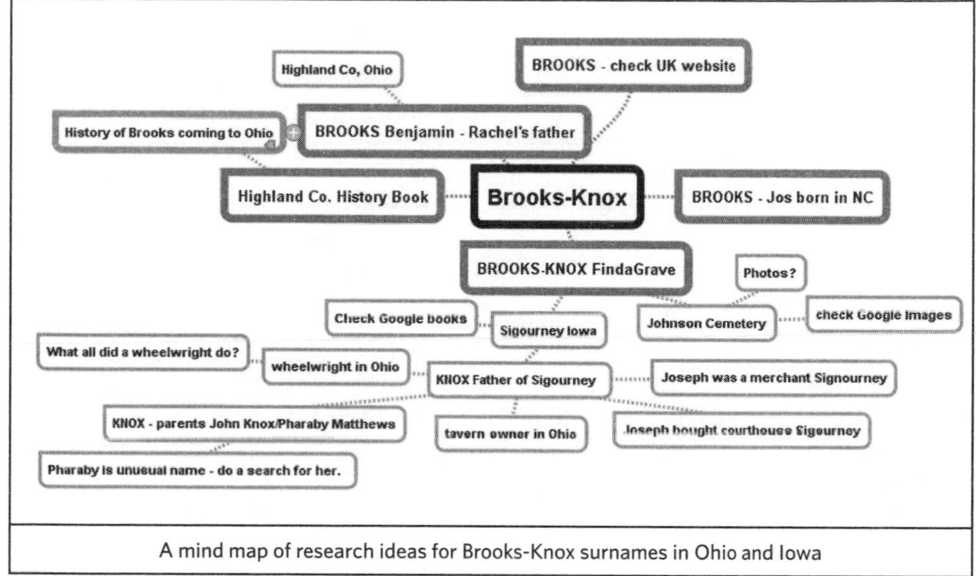

A mind map of research ideas for Brooks-Knox surnames in Ohio and Iowa

for permission to use their photo. While waiting, I launched Google Earth and flew to the cemetery, then captured a screenshot from the aerial view.

NOTE: Per Google, pictures such as the one I want of the cemetery can be used for noncommercial purposes. If you want to use an image in a book that you're going to sell, check the Google website for permission guidelines.

TAKE AWAY: Think "aerial" if you can't find a ground-level photo.

TECHNIQUE 4: COMPLEX GOOGLE SEARCHES

In chapter three you discovered "search-engine math"—that algebraic-looking way of crafting a complex search. Here, I'll use this technique to track down information on my fourth-great-grandparents, Joseph Knox and Rachel Brooks.

First, I did a search for: *""Joseph Knox" "Rachel Brooks""*.

The first result was a Find A Grave <findagrave.com> listing for Joseph and Rachel at the Johnson Cemetery, Sigourney, Keokuk County, Iowa. I was surprised to read that Joseph was considered "The Father of Sigourney." My sister reminded me that our great-aunt had lived in Sigourney, but we had no idea the family connection went back further. Among the Google search results, I also found Rachel's father, Benjamin, and a Highland County, Ohio, connection.

Because Joseph Knox was born in North Carolina, I wanted to do another search but omit the North Carolina results just to see what I could find that was more Iowa-centric: *""Joseph Knox" Sigourney Iowa -"North Carolina""*.

This search led to several gems, including information about Joseph's house and his position as a leading merchant of Sigourney. I also learned the exact location of Joseph and Rachel's burial plots.

I followed another search results to the Keokuk County pages of the USGenWeb <usgenweb.com>. There I read that "On the removal of the county-seat to Lancaster the court-house became the property of Mr. Joseph Knox who was one of the most successful merchants of early days, and after his day it fell into other hands and continued in use till 1873, when it was removed two miles east of Sigourney and is now doing duty as a cow stable on the farm of Mr. Win. Bineman."

Another search result link took me to a user-uploaded GEDCOM on the WorldConnect Project <wc.rootsweb.ancestry.com>; the GEDCOM included information on Joseph's siblings and parents (John Knox, Phereby [Pharaby] Matthews).

Now back to Rachel's father, Benjamin, and Ohio. I tried this search formula: *""Rachel Brooks" Benjamin Highland Ohio "Joseph Knox""*.

This search garnered information on Joseph as a wheelwright in Ohio as well as tavern owner. The post, found on GenForum.com, also noted that the family moved to Wells County, Indiana, but later left when the Blackhawk War broke out.

Another search of *""Benjamin Brooks" Highland Ohio"* included a Brooks family website, based in the U.K. This means cousins I can contact for networking (chapter 13).

The mind map for this technique covers research idea in Ohio and Iowa. Also, because of the unusual name "Pharaby Matthews," I will search that too (much easier than looking for "John Knox"!)

TAKE-AWAY: Be creative in your Google searches; remember to add and subtract phrases and keywords. Follow the clues in the relevant search results.

TECHNIQUE 5: GOOGLE BOOKS

While my Google searches provided me with great web results, I'm wondering if there are any books that have information about Joseph Knox and Rachel Brooks. I can find the answer to this on Google Books <books.google.com>. I entered the search-engine operators *""Rachel Brooks" Benjamin Highland Ohio "Joseph Knox""*.

The results include several mentions of Joseph in a history of Highland County, Ohio. The same book also has a history of Benjamin Brooks and his family's travels from Pennsylvania to Ohio. Further, I learned that one of Rachel's brothers had been a surveyor of the Northwest Territory with Gen. Massie.

If I had wanted to limit my results to return only books and documents that can be read in their entirety, I could have selected the advance search option and selected the filter for "full view."

TAKE-AWAY: Google Books can provide an invaluable glimpse into the past—including your ancestors' names, occupations, towns, and events.

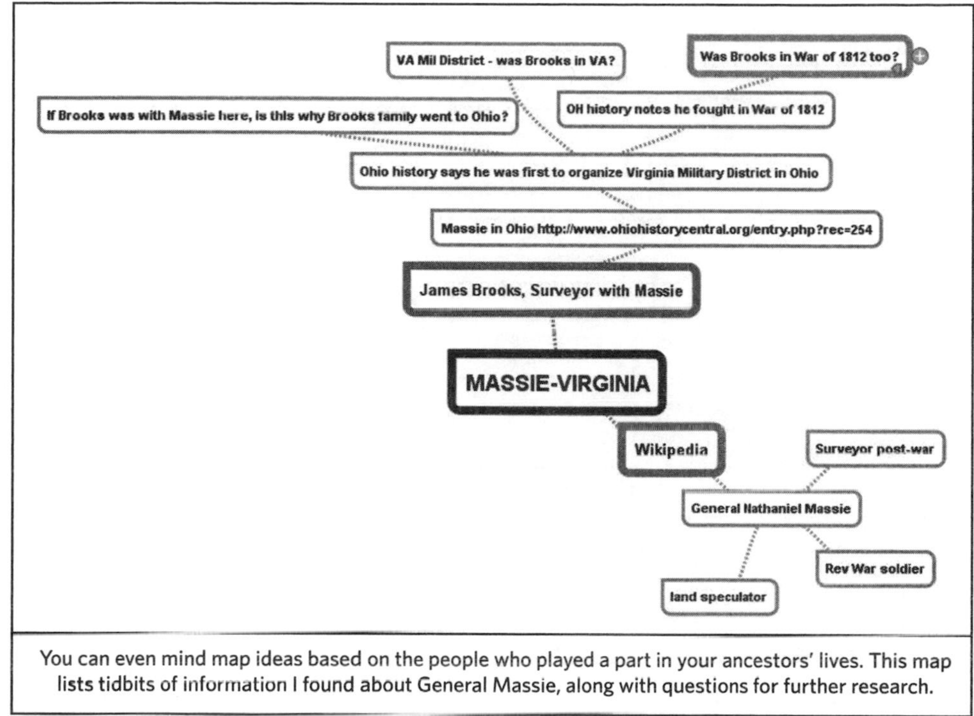

You can even mind map ideas based on the people who played a part in your ancestors' lives. This map lists tidbits of information I found about General Massie, along with questions for further research.

TECHNIQUE 6: RESEARCH FAMOUS FIGURES CONNECTED TO YOUR FAMILY

The Highland County history book says one of Benjamin Brooks's sons had been a surveyor of the Northwest Territory with General Massie. To learn more about this ancestor's life, I need to research Gen. Massie.

I first did a Wikipedia and then a Google search for Gen. Massie. There is a tremendous amount of information on him online, including his Revolutionary War service, his surveying days, his being a congressman from the new state of Ohio, and serving in the War of 1812.

Because Rachel's brother, James, is so vividly described as a bigger-than-life character in the history of Highland County, Ohio, I wondered if James had been in the War of 1812 as well.

Because Gen. Massie was from Virginia, I searched for Benjamin Brooks in Virginia, as a Revolutionary War soldier. My search took me to fold3.com <fold3.com>, Ancestry.com <ancestry.com>, and the Bounty Land and Pension records at FamilySearch.org <familysearch.org>. I had no trouble finding Revolutionary War Benjamin Brooks from Virginia, but I have no proof that any one of the Benjamins is my Benjamin. However there are many possibilities to follow.

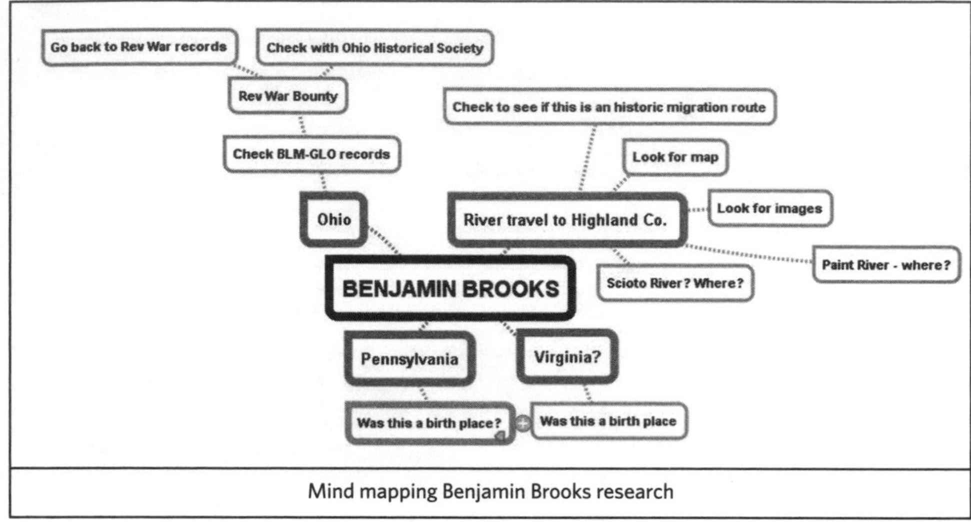

Mind mapping Benjamin Brooks research

TAKE AWAY: Search for people your ancestors worked or served with.

TECHNIQUE 7: LOOK FOR LAND RECORDS

The Highland County history included Benjamin Brooks's route from Pennsylvania to Ohio. According to the history, his route took him down the Ohio River to the mouth of the Scioto River and later to the mouth of the Paint River.

I typed *Ohio map with rivers* to visualize this route. I found a very helpful map in the results: <geology.com/lakes-rivers-water/ohio.shtml>.

My next question is did Benjamin own land in Ohio? Using the techniques explained in chapter eight, I went to the Bureau of Land Management, General Land Office (GLO) website <www.glorecords.blm.gov> and searched for Benjamin Brooks in Ohio. The results included four land warrants, three of them in conjunction with Nathaniel Massie (the same General Massie of the American Revolution). Of those three, the GLO site notes:

> *Due to the lack of precise information on where the land was located, it was not possible to tie this record to a specific land description. In the late 1790's and early 1800's, several dozen volumes of Ohio military bounty warrants were issued to Virginia veterans of the Revolutionary War. The lands were in the Virginia Military District in central Ohio (between the Scioto River and Little Miami River). We recommend you contact the Ohio Historical Society State Archives once you have a specific warrant number. They may be able to help you obtain a more precise location of the land.*

This information seems to verify the information in the Highland County history. It also creates another Virginia and Revolutionary War connection for Benjamin Brooks.

TECHNIQUE 8: FAMILYSEARCH ORIGINAL SITE

I returned to FamilySearch.org, but this time clicked the "go to previous site" link. In searching for Benjamin Brooks, there was one listing in the Ancestral File. It showed a Benjamin, son of Robert Brooke, with brothers William and Thomas.

I had read on a GenForum.com post that three of Benjamin's brothers were with Daniel Boone at Boonesborough.

In looking back at the Boonesborough information, two of the three Brooks brothers with Daniel Boone were William and Thomas. Could this be the same family?

What really caught my attention was a note attached to this file stating that Benjamin Brooks's will was probated on June 8, 1809, in Highland County, Ohio. It also lists Benjamin's place of birth as Virginia.

Using the Family History Library catalog, I located the microfilm for 1809 Highland County, Ohio, wills. I logged into FamilySearch.org and ordered the microfilm. I'm hoping the will provides more information to help me push this family back one more generation.

In the past, you had to physically go to a FamilySearch Center to order microfilms. You can now order them online and have them delivered to your nearest FamilySearch Center.

To order, click Sign In from the FamilySearch.org Home page. If you don't have an account (they're free), you'll set one up now. Once you have an account, go to <familysearch.org/films>. You'll be asked to choose a default Center; next enter the ID number of the film or fiche you want to order. You can pay with a credit card or PayPal.

TIP

If you're new to FamilySearch.org, you may not know about the Ancestral File. These are files that contain lineage-linked names, dates and places for birth, marriage and death of millions of individuals. Records in the Ancestral File were member submitted prior to 1991. No notes or source information is given. The information you find here needs to be verified, but can be used as a starting point in your research.

While waiting for the microfilm, I decided to search the public member trees at Ancestry.com. Wouldn't you know it—there, in one of the trees, was a transcript of Benjamin Brooks's will, including mention of his wife, Nancy. Now I had one more important clue (the name of his wife)—and hopefully can find a marriage record using this information.

TAKE-AWAY: Note every scrap of information, then decide how to begin researching for verification (unless the material has a source).

TECHNIQUE 9: FOLLOWING THE CLUES—FREE AND FEE SITES

I'm going to stick with the Knox-Brooks line and see what clues I can pick up along the way. I may not reach a final conclusion, but I'm confident that I'll find several leads.

Per the GEDCOM I found on WorldConnect, Joseph and Rachel had fifteen children; the oldest was John, who married Isabel Bay. One of John and Isabel's children was James, my great-great-grandfather.

One of the stories I remembered hearing from my grandmother was that her grandfather (James Knox) had been wounded in the knee during the Battle of Shiloh. Since I knew he was a Civil War veteran, I went to fold3.com and searched the Compiled Civil War Service Records.

From fold3.com's home page, select the Browse option, then Civil War as the category, and from there scroll down to find the Union Service Records. You can then further filter by state.

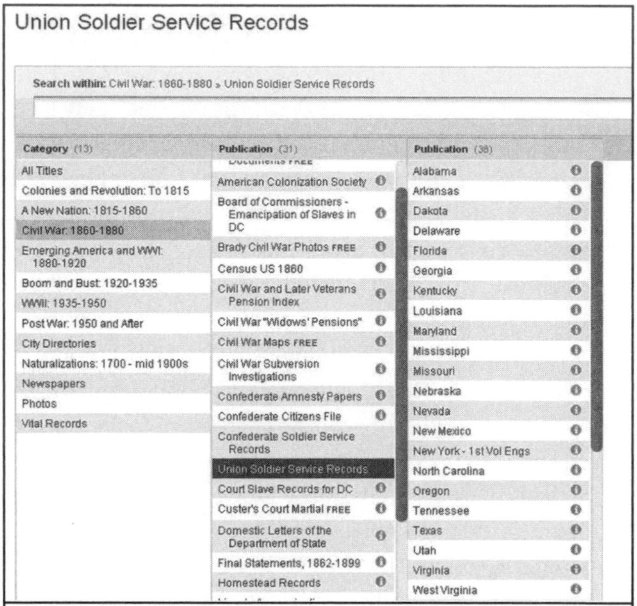

Filter Civil War records by type and state, fold3.com

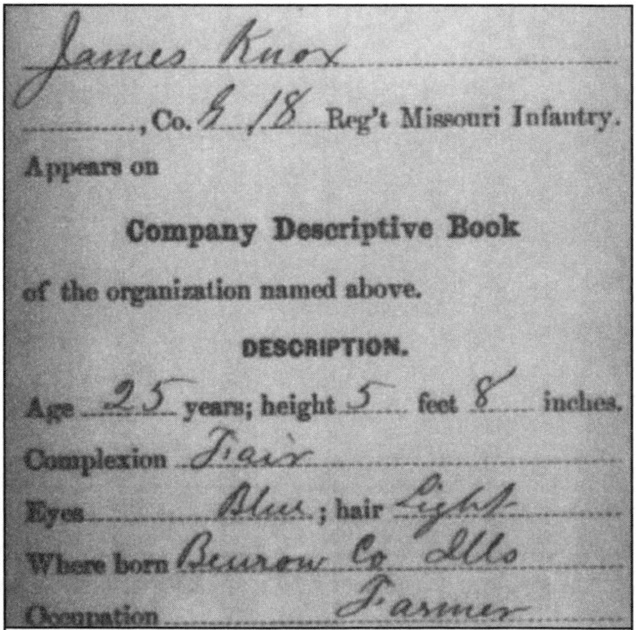

James Knox

........., Co. G 18 Reg't Missouri Infantry.

Appears on

Company Descriptive Book

of the organization named above.

DESCRIPTION.

Age 25 years; height 5 feet 8 inches.

Complexion Fair

Eyes Blue; hair Light

Where born Benrow Co Ills

Occupation Farmer

Civil War enlistment papers included a physical description, fold3.com

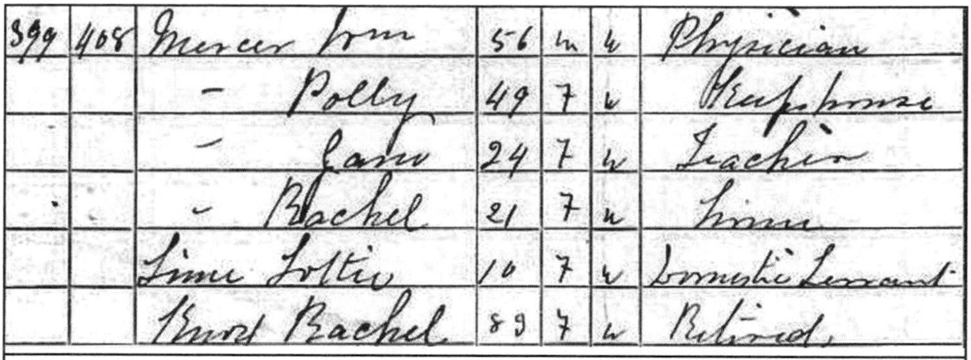

1870 census, Bureau County, Illinois, Ancestry.com

A search of fold3.com's Compiled Civil War Service Records found that James was born in "Beurow" [Bureau] County, Illinois.

When searching the 1870 federal census for Rachel Brooks Knox (I know that Joseph was no longer living in 1870), I found a Rachel living with the William and Polly Mercer family in Bureau County, Illinois.

Polly is Rachel's daughter (information gathered from another family researcher). The 1870 census shows Rachel as being blind and having been born in Pennsylvania.

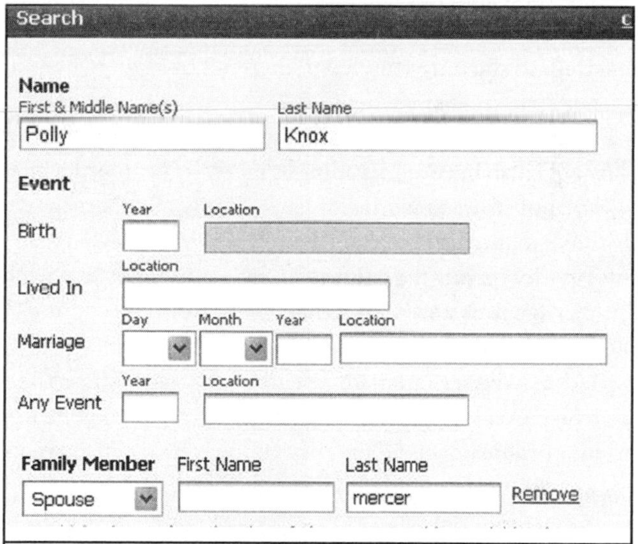

Marriage search, Ancestry.com

Two things to note: First, I don't have *absolute* proof that this Rachel is the one I'm looking for, although it's about as close as I'll get (name of daughter, son-in-law, place, age). Second, Rachel's birth in Pennsylvania is going to help me in tracking down the origin of the Brooks family. Even if Benjamin Brooks wasn't born in Pennsylvania, I know that he and his wife lived there.

Just to double-check the marriage, I went to Ancestry.com and found the marriage record for Polly Knox and William Mercer on 15 October 1840, Lee County, Illinois.

Illinois Marriages, 1790-1860 about Polly Knox

Name:	**Polly Knox**
Spouse:	William Mercer
Date:	15 Oct 1840
County:	Lee
State:	Illinois
Source:	Family History Library, Salt Lake City, UT
Microfilm:	0848652 items 4-6

Chicago marriage record, FamilySearch.org

Initially selecting the Birth, Marriage, and Death databases at Ancestry.com, I narrowed the search by choosing to search only within the Marriage and Divorce databases.

As you can see in the search to the right, I wasn't 100 percent sure where Polly was married, so the only search parameters I used were her name and Mercer as the surname for her spouse.

The search results gave me the name of bride and groom, the date, and county. As you can see, I also have a microfilm number, so I can order the film to see the original record.

I've now found records for Knox family members in two Illinois counties. Did the family move while they lived in Illinois? I went to USGenWeb <www.usgenweb.com> for more information about the counties. The county map at the Illinois pages of the USGenWeb <http://ilgenweb.net> shows that Lee and Bureau counties border one another, so the family likely did not move within Illinois.

TAKE-AWAY: Start with a search and then follow the clues, as each will prompt further research. Not only will you be delving into genealogy sites, you'll also be looking up biographies (Massie), maps (Ohio rivers), census records, land records, out-of-print books, military records, and local histories.

TECHNIQUE 10: GOOGLE NEWS ARCHIVE

In chapter three, you learned about finding a country of origin, such as the Broyles migration from Germany to the Germanna Colony in Virginia. And, in chapter seven, you learned about using Google's News Archives. Now, let's merge the two and see what can be learned about Germanna in the Archives.

A search for *Germanna Colony* <news.google.com/archivesearch> returned news articles on topics ranging from archaeological studies on the site to Civil War operations that had taken place in the area.

What I found especially fascinating, though, was that on searching the Archives for *"Broyles Germanna,"* there were several articles naming Broyles family members who still lived in the area. Again, another opportunity for networking.

TAKE-AWAY: Your research may uncover living relatives you didn't know you had. It's possible they can help in your search.

TECHNIQUE 11: USING FAMILYSEARCH.ORG

Chapter four was all about online databases, including the free site at FamilySearch.org. A quick search of this mega-site yielded surprising results.

In talking to a friend about her father, she mentioned that he didn't have a middle name and the only thing she knew about him was that he was born in Chicago.

Knowing that FamilySearch.org has a database of Chicago births (with images), I went directly to the site <familysearch.org>. There I clicked the USA, Canada and Mexico collections, then browsed down the list until I came to "Illinois, Cook County Birth Certificates, 1878–1922."

Next I entered her father's name, Donald Brooks, and found the birth certificate for her father, who was listed in the index as Donald J. Brooks. When I viewed the images of the certificate itself, it seems her father *did* have a middle name.

TAKE-AWAY: Browse through the list of FamilySearch databases, which are organized by state. Many now have images of the original documents. Also, until you see the original document, you never know what you'll find!

TECHNIQUE 12: SUBSCRIPTION SITES

This puzzle began at the Fort Rosecrans National Cemetery in San Diego, California. My sister and I were at the cemetery, taking photos to fulfill a Find A Grave <findagrave.com> request.

We drove into the older section of the cemetery and stopped to walk back through the stones—as genealogists often do. An old stone caught our eye because it showed that the deceased had served in the Mexican War, Civil War, and Indian Wars—a rarity.

The stone was that of Sgt. John Gallagher of Battery B, 4th U.S. Artillery. According to the inscription, Sgt. Gallagher died on July 18, 1879, aged 56 years, "a gallant soldier who faithfully served his adopted country."

His service in three wars and his foreign birth were too tempting to pass up doing a bit of research, even though he was not an ancestor.

My first stop was GenealogyBank.com. After entering Gallagher's name, date of death, and specifying California, I found a San Francisco article giving the date that

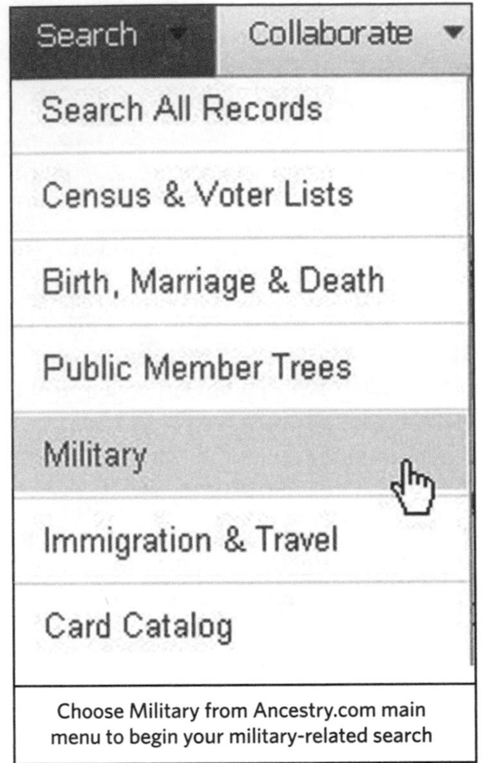

Choose Military from Ancestry.com main menu to begin your military-related search

Narrow your search by category or collection

Gallagher's estate went through probate and the names of the family members to whom he'd left money.

Most curious, though, was the fact that he left a sum of two hundred dollars to the men of Battery B for a "good dinner." He then directed that any monies left over after the disposition of his estate be used for the benefit of Battery B. Clearly his Army unit meant a great deal to him.

I e-mailed the coordinator at the San Francisco County USGenWeb page <cagenweb.com/sanfrancisco>, who gave me the e-mail address of a local researcher. The researcher reminded me that the will and probate file were not available; they were part of the official records destroyed in the Great San Francisco Earthquake of 1906, something I had failed to take into account.

Dead end.

Because there was no mention of a wife in Gallagher's obituary, I assumed that he was probably married to the Army, but I still checked the widows pension records at fold3.com <fold3.com>. There were none. The lack of a widow pension record doesn't mean John Gallagher never married; it just means I have no proof of a marriage at this time. It is possible his wife died before him and therefore wouldn't have collected a pension.

Next I went to Ancestry.com <ancestry.com> to search for Army records. I found several, including enlistments (and re-enlistments) in 1847, 1863, 1868, 1871, and 1876. I'm almost positive there was an earlier enlistment than 1847 as well as one in 1861, but I can't prove it with the records I have on hand.

Ancestry.com searches were used with a combination of the U.S. Civil War Soldiers database and the U.S. Army, Register of Enlistments, 1798–1914.

If you are looking for military records, such as these, once you've chosen Military from the Home page menu, you can either narrow by category or browse all of the military-related titles. In this case, I browsed the titles until I found the Register of Enlistments. Why that database? Gallagher's tombstone and obituary revealed he was in the 4th Artillery, which was a U.S. regiment as opposed to a state regiment. I didn't know this at the time, but it occurred to me that Civil War records typically show units as 20th Maine, or 18th Missouri—and since this unit was listed as 4th U.S. Artillery, I did a Google search and found this was a regular Army unit. That's why I wanted to check the Register of Enlistments, which is a register of enlistments in the U.S. regular Army from 1798–1914.

The Army records indicated Sgt. Gallagher was born in Derry, Ireland. I also learned he died of cancer in San Diego on July 18, 1879, the same date shown on his tombstone. Although what he was doing in San Diego, I don't know, because he was stationed at the Presidio in San Francisco.

The obituary mentioned that Gallagher had left "his lands and properties near Junction City, Kansas," to a nephew. I wondered at what period of time he had been in Kansas. When I saw his enlistment papers, it noted that from 1868 to 1871, the 4th Artillery was stationed in Fort Leavenworth, Kansas. A quick check on Google Maps <maps.google.com> shows the distance between Junction City and Leavenworth is 126 miles, not a hop, skip, and jump in 1868. I'm still wondering what brought Gallagher to Junction City.

After getting everything I could from the subscription sites, I expanded my search to general internet search engines. My research included following the 4th Artillery from the Mexican War through the Indian Wars (Modoc War, California). Because there are so many blogs and websites that are related to military units, it was fairly easy to do a simple search on the 4th Artillery. I found several websites with information on the 4th Artillery, including the U.S. Army Center of Military History <www.history.army.mil>.

When I searched the 4th's role in the Civil War, I discovered the battles in which they took part. Then I tried to pinpoint where Battery B had been on the battlefield so I could fly there on Google Earth.

I determined the battlefield placement by searching for online diaries, battle descriptions, and Google Books. I also did a search engine query for the *order of battle* at the major battles. For example, the order of battle at Gettysburg revealed that Battery B was in I Corps, under Col. Wainwright. Later, a Google search turned up Battery B's service throughout the entire Civil War <www.civilwarintheeast.com/USA/US/US4artB.php>.

Mysteries remain.

I have the name of Gallagher's brother-in-law and his nieces and nephew, but I don't have his sister's first name, nor do I know where the family lived in 1879. I see a search of the 1880 census on the horizon!

TAKE-AWAY: Without using GenealogyBank.com, I doubt I would have found the Gallagher obituary. And without the obituary I would have very little information to go on. Since most subscription sites have free trial periods, why not tackle your weighty problems during the trial period.

SUMMARY

Whether you're searching Google Books, the USGenWeb, Ancestry.com, fold3.com—or any internet website—a key to success is curiosity. Be curious, ask questions, put yourself in your ancestor's time and place. Then start asking yourself questions:

- Where was he buried?
- When did this state start keeping death records?
- Did he own land?
- Is it possible he was buried on a family farm?
- Does the farm cemetery still exist?
- Is there a local genealogy society I can contact?
- Would the USGenWeb county have a list of cemeteries?
- Where else can I look?
- Is there a volunteer who might check courthouse records for me?
- What wars were fought during his lifetime, and was he the right age to serve in the wars?
- What *was* the average age of soldiers in the wars fought during my ancestor's lifetime?
- If you find an occupation for your ancestor, do you understand the job title and what the job would have entailed?

You get the picture.

Don't be afraid to go back and forth between websites. It's rare that you'll find everything on a single site; rather, one site has clues that take you to another and then another.

Remember—just because it's online doesn't make it true. Clues are just clues, and what you find on a website is what someone else thinks is true. Take what you find and then try to prove it.

American Indian Resources by Geographic Region

NORTHEAST

WHERE: Canada on the north, Great Lakes on the west, Tennessee River to the south, the Atlantic Ocean to the east.

WHO: Tribes include Abenaki, Delaware, Huron, Kickapoo, Iroquois, Mohawk, Ottawa, Oneida, Shawnee, Tuscarora, Penobscot, Narragansett.

- Abenaki <native-languages.org/abenaki.htm>
- Delaware Tribe of Indians <delawaretribe.org/home.htm>
- Four Huron Wampum Records <archive.org/stream/cihm_06665#page/n5/mode/2up>
- Oneida Nation <oneida-nation.net>
- Oneida Nation of Wisconsin <oneidanation.org>
- People of the Standing Stone <peace4turtleisland.org/pages/oneida.htm>
- United Tribe of Shawnee Indians <unitedtribeofshawneeindians.org>
- Mohawk Nation Council of Chiefs <mohawknation.org>
- The Six Nations <ratical.org/many_worlds/6Nations/index.html>

- Mohawk and Iroquois <kahonwes.com/index1.htm>
- The Wampum Chronicles <wampumchronicles.com>

SOUTHEAST

WHERE: Area bordered by Kentucky and Virginia on the north, Mississippi River to the west, Gulf of Mexico and Atlantic on the south and east.

WHO: Five Civilized Tribes: Cherokee, Chickasaw, Choctaw, Creek (Muscogee), Seminole, plus Alabama, Natchez, Quapaw.

- The Quapaw Tribe of Oklahoma <quapawtribe.com>
- History of the Cherokee <cherokee.org/AboutTheNation/History/Facts/Default.aspx>
- Cherokee North Carolina <cherokee-nc.com>
- Chickasaw Nation <chickasaw.net>
- Choctaw Nation of Oklahoma <choctawnation.com>
- Muscogee (Creek) Nation <muscogeenation-nsn.gov>
- Seminole Nation of Oklahoma <seminolenation.com>
- Seminole Tribe of Florida <seminoletribe.com>
- Muscogee Nation of Oklahoma <genealogynation.com/creek>
- Cherokee Heritage Center <cherokeeheritage.org>
- Beginning Your Cherokee Research <tngenweb.org/cherokee_by_blood/cher3.htm>
- The Cherokee Messenger <powersource.com/cherokee/default.html>

GREAT BASIN, INTERIOR PLATEAU, NORTHWEST COAST

WHERE: Idaho, Nevada, Oregon, Washington and the western halves of Colorado, Montana and Wyoming.

WHO: Bannock, Klamath, Spokane, Paiute, Shoshone, Ute, Flathead, Kutenai, Nez Perce, Chinook, Clatsop, Haida.

- Klamath Tribes <klamathtribes.org>
- Southern Ute Indian Tribe <southern-ute.nsn.us>
- The Ute Indian Tribe <utetribe.com>
- Shoshone Indians <shoshoneindian.com>
- Confederated Tribes of Warm Springs (Paiute) <warmsprings.com>
- Nez Perce Tribe <nezperce.org>
- Confederated Tribes of the Umatilla Indian Reservation <umatilla.nsn.us>
- Yakama Nation <yakamanation-nsn.gov>

PLAINS/PRAIRIES AND WOODLANDS

WHERE: Extended from Canada to near Mexico. Southern portions of Alberta, Saskatchewan, Manitoba; eastern portions of Montana, Wyoming, Colorado, extreme eastern portion of New Mexico; North and South Dakota, Nebraska, Kansas, Oklahoma, Minnesota, Iowa, Arkansas, Texas. Woodlands bounded by Lake Michigan and Lake Superior on the east, Mississippi on the west, parts of Illinois, Wisconsin, Iowa.

WHO: Arapaho, Arikara, Assiniboine, Blackfeet, Cheyenne, Comanche, Crow, Kansa, Kiowa, Mandan, Omaha, Osage, Pawnee, Sioux, Chippewa, Fox, Illinois, Menominee, Ojibwa, Sauk, Winnebago

- Lakota Dakota Information Home Page <puffin.creighton.edu/lakota/index.html>
- Cheyenne Genealogy <cheyenneancestors.com>
- South Dakota Indian Tribes <accessgenealogy.com/native/southdakota/index.htm>
- Blackfeet Nation <blackfeetnation.com>
- Northern Cheyenne Tribe <cheyennenation.com>
- Mandan, Hidatsa, and Arikara Nation <mhanation.com/main/main.html>
- Fort Peck Assiniboine and Sioux History <fortpecktribes.org>
- Comanche Language and Cultural Preservation Committee <comanchelanguage.org>
- Great Sioux Nation <snowwowl.com/peoplesioux.html>
- Rosebud Sioux <rosebudsiouxtribe-nsn.gov>
- An Introduction to Dakota Culture and History <www.tc.umn.edu/~call0031/dakota.html>
- Pawnee Nation of Oklahoma <pawneenation.org>
- Great Lakes Inter-Tribal Council <www.glitc.org>
- Sault Tribe of Chippewa Indians <saulttribe.com>
- An Introduction to Ojibway Culture and History <www.tc.umn.edu/~call0031/ojibwa.html>
- The Illini Confederation <rfester.tripod.com>
- Menominee Indian Tribe of Wisconsin <menominee-nsn.gov>
- The Sac and Fox Nation <sacandfoxnation-nsn.gov>

SOUTHWEST AND CALIFORNIA

WHERE: Most of Arizona, New Mexico, part of western and southern Texas, California.

WHO: Chumash, Miwok, Modoc, Cahuilla, Havasupai, Mojave, Navajo, Papago, Pima, Yaqui, Yavapai, Yuma, plus the Pueblo tribes of the Hopi, Laguna, Taos, and Zuni.

- Chumash Indians <chumashindian.com>
- The Federated Indians of Graton Rancheria <gratonrancheria.com>
- Navajo Nation <navajo-nsn.gov>
- Hopi Cultural Preservation Office <nau.edu/hcpo-p>
- Hopi Information Network <hopiland.net>
- Indian Pueblo Cultural Center <indianpueblo.org/19pueblos/index.html>

MISCELLANEOUS RESOURCES

- U.S. Department of Interior American Indians and Alaska Natives <doi.gov/tribes/index.cfm>
- U.S. Department of Interior Indian Affairs <www.bia.gov>
- Native Web <nativeweb.org>
- Native American Tribes: Information Virtually Everywhere <www.afn.org/~native>
- Native American Resources <rootsweb.com/~usgwnar>
- Native American Genealogy Resources <distantcousin.com/Links/Ethnic/Native>
- Cyndi's List, Native American <cyndislist.com/native.htm>
- Federally Recognized American Indian Tribes <indians.org/Resource/FedTribes99/fedtribes99.html>
- Index of Native American Resources on the Internet <hanksville.org/NAresources/>

Tracing Jewish Ancestors

By Schelly Talalay Dardashti
From *Family Tree Magazine*

If you've started researching your Jewish ancestors, you might have heard that all the records were destroyed or that Ellis Island clerks changed your family's surnames, essentially cutting you off at the genealogical pass.

Don't believe the rumors. In reality, there's not a single documented case of an Ellis Island official changing an immigrant's surname (learn the truth behind this common mistake <familytreemagazine.com/article/ellis-island-myth>). Archives hold impressive collections of records, and a wealth of online resources can help you fulfill the goals you probably share with every Jewish family historian: to learn the fate of lost branches, create memorials for relatives without resting places, and connect with distant kin around the world.

That's not to say Jewish genealogy is easy. Cultural differences, language barriers, religious persecution, forced conversion, and genocide have created black holes in every Jewish family's history. But those roadblocks needn't stop you from discovering and honoring your past. With these seven research strategies to guide your genealogical journey, you'll find that your family's ties are stronger than any outside forces.

1. LEARN YOUR HISTORY.

Jewish history, unfortunately, is riddled with tragic events that complicate genealogists' work. Marauding Crusaders destroyed many European Jewish communities. Massacres, mass conversions, the Inquisition, and 1492 Expulsion shattered lives in Iberia. The Russian pogroms and the tragedy of the Holocaust affected our history forever. This Day in Jewish History <thisdayinjewishhistory.blogspot.com> documents historical events in detail.

Many actions spurred survivors to move elsewhere—sometimes to the next village or, more often, far from home. That means you'll need to cast a wide net to find information about your family. From the Middle Ages, Sephardic communities existed in major European cities (such as Hamburg, Vienna, and Warsaw), and some Ashkenazi families made their homes in the Mediterranean.

To understand and decipher Jewish records—from Hebrew tombstones to Jewish marriage contracts (ketubot)—it's useful to learn basic tenets and traditions of Judaism, such as life events and the Jewish calendar. Knowing the Jewish day ends at sunset, for example, helps you understand death records. An online calendar conversion tool such as Steve Morse's <stevemorse.org/jcal/jcal.html> lets you translate Jewish dates to the civil calendar. Remember, too, that Jews use BCE (before common era) and CE (common era) instead of BC and AD when referring to civil years.

2. FOLLOW THE GROUP.

Jews fall into two major groups—Ashkenazim and Sephardim—with further subdivisions. Because of each group's unique origins and migrations, your genealogical research will take different paths depending on which group your ancestors belonged to.

The first Jewish immigrants to the New World were Sephardim, who originated in the Iberian Peninsula. Ashkenazi Jews from Western Europe began arriving in the United States as early as the 1840s. About 95 percent of Jewish immigrants to America—predominantly Ashkenazi—came in a wave starting in 1881 following Russian pogroms, and then after each World War. Although Ashkenazim in much of Europe generally were assimilated and spoke secular languages, Yiddish was the lingua franca for those in Eastern Europe—Russia, Lithuania, Poland, and Germany.

Sephardim spoke Ladino, a mix of Hebrew, Spanish, and other languages sometimes called Judeo-Spanish or Judezmo. The term *Sephardic* generally describes any Jews not of Ashkenazi origin, including those who lived in the former Ottoman Empire, the Mediterranean, North Africa, the Middle East, the Balkans, and Asia. But Jews from Iran, Iraq, Afghanistan, and India are more correctly referred to as Mizrahi, Oriental, or Eastern Jews. Roman Jews make up the oldest Jewish community outside Israel, and the Romaniote Jews have resided in Greece for more than two millennia.

Ladino-speaking Sephardim began to arrive in the New World in the late 1500s as *conversos*—the Spanish word for those forced to convert to Catholicism during the Inquisition. Columbus's ships included converso crew. Sephardim settled in Brazil, the Caribbean, and New Amsterdam. Get more information on conversos at <familytreemagazine.com/article/Conversos-Connections>.

3. BREAK DOWN LANGUAGE BARRIERS.

Jewish records can appear in Hebrew, Yiddish, Ladino, German, Polish, Russian, French, Italian, Spanish, Catalan, Hungarian, Romanian, and more—whatever language was spoken wherever a Jewish community existed. Vital records kept by Jewish communities are likely to be in Hebrew, Yiddish, or Ladino, as well as the secular language, which may have changed as borders changed. You'll want to examine dual-language records carefully, because certain details might appear in only one language.

Sephardic records are especially challenging. Turkey is an excellent example of how convoluted the quest can be. Ashkenazi and Sephardi communities have existed side by side in what's now Istanbul since the 1400s. Turkish was originally written with Arabic letters; since 1928, it's employed the Latin alphabet. Sephardic records were written in Turkish, Hebrew, Ladino, and solitreo, an obsolete script, while Ashkenazi and civil records are found in Turkish, Hebrew, Yiddish, and Eastern European languages. (The Ashkenazi community kept its communal records in the language it knew best.)

To learn more about Jewish languages worldwide, visit Jewish Language Research <jewish-languages.org> for maps, text, audio samples, and additional links. As you trace your family into areas whose languages you don't speak, FamilySearch's Research Helps <familysearch.org/eng/search/rg/frameset_rhelps.asp> can give guidance for writing to foreign repositories.

4. TRACE THE NAMES.

In Jewish families, given names offer clues to past generations—sometimes more so than surnames. Ashkenazim generally name children after recently deceased relatives, so you can try to estimate Ashkenazi relatives' years of death by matching infants to ancestors. Sephardim name offspring after the living as well as the dead.

Ashkenazi given names often changed as families migrated—Hebrew or Yiddish names gave way to colloquial diminutives or secular versions. The JewishGen Given Names Database <jewishgen.org/databases/givennames> helps you find alternate forms of monikers based on local and Jewish vernaculars. For example, searching for the name David turns up possible Yiddish nicknames of Debele, Dovitke, Tevele, and Dovet.

The roots of European Jewish surnames are relatively recent, following civil laws passed in the late eighteenth century that required Jews to take fixed surnames. Many unrelated families adopted common names, so knowing the name of the ancestral village is often more helpful than searching for a surname.

Sephardic surnames, on the other hand, can be ancient—some appear in Spanish archival records as early as the tenth century. Many modern Sephardic names bear close resemblance to their original forms, indicating descent from a particular family. In Sephardic research, the surname is key to finding family in Spain or Portugal as well as Italy, Greece, and Turkey.

Sephardic given names often follow established patterns. The eldest son is traditionally named for the paternal grandfather; eldest daughter for the paternal grandmother; second male child for the maternal grandfather; second female child for the maternal grandmother; next child for a paternal uncle or aunt; and the next child for a maternal uncle or aunt. But a recently deceased grandparent or sibling often takes precedence over a living relative. Some Sephardim commonly name children after their own living parents—a great honor.

Try the Sephardic name search engine at Sephardim.com <jewishgen.org/databases/givennames>. The Jewish History Channel Blog <ha-historion.blogspot.com> has good information on Sephardic names.

5. REVIEW AVAILABLE RECORDS.

Both Ashkenazi and Sephardic Jews have lengthy paper trails to follow—once you've identified your family's ancestral town. You might find this in immigration records, draft registration cards, Social Security applications, or other documents. When you know the town, you can determine where its documents are located today. JewishGen's Community Database <jewishgen.org/communities> can help you find a town with phonetic searches and maps. Records may be in surprising locations. In Morocco, for example, civil registration wasn't required until the twentieth century, and with major immigration to France and Israel, many communal records were sent to those countries.

Some resources and documents are specific to Ashkenazim or Sephardim, but marriage, divorce, birth, and circumcision records exist for both groups. They may provide three generations of names in one record through the use of patronymics (the child's name derives from the father's name, such as Moshe Leib ben David Leibovich, indicating the father's and grandfather's names). Many of these European records have been microfilmed and are available at the Family History Library <familysearch.org>. Other records, such as circumcision, may have been kept privately by the mohel, the person who performs the circumcision. But some communities kept mohel registers, which indicate the date of circumcision, the parents, and the mohel.

Jewish birth records include the baby's name, sex, date (civil and Hebrew), names and residence of parents and grandparents, and sometimes the mother's maiden name, relatives' occupations, and name of the mohel.

A Jewish marriage record will generally show the date, place, the names of the bride and groom, the dowry, parents (with patronymics giving you another generation), and sometimes occupations and previous residences. In England, many synagogues kept separate marriage registers, now transcribed and published, for both Sephardic and Ashkenazi congregations. Iberian marriage contracts will normally list several generations for both bride and groom. And don't overlook Christian records—because of forced conversion, they might document your ancestor's union.

Gravestones show the death date, the deceased's given name, and his or her father's name. Some Sephardic stones contain much more information. Cemetery registers, if they still exist, may also be useful.

Holocaust records are valuable for both Ashkenazi and Sephardic research. Some Sephardic communities were nearly destroyed in addition to the decimated Eastern European Ashkenazi communities. See the next section for more information on the repositories that hold records of the Shoah.

Records specific to Eastern Europe include cadastral records and maps—real estate maps showing where families lived in a town or village, sometimes for generations. Depending on the time period, Jewish records might have been kept by the parish church. So if you're searching prior to civil registration, your Jewish ancestor's vital records might be within the church records.

For Sephardic researchers, records may go back to the tenth century. Note that many smaller Spanish archives are only now beginning to go digital. In Lerida a few years ago, for example, the archive had just one computer and was attempting to catalog more than ten thousand documents. Inquisition records are maintained in dedicated archives, but notarial records identify accused or sentenced individuals as Jew or converso and can provide other details.

Every Spanish town's archives holds notarial records. These extremely detailed files might include records of debts, real estate transfers, marriage settlements, and divorces. Jews and conversos are noted, and variations of names can appear, as well as other towns of residence. Because of conversions, Catholic Church records are a next stop for baptism, marriage, and death records.

6. RESEARCH IN REPOSITORIES.

You'll find Jewish records in a number of different places, from Web sites to centuries-old archives. The worldwide Jewish genealogy community is made up of many dedicated volunteers who are transliterating and translating records. Projects might be as narrow as births from one small town or as gigantic as the three million Pages of Testimony at the Yad Vashem Holocaust Memorial.

JewishGen hosts many databases, some of which are searchable for free on Ancestry.com. You may also have luck with Jewish Records Indexing Poland <jri-poland.org>, which has some three million vital records. The Family History Library holds microfilm of original records used by Jewish volunteers to create accessible, searchable databases, while other groups work directly with Eastern European archives to create indexes. You can search many of these on JewishGen.

Yad Vashem: The Holocaust Martyrs' and Heroes' Remembrance Authority <yadvashem.org> holds International Tracing Service (ITS) documents, concentration camp records, a comprehensive library, and a database of Shoah victims' names. The U.S. Holocaust Memorial Museum <ushmm.org> also has ITS records.

The Center for Jewish History <cjh.org> in New York City holds records and library resources of the American Jewish Historical Society <ajhs.org>, YIVO Institute <yivoinstitute.org>, Leo Baeck Institute <lbi.org>, American Sephardi Federation <americansephardifederation.org>, and the Jewish Genealogical Society <jgsny.org>.

The Central Archives for the History of the Jewish People Jerusalem <sites.huji.ac.il/archives> holds the collections of hundreds of Jewish communities, as well as local, national, and international Jewish organizations. The Central Archives has a large collection of vital record registers from Germany from the end of the eighteenth century onward, as well as registers from France, Italy, and Poland.

Sephardim.com <sephardim.com> has an extensive name index and an active discussion group. Sephardicgen <sephardicgen.com> has links to sources, names, news lists, and country resources, plus information on Spanish notarial records, Inquisition archives, and ketubot. JewishGen also has Sephardic information at <jewishgen.org/infofiles/sefard5.htm> and <jewishgen.org/sephardic/names.htm>.

7. GO GENETIC.

The most advanced genealogy tool—DNA testing—is raising as many questions as answers. My family is Ashkenazi with Sephardic roots; New Yorker Judy Simon had a similar story. "My grandfather always said we were marranos," says Simon, using a derogatory term for Jews that refers to swine. "It was a story carried through the generations that our family left Spain during the Inquisition."

In 2007 Simon and I co-founded the Iberian Ashkenaz Y-DNA project <familytreedna.com/public/IberianSurnamesofAshkenaz/default.aspx> to find more people like us.

Simon and I discovered Ashkenazi families from Eastern, Western, and Central Europe with indicators of Sephardic heritage, such as Spanish or Portuguese surnames, an oral history of Sephardic ancestors, children named after living grandparents, or Mediterranean genetic disorders. The families couldn't verify possible Sephardic roots through archival records, so we used DNA.

Simon's male cousin was tested, and his matches were Ashkenazi Jews from villages near his own, where Latvia, Belarus, and Lithuania meet. Two Hispanic men in Mexico and Texas matched him, too. Of the Ashkenazim who found matches, none had any idea they had paternal Sephardic roots.

The most important element of DNA testing for investigating Jewish ancestry is the size of the comparative database (that is, how many other samples your profile will be compared to). FamilyTreeDNA <familytreedna.com> has the largest Jewish comparative databases and the largest general DNA database, according to founder Bennett Greenspan, with records for Ashkenazim, Sephardim, Levites, and Kohanim. JewishGen links to FamilyTreeDNA studies <jewishgen.org/DNA/genbygen.html>. Another study, the DNA Shoah Project <dnashoah.org>, aims to reunite families separated by the Holocaust. It's free to join, and more than one thousand samples are already in the collection—all potential ties to your past.

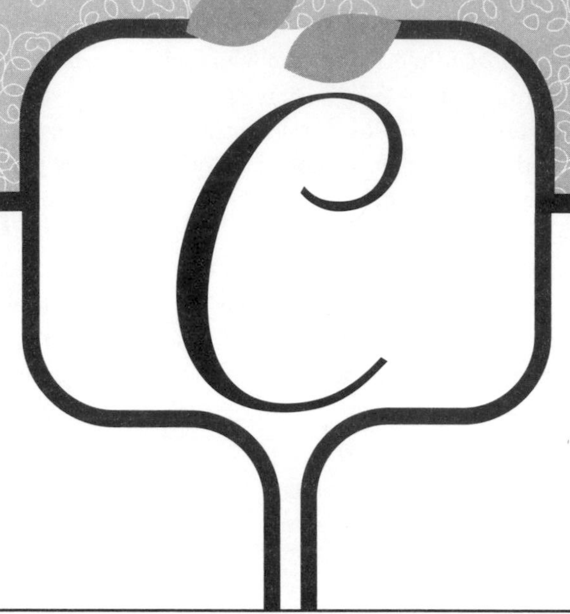

Tracing Slave Ancestors

By Kenyatta D. Berry
From *Family Tree Magazine*

My third-great-grandfather Lewis Carter was born about 1817 in Virginia and spent most of his life there. The 1870 census shows him living in that state's Madison County with his wife and six children. He was a farmhand with real estate valued at $4,700 and personal property worth $1,150.

Such substantial holdings aren't bad for a "mulatto" so soon after the end of slavery. Was Lewis Carter freed before the Emancipation Proclamation took effect in 1863? Did a former master reward his work with this land? Had my third-great-grandfather scraped together enough money to buy property?

My search for the truth about Lewis Carter arose from a curiosity familiar to many African-Americans: Where did my ancestors come from? What were their experiences in slavery? Slavery has clouded the answers to these questions, but it hasn't erased them entirely. These resources and strategies will help you learn who your enslaved ancestors were and reconnect with your family's history.

STUDYING SLAVE COMMUNITIES

The enslavement of Africans in the United States began in 1619, when a Dutch trader sold slaves to settlers at Jamestown, Virginia. Millions of Africans were forced to cross the Atlantic over the next two hundred years—a branch of the slave trade known as the Middle Passage.

The website Voyages <slavevoyages.org> details this trade. Britain and the United Stated outlawed importing (but not owning) slaves in 1807, though the practice continued illegally for years.

Not every white Southerner owned slaves, and whites weren't the only slave owners. Little has been written about African-Americans who owned slaves, but it appears the practice was common in Louisiana, South Carolina, Maryland, and Virginia. Anthony Johnson, a free African and former indentured servant, won a court case in 1654 that, ironically, declared his servant a slave for life. You can learn more about this phenomenon in *Black Slaveowners: Free Black Slave Masters in South Carolina, 1790–1860* by Larry Koger.

Whether someone was a slave depended on his or her mother's status: If the mother was a slave, her children were slaves; if the mother was free, so were her children. A slave community could consist of a large plantation with more than one hundred slaves, or it could be a small farm with just a few slaves.

To research your slave ancestors, you'll first need to trace your family tree back from yourself to the time slavery ended in 1865, documenting your ancestors in as many historical records as possible. For help with this, see the November 2007 *Family Tree Magazine*, <familytreemagazine.com> as well as *A Genealogist's Guide to Discovering Your African-American Ancestors* by Franklin Carter Smith and Emily Anne Croom. Try to learn your ancestors' names and where they settled after slavery ended.

Researching enslaved ancestors involves the same basic genealogical principles as any other family history quest, with this difference: You'll need to study both the slave family and the owner's family. Your goal is to reconstruct relationships in the slave-holding family and their process of acquiring slaves. The slave and white families were bound together not just as property and owner, but also as a community and a family unit. Their children played together, black women cared for white children, and the owners and slaves sometimes worked side by side. But more important, slaves were often "kept in the family." As legal property, they could be passed down through inheritance, loaned out, and given away as gifts to children. All of these actions could generate records under the slave family's name.

Identifying your slave ancestor's owner is a process. You might take an educated guess that proves untrue as you research that family. Don't be discouraged from rechecking your research, forming another theory, and trying again.

DISCOVERING THE SLAVEOWNER FAMILY

You probably already know slaves didn't use last names. Your newly freed ancestor could have chosen a particular surname for a variety of reasons, so don't assume your ancestor took his most recent master's name. But because many freedmen did, start by researching white families with the same surname in your ancestors' community, especially if it was an uncommon surname.

First, focus on the county where your ancestors lived in 1870. Look at county histories and find your family in the 1870 census (the first census to include former slaves' last names). Next, examine the white families living in the same enumeration district as your ancestors. A few things to ask yourself: How many whites with the same surname lived in the district? Did they live near my ancestors? Can I find them in the 1860 U.S. census? In the 1850 census? Are they listed as slave owners on 1850 or 1860 slave schedules? In 1850 and 1860, African-Americans were included on a supplemental slave schedule. Schedules are organized by the slave master's name and list the slaves' color, sex, and age—not their names, but you still can use the ages to hypothesize about your ancestral family. Information also includes whether the slave was a fugitive or deaf, dumb, insane, or idiotic; the total number of slaves the owner manumitted (freed); and the number of slave houses on the owner's property.

Here's an example: Prince Ailes was born about 1845 in Arkansas, the son of a slave named Charlotte, born about 1815 in Mississippi. His brother Frank was born about 1851 in Arkansas. To identify Prince's last owner, I first found Prince in the 1870 census, in Union County, Arkansas, with his wife, two children, mother, and brother. In the same county were two white households with Aileses: Martin Ailes and Ackley Ailes. I searched for both in the 1860 census. I found "Auckley" living with her parents, Walker and Martha Aills, in Union County. Walker owned six slaves in 1860; two were within the right age range for Prince and Frank. I also noticed Auckley was born in Mississippi—as was Prince's mother, Charlotte. In 1850, Walker and Martha lived with their five children and seven slaves in Union County. The 1850 Union County slave schedule lists two slaves about the ages Prince and Frank would've been.

Freedmen's Bureau records may not only contain valuable information for finding ancestors post-slavery, but they also might hold clues to former owners' names. The bureau, created after the Civil War under the purview of the War Department, became the primary structure through which freed slaves sought aid, protection, and assistance. These records, generated between 1865 and 1872, include:

- labor contracts between planters and freedmen
- registers of transportation
- school records
- correspondence and registers of outrages and violence against freedmen
- marriage registers

- bounty applications for soldiers discharged for the U.S. Colored Troops
- registers of payment claims (related to Civil War service) of Colored Troops veterans, their families, and others
- correspondence from bureau field agents and local residents

Records from Freedmen's Bureau field offices are available on microfilm at the National Archives and Records Administration (NARA) <archives.gov> in Washington, D.C., and its regional facilities, as well as through the Church of Jesus Christ of Latter-day Saints' Family History Library (FHL) <familysearch.org> in Salt Lake City. (You can borrow FHL microfilm through a FamilySearch Center near you. Some state libraries and archives also have records for their states. Check your state archives and see NARA's online guide <archives.gov/research/african-americans/freedmens-bureau>.

Freedmen's Bureau records at the Library of Virginia <www.lva.virginia.gov> might have helped me find the owner of my third-great-grandfather Lewis Carter. Since the 1870 census listed Lewis as a farmhand, rather than a farmer, I thought perhaps he worked for someone. Freedmen's Bureau records contained a labor contract dated January 5, 1866, between Carter and a Dr. John W. Taylor of Madison County, Virginia. For farming Taylor's land, Carter would receive half the crops. That was a standard sharecropping agreement after the Civil War, common between freed slaves and their former owners.

In 1860, John W. Taylor lived in Madison County with his wife and four children. He owned real estate worth $12,500 and personal property worth $20,570, which included twenty slaves. Of those, one, "a mulatto male, age 43," matched Lewis Carter's age and description. But none of the slaves matched the age, race, and sex of Lewis's wife and children, so I'll need to keep researching the Taylor family and their associates.

Records of the Freedman's Savings Bank & Trust Co., or Freedman's Bank, which operated from 1865 to 1874 for former slaves and their descendants, also can help you learn about your family's whereabouts when slavery ended. Surviving records include depositors' names, birthplaces, occupations, and residences. Records are on microfilm at NARA and the FHL, and on CD at FamilySearch Centers. Search digitized versions on FamilySearch, on the subscription site Ancestry.com, and on HeritageQuest Online (free through subscribing libraries) <heritagequestonline.com/hqoweb/library/do/index>.

RESEARCHING THE SLAVE-HOLDING FAMILY

Create a basic genealogy of both your family and the slave-owning family. Include collateral lines—relatives such as siblings, aunts, uncles, and cousins.

CENSUS RECORDS: Searching the 1840 and 1830 census, I noted Walker Aills lived in Amite County, Mississippi, before he migrated to Arkansas. He had one slave whose age was in the range of Prince and Frank's mother. But what happened to Charlotte in 1850 and 1860? During those two years, Martin's son owned two female slaves, ages thirty-five and age seven. The thirty-five year old could have been Charlotte.

PROPERTY RECORDS: Because slaves were considered property, many records that name them are with the slave owner's other property-related records: Wills, probate files, inventories, account books, deeds, and tax records can help you discover your enslaved ancestors. Typically, slaves are identified by first name and color (such as black or mulatto). A few of these records are online, either digitized or as indexes that will tell you the name of the repository holding the original. Afro-Louisiana History and Genealogy <ibiblio.org/laslave> catalogs information about slaves in Louisiana from 1719 to 1820. AfriQuest <afriquest.com> has a variety of wills and court records.

Most property-related records, though, are in county courthouses, local libraries, historical societies, and state archives. Look up your ancestor's county in a genealogy reference such as *Red Book: American State, County and Town Sources* or the *Family Tree Sourcebook* to see where old records are kept.

If you live near the repository, it's just a matter of calling to ask about research hours. If not, you can write to request copies or see if the records are microfilmed at the FHL. Search the online catalog <familysearch.org/eng/library/fhlc/frameset_fhlc.asp> by choosing Place Search and entering the county and state where your ancestor lived. (Some county names have changed over the years—enter the name during your ancestor's lifetime.) Look for topics such as court records, wills, deeds, and probate, and see if records cover the right time period. These records also could tell you about your ancestors.

PROBATE RECORDS: These are all the court records associated with the settling of a deceased person's estate, so they may help you learn what happened to slaves he or she owned. A probate file might include a will spelling out who was to get which slaves, property inventories, deeds, account books, and correspondence. These records are often found at county courthouses and state archives.

For example, the estate papers of Clark J. Cook, a white man I believe is the father of a mulatto man named George Dwelle, showed how the profits from selling Cook's property were divided among his siblings. After Cook's death, auctioneer Augustus Lafayette sold George and his mother, Mary, to Milo Hatch on September 2, 1851, for $2,300.

INVENTORIES: Also often part of estate papers, inventories itemized all the deceased's property at the time of death. Slaves would be listed with sex and age.

ACCOUNT BOOKS: The executor of the estate kept account books, which may record when the deceased's slaves were sold and to whom. You might find them in probate file collections or on their own at historical societies, state archives, and in collections of family papers.

DEEDS: These papers record the transfer of property on the basis of a sale, gift, or trust. Slaves were sometimes transferred via deeds. Deeds are usually in county courthouses, but might have been transferred to state archives. You'll also find some on FHL microfilm. Run a search on your ancestor's county and look for the Deed Records heading.

MANUMISSION PAPERS: An owner or a court could issue these papers to document a slave's freedom when the owner granted it (sometimes in a will) or the slave purchased it. The papers are often located at historical societies and state archives, and in manuscript collections held in state and local libraries (see below). NARA has Washington, D.C., manumissions from 1857 to 1863 on microfilm M433.

MANUSCRIPT COLLECTIONS: Typically, larger plantations kept meticulous records regarding expenses for clothing or medical care. For these slaveholders, manuscript collections of account books and business and personal papers can prove valuable resources. Manuscript collections can be in various locations: city, county, or state historical or genealogical societies; state archives; and public or university libraries. Most societies and libraries publish manuscript collection guides on their websites, so search Google on the slave-owning family's name. See the March 2009 *Family Tree Magazine* for more techniques for finding resources in libraries.

Don't forget to ask for help. Testing my theory that Walker Ailes owned Prince Ailes, I posted my research and assumptions to the Aills mailing list on RootsWeb <rootsweb.com>. I was thrilled to receive a response from the descendants of Walker Ailes, who had records showing the Aileses indeed owned Prince. They even sent photos of Prince and Walker Ailes.

I'm hoping for equally satisfying results to my ongoing search for my ancestor Lewis Carter. As I continue to discover my heritage and learn more about my ancestors, I'm reminded of the challenges and connections that bind families across generations—and the uniqueness of African-American genealogy.

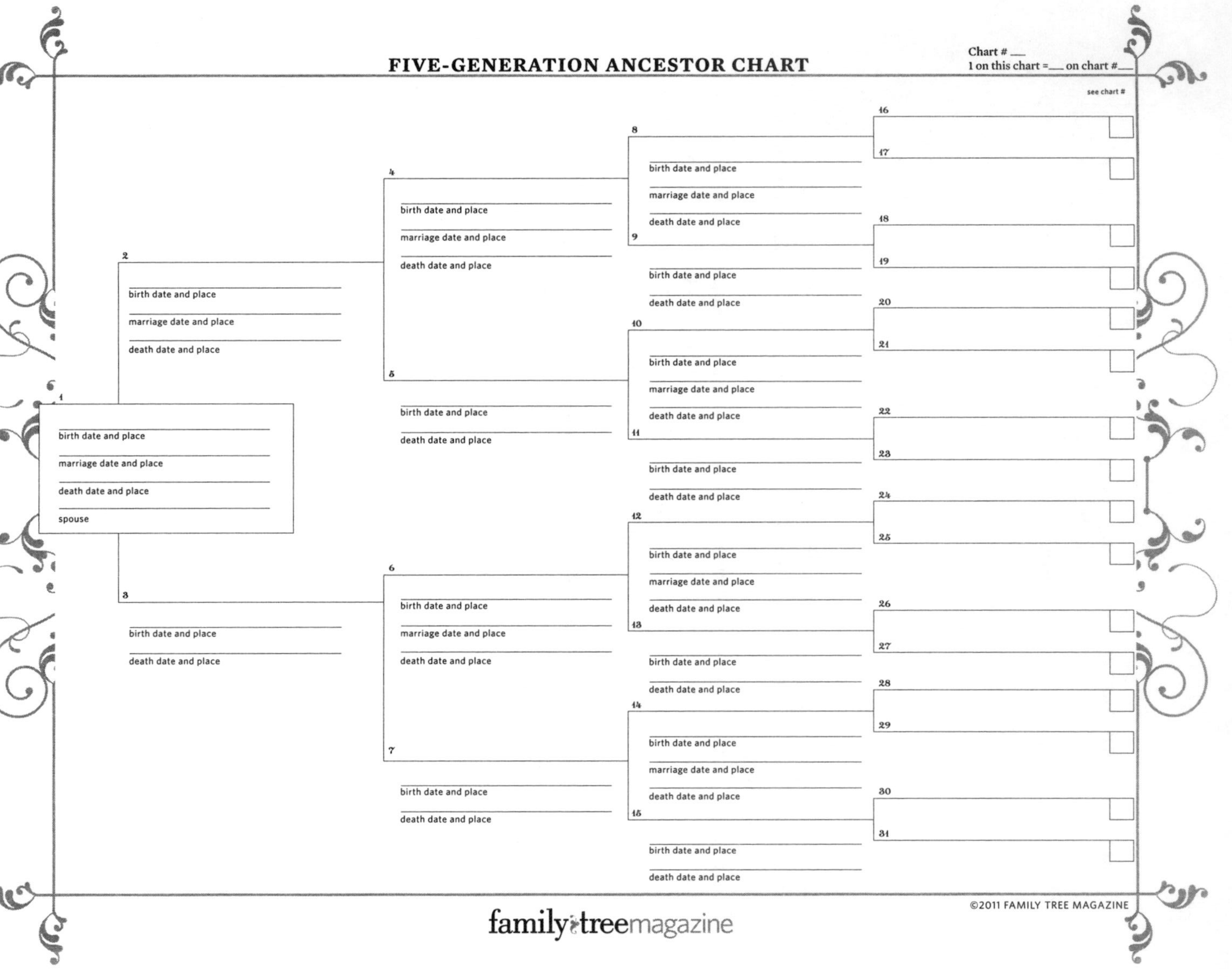
FIVE-GENERATION ANCESTOR CHART
Chart # ___
1 on this chart = ___ on chart # ___
see chart #
1
birth date and place
marriage date and place
death date and place
spouse
2
birth date and place
marriage date and place
death date and place
3
birth date and place
death date and place
4
birth date and place
marriage date and place
death date and place
5
birth date and place
death date and place
6
birth date and place
marriage date and place
death date and place
7
birth date and place
death date and place
8
birth date and place
marriage date and place
death date and place
9
birth date and place
death date and place
10
birth date and place
marriage date and place
death date and place
11
birth date and place
death date and place
12
birth date and place
marriage date and place
death date and place
13
birth date and place
death date and place
14
birth date and place
marriage date and place
death date and place
15
birth date and place
death date and place
16
17
18
19
20
21
22
23
24
25
26
27
28
29
30
31
©2011 FAMILY TREE MAGAZINE
familytreemagazine

FAMILY GROUP SHEET OF THE

_______________ Family

	Source #		Source #
Full Name of Husband		Birth Date and Place	
His Father		Marriage Date and Place	
His Mother with Maiden Name		Death Date and Place Burial	
Full Name of Wife			
Her Father		Birth Date and Place	
Her Mother with Maiden Name		Death Date and Place Burial	
Other Spouses		Marriage Date and Place	

Children of This Marriage	Birth Date and Place	Death Date, Place and Burial	Marriage Date, Place and Spouse

family tree magazine

RECORDS CHECKLIST

Refer to this handy roster of source types to ensure you've checked all ancestral records.

Business and Employment Records

- ☐ apprentice and indenture records
- ☐ doctors' and midwives' journals
- ☐ insurance records
- ☐ merchants' account books
- ☐ professional licenses
- ☐ railroad, mining and factory records
- ☐ records of professional organizations and associations

Cemetery and Funeral Home Records

- ☐ burial records
- ☐ grave-relocation records
- ☐ tombstone inscriptions

Censuses

- ☐ agriculture schedules (1850 to 1880)
- ☐ American Indian (special censuses)
- ☐ Civil War veterans schedules (1890)
- ☐ defective, dependent and delinquent schedules (1880)
- ☐ federal population schedules (1790 to 1930)
- ☐ manufacturing/industry schedules (1810, 1820, 1850 to 1880)
- ☐ mortality schedules (1850 to 1880)
- ☐ school censuses
- ☐ slave schedules (1850, 1860)
- ☐ social statistics schedules (1850 to 1880)
- ☐ state and local censuses

Church Records

- ☐ baptism and christening records
- ☐ confirmation records
- ☐ congregational histories
- ☐ meeting minutes
- ☐ membership, admission and removal records
- ☐ ministers' journals

Court Records

- ☐ adoption records
- ☐ bastardy cases
- ☐ civil records
- ☐ coroners' files
- ☐ criminal records
- ☐ custody papers
- ☐ estate inventories
- ☐ guardianship papers
- ☐ insanity/commitment orders
- ☐ licenses and permits
- ☐ marriage bonds, licenses and certificates
- ☐ military discharges
- ☐ minute books
- ☐ name changes
- ☐ naturalizations
- ☐ property foreclosures
- ☐ voter registrations
- ☐ wills
- ☐ wolf-scalp bounties

Directories

- ☐ biographical
- ☐ city
- ☐ professional/occupational
- ☐ telephone

Home Sources

- ☐ baptism and confirmation certificates
- ☐ birth certificates and baby books
- ☐ checkbooks and bank statements
- ☐ death records and prayer cards
- ☐ diaries and journals
- ☐ family Bibles
- ☐ funeral/memorial cards
- ☐ heirlooms and artifacts
- ☐ letters and postcards
- ☐ marriage certificates and wedding albums
- ☐ medical records
- ☐ photographs
- ☐ recipe books
- ☐ school report cards, yearbooks and scrapbooks
- ☐ wills

Immigration Records

- ☐ alien registration cards
- ☐ citizenship papers
- ☐ passenger lists
- ☐ passports

Institutional Records

- ☐ almshouse
- ☐ hospital
- ☐ orphanage
- ☐ police
- ☐ prison
- ☐ school
- ☐ work-farm

Land and Property Records

- ☐ deeds
- ☐ grants and patents
- ☐ homestead records
- ☐ mortgages and leases
- ☐ plat maps
- ☐ surveys
- ☐ tax rolls
- ☐ warrants

Military Records

- ☐ Colonial wars
- ☐ Revolutionary War and frontier conflicts (War of 1812, Indian wars and Mexican War)
- ☐ Civil War
- ☐ Spanish-American War
- ☐ World War I
- ☐ World War II
- ☐ Korean War
- ☐ Vietnam War
- ☐ draft records
- ☐ pension applications
- ☐ records of relocations and internment camps for Japanese-Americans, German-Americans and Italian-Americans during World War II

Newspapers

- ☐ birth announcements
- ☐ classified advertisements
- ☐ engagement, marriage and anniversary announcements
- ☐ ethnic newspapers
- ☐ family reunion announcements
- ☐ gossip and advice columns
- ☐ legal notices
- ☐ local news
- ☐ obituaries
- ☐ runaway notices (slaves, indentured servants, wives)
- ☐ unclaimed-mail notices

Published Sources

- ☐ compiled genealogies
- ☐ genealogical periodicals
- ☐ local and county histories
- ☐ record abstracts and transcriptions

Vital Records

- ☐ birth
- ☐ death
- ☐ divorce/annulment
- ☐ marriage

ACKNOWLEDGEMENTS

I want to thank Allison Dolan, head honcho at *Family Tree Magazine* for prompting me to write this book.

We first considered updating my original genealogy book, *Finding Your Roots Online*, but the internet has changed so much since *Finding* was first written that an update just wouldn't do. What you're holding in your hands is a brand new creation, with new sources, techniques, and real-life examples.

Next, I want to thank Diane Haddad, who has edited many of my articles for *Family Tree Magazine*—and always makes me look like a far better writer than I am. The same goes for Jackie Musser, who had infinite patience in editing this book.

Thanks also to Grace Dobush, who, until the last few months, was the driving force at Family Tree University. We miss you, girl.

And of course a big thanks to all of my students at Family Tree University, my friends, and the readers of my blog. I'm especially grateful for all of the thorny research problems that were sent to me for inclusion in this book. Some I solved, some I didn't—but I had fun trying them all!

Lastly, and most importantly—thank *you* for purchasing *Discover Your Family History Online*. I hope it brings you hours of good reading and hundreds of new ancestors.

See you on Twitter!

Nancy Hendrickson

San Diego, California

Twitter: @genealogyteach

AncestorNews.com

Published by Family Tree Books, an imprint of F+W Media, Inc., 10151 Carver Road, Suite 200, Blue Ash, Ohio 45242. (800) 289-0963. First edition.

ISBN: 978-1-4403-1850-4

Other Family Tree Books are available from your local bookstore and online suppliers. For more genealogy resources, visit <**shopfamilytree.com**>.

16 15 14 13 12 5 4 3 2 1

DISTRIBUTED IN CANADA BY FRASER DIRECT
100 Armstrong Avenue
Georgetown, Ontario, Canada L7G 5S4
Tel: (905) 877-4411

DISTRIBUTED IN THE U.K. AND EUROPE BY
F&W Media International, LTD
Brunel House, Forde Close,
Newton Abbot, TQ12 4PU, UK
Tel: (+44) 1626 323200,
Fax (+44) 1626 323319
E-mail: enquiries@fwmedia.com

DISTRIBUTED IN AUSTRALIA BY CAPRICORN LINK
P.O. Box 704, Windsor, NSW 2756 Australia
Tel: (02) 4577-3555

PUBLISHER/EDITORIAL DIRECTOR: Allison Dolan
EDITOR: Jacqueline Musser
DESIGNER: Christy Miller
PRODUCTION COORDINATOR: Mark Griffin